ASUS Eee PC For Dummies®

Cheat Sheet

Eee PC Function and Control Keys

Fn+F1	Puts the Eee PC in standby mode. Press the Power button to resume.
Fn+F2	Turns the wireless card on and off. On models with Bluetooth, also toggles Bluetooth on and off.
Fn+F3	Decreases the screen brightness.
Fn+F4	Increases the screen brightness.
Fn+F5	Toggles the display mode between the Eee PC screen, an attached VGA device (monitor or projector), or both.
Fn+F6	Runs the Task Manager.
Fn+F7	Mutes the speaker.
Fn+F8	Decreases speaker volume.
Fn+F9	Increases speaker volume.
Fn+F11	Turns keyboard Num lock on and off.
Fn+F12	Turns keyboard Caps lock on and off.
Fn+Ins	Runs the Print Screen program in Linux. Saves a copy of the screen to the clipboard in Windows.
House	Shows the Linux desktop.
Ctrl+Alt+Del	In Windows, brings up the Task Manager and allows you to reset your computer.
Ctrl+Alt+Backspace	In Linux performs an immediate system reset.

Essential Eee PC Web Sites

Official Eee PC site — `http://eeepc.asus.com`

ASUS support site (including downloads) — `http://support.asus.com`

EeeUser.com Forums — `http://forum.eeeuser.com`

EeeUser.com Wiki — `http://wiki.eeeuser.com`

ASUS Eee PC For Dummies®

Cheat Sheet

Eee PC Models — Basic Specifications

Model	CPU	Screen	Larger Keyboard	Drive Space	OS
2G Surf (700)	800 MHz Celeron	7", 800x480	No	2GB SSD	Linux
4G Surf (701)	900 MHz Celeron	7", 800x480	No	4GB SSD	Linux
4G (701)	900 MHz Celeron	7", 800x480	No	4GB SSD	Linux
8G (701)	900 MHz Celeron	7", 800x480	No	8GB SSD	Linux
900	900 MHz Celeron	8.9", 1024x600	No	12GB SSD 16GB SSD 20GB SSD	Linux or Windows XP
901	1.6 GHz Intel Atom	8.9", 1024x600	No	12GB SSD 20GB SSD	Linux or Windows XP
904HD	900 MHz Celeron	8.9", 1024x600	Yes	80GB HDD	Windows XP
1000	1.6 GHz Intel Atom	10.2", 1024x600	Yes	20GB SSD	Linux
1000 H	1.6 GHz Intel Atom	10.2", 1024x600	Yes	80GB HDD	Linux or Windows XP
1000 HD	900 MHz Celeron	10.2", 1024x600	Yes	80GB HDD	Linux or Windows XP

Note: SSD = Solid State Drive, HDD = Hard Disk Drive.

Eee PC Preinstalled OpenOffice Programs

Program	Function
OpenOffice Writer	Word Processor
OpenOffice Calc	Spreadsheet
Open Office Impress	Presentations (similar to PowerPoint)
OpenOffice Draw	Vector graphics editor
OpenOffice Base	Database
OpenOffice Math	Mathematical equation editor

For more information, visit: www.openoffice.org.com

For Dummies: Bestselling Book Series for Beginners

ASUS Eee PC
FOR
DUMMIES®

by Joel McNamara

WILEY

Wiley Publishing, Inc.

ASUS Eee PC For Dummies®

Published by
Wiley Publishing, Inc.
111 River Street
Hoboken, NJ 07030-5774

www.wiley.com

For general information on our other products and services, please contact our Customer Care Department within the U.S. at 877-762-2974, outside the U.S. at 317-572-3993, or fax 317-572-4002.

For technical support, please visit www.wiley.com/techsupport.

Wiley also publishes its books in a variety of electronic formats. Some content that appears in print may not be available in electronic books.

Library of Congress Control Number:

ISBN: 978-0-470-41154-4

Manufactured in the United States of America

10 9 8 7 6 5 4 3 2 1

WILEY

About the Author

Joel McNamara started using computers in the Dark Ages (1980 to be precise), and if the words NorthStar Horizon, ARPANET, PDP-11, Kaypro, and Apple Lisa mean anything to you, like in the movie *Zelig*, he was there. Over the years Joel has worked, among other things, as a programmer, technical writer, and manager for a number of companies in the high-tech sector. He currently writes and consults on technology he finds interesting (like little Linux laptops).

Joel is also the author of *GPS For Dummies, Geocaching For Dummies*, and *Secrets of Computer Espionage: Tactics & Countermeasures* (all published by Wiley).

Acknowledgments

First, thanks to ASUS for starting the mini-laptop/netbook revolution and providing support for this book.

Next, I'd like to thank the members of the band. On bass (my Wiley acquisitions editor) Kyle Looper, on drums (technical editor) Charlton Ho, on guitar, copy editor Mary Lagu, and on keyboard, the man who brings it all together, Marvelous Mark Enochs (project editor maximus). Also, everyone else at Wiley who did background vocals. One day I hope to have the pleasure to meet you all in person.

Thank you. Thank you very much.

Publisher's Acknowledgments

We're proud of this book; please send us your comments through our online registration form located at http://dummies.custhelp.com. For other comments, please contact our Customer Care Department within the U.S. at 877-762-2974, outside the U.S. at 317-572-3993, or fax 317-572-4002.

Some of the people who helped bring this book to market include the following:

Acquisitions and Editorial

Senior Project Editor: Mark Enochs

Acquisitions Editor: Kyle Looper

Copy Editor: Mary Lagu

Technical Editor: Charlton Ho

Editorial Manager: Leah Cameron

Editorial Assistant: Amanda Foxworth

Sr. Editorial Assistant: Cherie Case

Cartoons: Rich Tennant
(www.the5thwave.com)

Composition Services

Senior Project Coordinator: Kristie Rees

Layout and Graphics: Reuben W. Davis, Nikki Gately, Christin Swinford, Ronald Terry

Proofreaders: John Greenough, Nancy L. Reinhardt

Indexer: Infodex Indexing Services, Inc.

Publishing and Editorial for Technology Dummies

    Richard Swadley, Vice President and Executive Group Publisher

    Andy Cummings, Vice President and Publisher

    Mary Bednarek, Executive Acquisitions Director

    Mary C. Corder, Editorial Director

Publishing for Consumer Dummies

    Diane Graves Steele, Vice President and Publisher

Composition Services

    Gerry Fahey, Vice President of Production Services

    Debbie Stailey, Director of Composition Services

Contents at a Glance

Table of Contents

Introduction

I've used a lot of personal computers over the years. The Apple II, Northstar Horizons, IBM and clone PCs, Macs, Palm Pilots, and a host of other machines long gone and forgotten. (Saying all this is suddenly making me feel pretty darn old.) Having seen lots of technology come and go, I must admit I can be a bit jaded when new products hit the market; especially those that arrive with an overabundance of hype.

When I first heard all the buzz about the Eee PC, I was skeptical. The Internet is filled with vocal fanboys for just about any product you can think of, and I figured this was yet another example. Then I got my hands on an Eee PC. And after a couple of days, the jaded skepticism turned into surprise and satisfaction as I found myself using the little laptop more and more.

Light and small (right around two pounds and about the size of this book), durable enough not to mind getting knocked about a bit, and considerably cheaper than a MacBook Air or high-end Ultra Mobile Portable Computer, it boots up in less than half a minute with a solid state hard drive. Eee PC is loaded all the hardware and software (a friendly version of Linux comes with lots of programs) that you need to access the Net and do personal, work and entertainment-related tasks from home or on the road. Sweet!

But aside from all the technical goodness, one of the things that impressed me the most was the Eee PC's functional simplicity. We are living in a time of over-complexity. The world around us is becoming ever complicated; especially the electronic gadgets we use on a daily basis. The Eee PC was a refreshing digital breath of fresh air. It is *easy* to use (that's what one of the Es in Eee PC stands for by the way) and almost more of an appliance than a traditional personal computer.

Now I won't kid you. The Eee PC isn't a perfect computer (if such a thing even exists). On most models the keys are small and I certainly wouldn't want to write the great American novel on it (although I did work on this book with the little laptop when I was away from home). Battery life is okay, but not stellar. Xandros, a version of Linux, has its quirks. Hard drive space is limited.

But these are really minor nits, because the Eee PC works incredibly well for what it was designed to be — an affordable, highly-mobile, easy-to-use computer you can use anywhere, inside or outside the home or office.

As you already guessed from the title, this book is about the Eee PC. I tell you everything you need to know about ASUS' Lilliputian wonder; its capabilities, limitations, and how to get the most from it.

Who This Book Is For

If you're browsing through this book at your favorite bookstore right now and are trying to decide whether this book is for you, ask yourself these simple questions:

- ✔ Are you thinking about buying an Eee PC?
- ✔ Have you recently purchased an Eee PC (or lucky you, gotten one as a gift)?
- ✔ Have you owned an Eee PC for a while, but want to get more out of it?

If you answered yes to any of these questions, stop reading and immediately proceed to the cash register because this book is indeed for you. (If you're still not convinced, feel free to continue flipping through the pages to see what I mean.)

Although the user manual that comes with the Eee PC manual covers the basics, it doesn't go into a whole lot of depth (which is perfectly understandable from ASUS' perspective; you don't want a voluminous user manual when you're interested in producing an affordable computer).

With this book I take you beyond the user guide and the online help, expanding on topics and programs, presenting a variety of subjects that aren't covered, and pointing out places to get more information on the Internet. All in the trademarked *For Dummies'* easy-to-read-and-understand style.

When the Eee PC first debuted, it was only available in models that ran a version of the Linux operating system (you could install Windows XP if you had a copy). Now Windows XP comes preinstalled on certain models.

Considering this, *ASUS Eee PC For Dummies* is written especially for the Linux newbie (there's no shame in that, we all had to start to somewhere). The Eee PC is a great computer to get a taste of what Linux is all about. The icon-based Xandros version of Linux that comes installed on the Eee PC is simple to use, and you don't need to worry about any scary command-line prompts that Linux is known for. I step you through using the operating system and installed programs, which is, honestly, a lot like using Windows. If you want to go beyond the icons and menus, I also gently introduce you to some of the more technical aspects of Linux.

Setting Some Expectations

Before getting started, I'd like to set a few expectations about the content you'll be reading, just so we're all on the same page:

- As I just mentioned, the Eee PC comes with either Linux or Microsoft Windows XP. I am not going to take sides (remember those fanboys I mentioned earlier?), but will objectively point out advantages and disadvantages of each operating system.

- Because Windows is so widely known and used, I spend more time discussing the Linux aspects of the Eee PC. If you own or are interested in a Windows model, I do have several chapters devoted to the Microsoft operating system. The chapters on hardware and Internet resources are useful for both operating systems. Even if you're a diehard Windows user, you might be interested in reading the Linux chapters just to see how the other half lives. You might even want to try running Xandros to see what it's like.

- Although I spend a fair amount of time talking about the Linux operating system and applications that come with the Eee PC, this book is not meant to be a manual on how to use Linux. Although I introduce you to the basics of using command-line Linux (which you need to know a little about if you want to go beyond the default Xandros user interface), it's not my goal to turn you into a Linux guru.

How This Book Is Organized

This book is conveniently divided into several different parts. The content in each part tends to be related but, by all means, feel free to skip around and read about what interests you the most.

Part 1: Getting Started with the Eee PC

This part of the book introduces you to the Eee PC. I tell you all about the laptop, describing available models and where to get them, walking you through the default hardware and software, and explaining what the Eee PC is (and more important, what it is not). In addition to descriptions, I also provide you with practical advice on using the Eee PC for the first time, including navigating through the basic user interface and connecting to the Internet and Windows networks.

Part II: Day to Day with the Eee PC

Linux versions of the Eee PC have a simple tabbed desktop user interface. You click a tab and available programs in a category are displayed. The tabs are Internet, Work, Learn, Play, Settings, and Favorites. For example to browse the Web, you click the Internet tab and then click a browser icon. In Part II, I devote chapters to each of the tabs and their associated programs. I describe the programs and give you helpful tips for using them and where to find more information. I close the part with a discussion of Windows XP on the Eee PC, including how it differs from Linux, what comes preinstalled on Windows models, and how to install your own copy of Windows XP on an Eee PC running Linux.

Part III: Adding Software to the Eee PC

After you have a grasp of the basics from the previous sections, you may be interested in installing different software titles on your Eee PC. I'll walk you through the installation basics in the first chapter of Part III. Chapter 13 covers popular Linux programs and how to install them. Chapter 14 is devoted to what I consider the best free Windows programs around (along with a few Eee PC specific utilities).

Part IV: Hardware and Accessories for the Eee PC

With a cutting-edge solid-state drive, 802.11 wireless, an Ethernet jack, and Web cam (on most models), you might think the Eee PC is all ready to go. *Au contraire*. You'll definitely want to expand the storage with SD cards, maybe add a DVD player/writer, perhaps charge the laptop in a car or plane, or connect any number of different peripherals to the USB and VGA ports. Part IV is about add-on Eee PC hardware and accessories, and I discuss everything from adding internal memory to appropriate carrying cases to using solar panels to powering the laptop off the grid.

Part V: Eee PC Advanced Topics

Up to this point in the book, I haven't really gotten all that techy, but in this part I do. Here you find chapters on backing up and restoring the Eee PC, how to install Advanced Desktop mode in Linux (which gives you more of a Windows-like desktop environment), the ins and outs of using the console and the Linux command line, and customizing the Xandros user interface.

Part VI: The Part of Tens

All *For Dummies* books have a part called The Part of Tens, and this one is no exception. In Part VI, you find a chapter devoted to troubleshooting tips and a chapter listing what I consider to be the best Eee PC Web sites, blogs, and forums on the Internet.

Bonus Chapters

In addition to the chapters you have here in the book, there are two bonus chapters on the companion Web site (www.dummies.com/go/asuseee pcfd). The first provides information about installing other Linux distributions on the Eee PC. The second bonus chapter offers a handy collection of power-saving tips to keep your Eee PC going, and going, and . . .

Icons Used in This Book

If you've ever read a *Dummies* book before, you probably know that all sorts of icons are scattered through the book. This one is no different and some of the icons you'll encounter include:

This is just a gentle little reminder about something of importance. Because I can't be there to mention it in person, this icon will have to do.

You can easily use only the programs that come with the Eee PC and be perfectly happy (I'm a self-admitted geek, and after much experimenting, I found myself going back to using the default Easy Mode just like it came out of the box). However, because the Eee PC is running Linux, sometimes technical stuff does creep in. In such cases I'll either give you a plain-English explanation or point you off to a Web site where you can get additional details.

This is good stuff designed to make your life easier; usually gained from practical experience and typically not found in the user guide or online help; or if it is there, it's buried deep in some obscure paragraph.

The little bomb icon signifies some potential bad juju. When you start tinkering with Linux, especially if you don't know what you are doing and just blindly start typing in commands, there's a chance you can mess things up. (The good news is the Eee PC is quick and easy to restore.) When you see the bomb, pay attention! There might be something lurking in the shadows that causes mental, physical, emotional, or monetary suffering of some degree.

When I started writing this book, ASUS only offered a few Eee PC models. But very quickly many more models became available, and with the Eee PC 901, ASUS rolled out their second generation of mini-laptops. The 901 and later models have a few differences compared to their predecessors (first generation models are still valuable by the way, and are great values). When you see this icon, I point out noteworthy differences between newer and older models.

Some Things to Keep in Mind

Before you get going with the rest of the book, and I know you can't wait, I'd like to mention a couple of things:

- ✔ Although this book has a whole lot more information in it than the Eee PC user manual, it's a good idea to read through the manual to get the official ASUS word on things.

- ✔ Linux Eee PCs come bundled with a lot of software. Many of these programs have entire books devoted to their use. My goal is to introduce you to the programs, get you going with them, and show you where to go to get more information.

- ✔ There are lots of references to Web sites in this book. Unfortunately Web sites change just about as fast as the latest celebrity scandals. If for some reason a link doesn't work, you should have enough information to find what you're looking for by using common sense and Google.

- ✔ You're not going to find every Eee PC–compatible program in existence mentioned in the book. I've tried to list and describe many of the more popular programs, but the realities of page-count constraints prevents this book from turning into an encyclopedia. So please don't get upset if I didn't mention a program you use or feel slighted because I ended up talking about one program more than another.

- ✔ When it comes to technology, it's a given that after you commit something to paper it changes. I personally think there's a conspiracy by hardware and software manufacturers to immediately make changes to their products the minute a book or two is published about them. So if what's on your Eee PC screen doesn't match how I describe it a couple of months after this book comes out, remember, it's a conspiracy. I'll take my tinfoil hat off now, thank you.

- ✔ Finally, the Eee PC is a wonderful little computer for kids and adults of all levels of technical proficiency. I've written this book so that if you have an Eee PC, you can easily follow along, doing the things I describe. But don't spend all your time with your nose glued to the book. Use it as a guide to learning about the Eee PC and then, as my mentor told me years ago when I first started working with computers, "Get your fingers dirty on the keyboard." Discover, experiment, and have fun!

Part I

Getting Started with the Eee PC

"I tell him many times — get Eee PC. It lighter and more durable than his laptop. But him think he know better. Him say, 'Me Tarzan, you not!' That when vine break."

In this part . . .

In the fall of 2007, a small laptop appeared on the market that took the world by storm. Manufactured by Asian computer powerhouse ASUS and dubbed the Eee PC, the Lilliputian laptop ushered in a new era of affordable and ultra-mobile personal computing. Go-anywhere, do-anything PCs had been around for years, but ASUS found the just right, magic combination of size, price, and performance; and customers eagerly opened their wallets and purses.

This part introduces you to the Eee PC and explains why the laptop is so popular. You learn all the basics about the Eee PC, including differences between available Linux and Windows XP models, navigating the Linux user interface, and how to get started using the computer. Because the Internet and the Eee PC go together like Bogart and Bacall, I also provide everything you need to know about connecting the laptop to the Net.

Chapter 1

Meet the Eee PC

*T*his chapter introduces you to the ASUS Eee PC. (Eee PC is pronounced with a single E, not multiple EEEs, as in "Eeek, a mouse!") If you're wondering where all those Es came from, it's from a marketing campaign that states the computer is "Easy to learn, easy to work, and easy to play."

In this chapter, I tell you what the Eee PC is — and just as important, what it isn't. I then list available models, describe their specifications, and conclude by giving you tips on selecting and purchasing an Eee PC.

Eee PC: Not Your Average Laptop

The Eee PC (see Figure 1-1) has been called a mini-laptop, a subnotebook, a *Mobile Internet Device* (MID), and a *netbook* (a catchy marketing buzzword for small, Internet-centric laptops). Whatever you call it, the Eee PC is a shrunk-down, lightweight laptop that has these key features:

✔ **Small** — At just a bit over two pounds and roughly the size of this book, the 7-inch and 8.9-inch screen models are designed to be go-anywhere, do-anything personal computers. To fit in such a small package, keys on the Eee PC are smaller than those found on a typical laptop keyboard — right around 83 percent of normal. After you get used to the small size it's possible to touch type with some practice. ASUS also offers several Eee PC models with larger cases (weighing around three pounds) that feature more usable keyboards — around 95 percent of normal size.

To see how the Eee PC compares in size to other laptops, visit a great Web site called sizeasy (http://sizeasy.com) that compares physical dimensions of various products. Do a search for Eee PC.

✔ **Easy to use** — The Eee PC comes with a version of Linux that features a simple Linux user interface — it's great for kids or adults with limited computer experience. Don't let the big icons and child-like appearance fool you, however, because the full Linux operating is available under the hood. Eee PCs with Microsoft Windows XP are also available. (Although it's possible for a user to load her own copy of Vista on an Eee PC, the current models just don't have enough processor horsepower to run Microsoft's latest operating system.)

✔ **Quick power up and shutdown** — With the preinstalled version of Linux, the Eee PC boots up and is ready to use in less than 30 seconds — and shuts down in about half that amount of time. The laptop accomplishes this by doing two things:

• **Using a Solid State Drive (SSD)** — Instead of relying on spinning platters found in standard hard drives, an SSD uses memory to store data. SSDs don't have any mechanical parts — making them more robust and less prone to failure. They start up and power down very quickly, are quiet, and have fast read and write times. SSDs are the wave of the future for laptops, but at present they are more expensive than traditional hard drives. (ASUS has also recently added conventional hard drive models to its mini-laptop line.)

• **Loading a simplified user interface version of Linux** — The simple Linux interface doesn't require very many system resources and loads rapidly. In addition, some processes are still loading in the background when the interface comes up and is ready to use.

✔ **Expandable** — The Eee PC features three USB 2.0 slots, a Secure Digital (SD) card reader, and a VGA video out port. On most models, internal memory can be expanded.

✔ **Internet-enabled** — The Eee PC has an 802.11 b/g wireless card (some models feature 802.11 b/g/n wireless) and an Ethernet jack that makes accessing the Internet a snap.

✔ **Entertainment-ready** — Sound card, built-in speakers, and microphone (as well as jacks for external speakers and microphone), a Web cam (on most models), and a processor and graphics chip capable of playing videos turn the Eee PC into a portable entertainment device.

✔ **Lots of useful, preinstalled software** — The Linux version of the Eee PC comes installed with all the software you need including:

• Open Office

• Firefox (Web browser)

- Thunderbird (e-mail)

- Acrobat Reader (PDF viewer)

- Amarok (a music player)

- Pidgin (an IM client)

- Skype (Internet phone calls)

- MPlayer (a media player)

- A photo manager

- Graphics programs

- Educational programs

- Several utilities

The Windows XP version comes with everything that's normally included with Windows in addition to Microsoft Works, Star Office, and a few other utility programs.

✔ **Affordable** — Even with all its features, the Eee PC is designed to be a low-cost, affordable computer. Depending on its features, models are available from around $250 to $600.

Figure 1-1:
The Eee PC.

Who's ASUS?

Eee PCs are manufactured by ASUS (pro-nounced ah-sooss). ASUSTek (www.asus.com) is a Taiwan-based company that makes computer components, peripherals, cell phones, PDAs, and notebook computers. The firm has been around since 1989, and its name comes from Pegasus, the mythological winged horse. In addition to its own products, the company also produces components for Sony (PlayStation), Apple (iPods and MacBooks), HP, and Compaq.

When you see an Eee PC for the first time, don't let the toy-like appearance of the mini-laptop fool you. This is a real computer, and for the most part it can do just about anything a normal PC can (with a few exceptions, which I discuss later).

Because of its small size and portable nature, the mini-laptop can get a lot of use while on the road or around the house. I find the Eee PC especially useful for the following:

- ✔ Checking and sending e-mail
- ✔ Browsing the Web
- ✔ Watching videos
- ✔ Listening to music
- ✔ Instant messaging and Skyping
- ✔ Working on word processing and spreadsheet documents when away from a primary computer
- ✔ Viewing digital photos
- ✔ Traveling (especially on airplanes, trains, and buses)

Popular Eee PC Misconceptions

If you read the preceding section, you should have a pretty good idea of what the Eee PC is. But how about what it isn't? To set the record straight, I'd like to spend a moment or two discussing popular misconceptions about the mini-laptop. In no particular order, here is what the Eee PC wasn't meant to be:

Eee PC and the OLPC XO

The origins of the Eee PC can be traced to the One Laptop Per Child (OLPC) initiative started by Nicholas Negroponte. OLPC's (`www.laptop.org`) goal was to design an educational laptop that would cost $100 and make it available to children throughout the world; especially those in developing countries. The result was the OLPC XO-1, a technologically advanced Linux mini-laptop with a user interface called Sugar, expressly developed for kids and education.

Unfortunately, the $100 price point has yet to be realized, and various politics have mired down OLPC's ambitions (the project may get a jump start, however, with Microsoft's recent announcement that Windows XP would be available on the XO-1). On a positive note, the OLPC project spurred interest in small, functional, inexpensive laptops, which led to the Eee PC and a growing number of similar computers.

✔ **Your primary computer** — The Eee PC isn't a replacement for your primary desktop PC or laptop. On most Eee PC models, the screen and keyboard size, slower processor, and limited internal storage space pale in comparison to current PCs. Think of the Eee PC as a secondary or accessory laptop versus a primary computer — even new Eee PC models with larger keyboards, screens, and drives are limited by a relatively slow processor (performance of the Intel Celeron and Atom chips are comparable).

✔ **An oversized PDA** — An Eee PC is a real computer. Unlike Palms, Pocket PCs, and smart phones, it can run most Linux and Windows programs.

✔ **Yet another cheap laptop** — I've often heard, "Why buy an Eee PC when I could get a real laptop for the same price or a little more?" Yes, in the same general price range you can buy a cheap, full-size laptop that has a DVD drive, more memory, a real keyboard, a large screen, and more storage. But this is like comparing apples and oranges. The Eee PC is designed to be used in places where lugging around a six pound plus, full-size laptop is a hassle.

✔ **A high-horsepower workstation or gaming machine** — The processor and graphics card inside the Eee PC really don't have enough oomph to play graphics-intensive games or perform tasks such as video editing or complex image rendering.

Eee PC Models

When the Eee PC was first introduced in the fall of 2007, only a handful of models were available. Now a year later, you can choose from over a dozen Eee PC models — and according to the rumor mill, even more are on the way.

ASUS has been incredibly aggressive in announcing and releasing new models, and it can be a little bewildering trying to keep track of them all. To help you sort through what's available, here is a brief overview of all models currently on the market. For quick reference, Table 1-1 provides the basic specifications and prices, and Table 1-2 lists key features by model.

Be sure to check the ASUS Eee PC Web site at `http://eeepc.asus.com` for the latest information on available models and specifications — just in case some new mini-laptops are introduced after this book goes to press.

The prices I list are in U.S. dollars and are current as of the summer of 2008. I wouldn't be surprised to see prices drop because of increased competition in the mini-laptop market. These days, just about everyone is offering his own version of an Eee PC-type laptop.

Eee PC 2G Surf

The Eee PC 2G (as in 2GB for the drive) Surf is the most basic and inexpensive Eee PC. It runs Xandros Linux (check out the "Linux, Xandros, KDE, and Windows" sidebar in Chapter 11 for more information) and comes with a 7-inch screen, a 900 Mhz Celeron processor, 512K of non-expandable RAM, and a small 2GB Solid State Drive. It doesn't have a Web cam and uses a fairly low-capacity battery (expect about 2 hours, 45 minutes of run time). It is available in white, black, blue, green, and pink. Retail price is $299.

ASUS formerly called the Eee PC 2G Surf the 700 model and designated the Eee PC 4G, 4G Surf, and 8G mini-laptops as the 701 models. If you see references to these numbers on the Internet, you'll know what people are talking about.

Eee PC 4G Surf, 4G

These models have the same case, keyboard, screen, and processor (although running at a slightly higher clock speed), as the Eee PC 2G, but offer expanded hardware — at a higher price point. The Eee PC 4G series have socketed RAM — which means memory can be expanded from the default 512K up to 2GB. Multiple colors are available, and you have your choice of either Linux or Windows XP. Models in the series include

- ✔ **Eee PC 4G Surf** — Similar to the 2G Surf, including the low-capacity battery, but with a 4GB Solid State Drive (SSD) and expandable memory.

- ✔ **Eee PC 4G** — 4GB SSD, Web cam, and higher capacity battery with a run time of around 3 hours, 30 minutes. Retail price is $349.

If you see references to an Eee PC 8G model on the Internet, this is a discontinued Eee PC 4G that comes with an 8GB SSD, 1GB RAM, Web cam, and higher-capacity battery.

The Eee PC is like most computers in that advertised hard drive size doesn't mean you have that much storage available out of the box. For example on a Eee PC 4G loaded with Linux, I had around 1.3GB of free space available, with the operating system and installed applications taking up the remainder of the space.

Eee PC 701SD

The Eee PC 701SD has the same specifications as the Eee PC 4G, but comes with an 8GB internal SSD and a 30GB USB external drive. If that's not enough space for you, ASUS also provides 10GB of online storage.

Eee PC 900 series

One of the downsides to Eee PC 2G, 4G, and 701 models is the tiny 7-inch (800-x-480) screen. Sure it's usable, but a little more screen real estate is nice, especially when browsing the Web.

ASUS bumped up the screen size in the 900 Eee PC series. The 900 models have an ever so slightly larger case, but retain most of the same features as the 7-inch screen models (including the small keyboard) with these notable exceptions:

- ✔ An 8.9-inch, 1024-x-600 screen
- ✔ 1GB of RAM
- ✔ Expanded drive space
- ✔ Higher resolution Web cam (1.3 versus .3megapixel found in the 701 series)
- ✔ Larger surface touchpad with MultiTouch support

Three Eee PC 900 series models are available:

- ✔ **Eee PC 900** — This is the base model. It comes with a 4GB primary SSD and a second SSD for storage (20GB for Linux models, 12GB for Windows XP models). Retail prices range from $499 to $549 depending on model.

✔ **Eee PC 900 16G** — This model comes with a single 16GB SSD — initial reports seem to indicate the drive isn't as speedy as the SSD found in the base model 900. Linux and Windows XP models are available, priced around $349.

✔ **Eee PC 900A** — The 900A is a Linux-only Eee PC. It features an energy efficient Intel Atom processor instead of the Celeron processor found in the other 900 series models. 8GB and 16GB of SSD storage are available. It uses a lower-cost .3-megapixel camera. The price of this new model has yet to be released.

Table 1-1			Eee PC Models — Basic Specifications			
Model	**Memory**	**Drive Space**	**Processor**	**Screen**	**OS**	**Price**
2G Surf	512K	2GB SSD	800 MHz Celeron M	7", 800x 480	Linux	$249
4G Surf	512K	4GB SSD	900 MHz Celeron M	7", 800x 480	Linux or Wind- ows XP	$299
4G	512K	4GB SSD	900 MHz Celeron M	7", 800x 480	Linux or Wind- ows XP	$349
701SD	512K	8GB SSD, 30GB exter- nal	900 MHz Celeron M	7", 800x 480	Linux or Wind- ows XP	*
900	1GB	12GB SSD (Wind- ows) 20GB SSD (Linux)	900 MHz Celeron M	8.9", 1024x 600	Linux or Wind- ows XP	$499 to $549
900 16G	1GB	16GB SSD	900 MHz Celeron M	8.9", 1024x 600	Linux or Wind- ows XP	$349
900A	1GB	8 or 16GB SSD	1.6 GHz Intel Atom	8.9", 1024x 600	Linux	*

Model	Memory	Drive Space	Processor	Screen	OS	Price
901	1GB	12GB SSD (Windows)	1.6 GHz Intel Atom	8.9", 1024x 600	Linux or Windows XP	$ 499
		20GB SSD (Linux)				
904HD	1GB (Windows)	80GB HD	900 MHz Celeron M	8.9", 1024x 600	Linux or Windows XP	*
	2GB (Linux)					
1000	1GB	40GB SSD	1.6 GHz Intel Atom	10", 1024x 600	Linux	$599
1000 H	1GB	80GB HD	1.6 GHz Intel Atom	10", 1024x 600	Windows XP	$475
1000 HD	1GB (Windows)	80GB HD	900 MHz Celeron M	10", 1024x 600	Linux or Windows XP	*
	2GB (Linux)					

* ASUS hasn't announced prices for these new models as this book goes to press. See the "Purchasing an Eee PC" section at the end of this chapter for several online retail sites you can check for current prices.

Eee PC 901

Shortly after ASUS released the Eee PC 900 model in late spring of 2008, the company announced the Eee PC 901 (see Figure 1-2). This is a second generation Eee PC with the same basic features as the 900, but with these additions:

- A new case (similar dimensions, but with a more upscale look including metal trim and a redesigned hinge).
- Built-in Bluetooth.

- ✔ 1.6 GHz Intel Atom processor (lower power consumption with roughly the same performance as the 900 MHz Celeron).

- ✔ 802.11b/g/n wireless card (faster speeds, greater range, better connectivity).

- ✔ Improved speakers.

- ✔ Enhanced touchpad.

- ✔ Additional function keys.

- ✔ 20GB of online, Internet storage

- ✔ Power-mode control (Super Hybrid Engine) that allows you to change the processor's speed to increase battery life.

- ✔ High-capacity battery. (Coupled with the Atom chip, expect battery life in the 4.5 to 5 hour range with WiFi on.)

For the extra features of an Eee PC 901, expect to pay around $499.

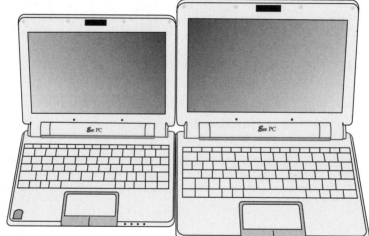

Figure 1-2:
901 (left)
and 1000
(right) model
Eee PCs.

Eee PC 904HD

During the summer of 2008, ASUS announced plans for a new Eee PC that is a cross between the Eee PC 901 and 1000 models — I discuss the 1000 series next. The Eee PC 904 HD is an Intel Celeron-powered laptop that combines the 8.9-inch screen of an Eee PC 901 with the case and larger keyboard of the 1000 series. The mini-laptop comes with an 80GB hard drive and is available in Linux and Windows XP models. A price has yet to be announced.

Eee PC 1000 series

Although the 900/901 models addressed the original Eee PC's small screen size, there was still the issue of the undersized keyboard. For some users, the small keys just didn't work.

Responding to customer demand, ASUS upped the ante again, and during the summer of 2008, it announced the Eee PC 1000 (shown in Figure 1-2 next to an Eee PC 901 for size comparison). This model is similar to the 901, but sports a larger 10-inch screen and a bigger, more usable keyboard (about 92 percent the size of a normal PC keyboard).

The 1000 series departs from the small form factor of the original Eee PC, and enters the mainstream subnotebook realm. These laptops are more expensive than their smaller ASUS siblings, but are still priced considerably less than traditional subnotebooks — just keep in mind they also don't have the performance and features typically found in costlier subnotebooks.

Three 1000 series models are currently available:

- ✔ **Eee PC 1000** — This is the top-of-the-line Linux-only model that comes with a 40GB Solid State Drive. With the larger screen and same size battery, expect run time to be a bit less than the 901. It's priced at $599.

- ✔ **Eee PC 1000 H** — The H stands for hard drive and this was the first Eee PC to come with a traditional hard drive — 80GB to be precise. It's cheaper than the Eee PC 1000 model with the Solid State Drive, is a little heavier, and only comes with Window XP or Linux preinstalled.

- ✔ **Eee PC 1000 HD** — The third model in the 1000 series is called the 1000 HD. It's just like the 1000 H with an 80GB hard drive, but instead of an Atom processor, it uses a 900 MHz Celeron CPU (and an 802.11 b/g instead of b/g/n wireless card). Battery life isn't as long, but the less-expensive hardware components mean a lower retail price.

Eee PCs come in a variety of colors including basic black (ASUS calls it Galaxy black) and a Macintosh-inspired white. Hues of blue, green, pink, and purple are available with some models. Unlike other laptops, your choice of color doesn't influence the price; although some colors tend to be more available than others.

Table 1-2 Eee PC Models — More Specifications

Model	Cam	Wireless	BT*	Larger Keyboard	Battery	Weight	Dimensions
2G Surf	None	802.11 b/g	No	No	4 cell, 4,400 mAh	2.04 lbs.	8.9" × 6.5" × 1.4"
4G Surf	None	802.11 b/g	No	No	4 cell, 4,400 mAh	2.04 lbs.	8.9" × 6.5" × 1.4"
4G	.3 MP	802.11 b/g	No	No	4 cell, 4,400 or 5,200 mAh	2.04 lbs.	8.9" × 6.5" × 1.4"
701SD	.3 MP	802.11 b/g	No	No	4 cell, 4,400 mAh	1.99 lbs.	8.9" × 6.5" × 1.4"
900	1.3 MP	802.11 b/g	No	No	4 cell, 4,400 mAh	2.19 lbs.	8.9" × 6.7" × 1.3"
900 16G	1.3 MP	802.11 b/g	No	No	4 cell, 4,400 mAh	2.19 lbs.	8.9" × 6.7" × 1.3"
900A	.3 MP	802.11 b/g	No	No	4 cell, 4,400 mAh	2.19 lbs.	8.9" × 6.7" × 1.3"
901	1.3 MP	802.11 b/g/n	Yes	No	6 cell, 6,600 mAh	2.43 lbs.	8.9" × 6.7" × 1.3"
904HD	.3 MP	802.11 b/g	No	Yes	6 cell, 6,600 mAh	3.09 lbs.	10.5" × 7.5" × 1.5"
1000	1.3 MP	802.11 b/g/n	Yes	Yes	6 cell, 6,600 mAh	3.2 lbs.	10.5" × 7.5" × 1.5"
1000 H	1.3 MP	802.11 b/g/n	Yes	Yes	6 cell, 6,600 mAh	3.2 lbs.	10.5" × 7.5" × 1.5"
1000 HD	1.3 MP	802.11 b/g	Yes	Yes	6 cell, 6,600 mAh	2.94 lbs.	10.5" × 7.5" × 1.5"

*BT = Bluetooth

Selecting an Eee PC

With the wide array of available models, if you're interested in an Eee PC, all the choices can leave you a little bewildered.

My first suggestion is to review Tables 1-1 and 1-2 to get a handle on features and specifications of different models. Figure out which features are important to you and narrow down your list from there.

If you're still feeling overwhelmed, here are some general suggestions for selecting an ASUS mini-laptop based on who will be using it:

- **Children** — The Eee PC 2G and 4G models make a great introductory computer for kids. They're relatively inexpensive and are fairly immune to minor bumps and drops. The smaller keyboard is perfect for little hands.

- **Students** — The first generation Eee PC 4G is still popular with students because of its small size and low price. If your budget allows, I'd look at the Eee PC 901 (or another model that uses the Atom processor), because of its longer battery life and bigger screen — Bluetooth is also a plus if you've got a compatible cell phone. Second choice would be the lower-priced Eee PC 900 model.

- **Business people** — The Eee PC 1000 series and the Eee PC 904HD offer more usably sized keyboards and screens. Keep in mind that with these models you're trading away size and portability — refer to Figure 1-2 to see the difference between the Eee PC 1000 and 901 models. If you want small, opt for an Eee PC 901. Go for an Atom processor for increased battery life.

- **Home computer users** — The Eee PC is a great second computer. If you have a wireless access point at home, the Eee PC's light weight and size make it perfect for accessing the Internet anywhere you want — kitchen, patio, bedroom, wherever. It's also convenient to toss in a bag or purse when you head to the coffee shop. If you're on a tight budget, I'd recommend an Eee PC 4G, followed by a Eee PC 900 or 901 if you have a little more to spend — the larger screen is better for browsing. If you don't mind a bigger case, an Eee PC 904HD offers a more usable keyboard.

- **Senior citizens** — For seniors I recommend an 8.9-inch or 10-inch screen model — they're much easier on the eyes. A larger keyboard might be a plus, depending on the person. If you're going to be using the mini-laptop mostly around home, you can opt for a lower-priced model with a Celeron processor because a power outlet is always nearby.

✔ **Techies** — Take your pick — depending on how much you've got to spend in your wallet or purse. The Eee PC's hardware and software both lend themselves to tinkering and customization.

You'll still need to decide whether you should get a model that runs Linux or Windows XP. I offer some advice on that decision in Chapter 11.

Purchasing an Eee PC

If you've made up your mind that you want an Eee PC, and are all set to buy a mini-laptop, where should you go to get one? You've got a few options.

The easiest way is to have your credit card ready and use the Internet. Eee PCs can be purchased from a number of large online retailers, including the following:

✔ **Amazon** — www.amazon.com

✔ **NewEgg** — www.newegg.com

✔ **Buy.com** — www.buy.com

If you want to check out an Eee PC in person before purchasing, your options are bit more limited. As of yet, ASUS doesn't have an extensive retail distribution network and, depending on where you're located, it may be tough to find an Eee PC for a hands-on evaluation. Larger retailers such as Best Buy (www.bestbuy.com) may stock the mini-laptop, but check around.

Before you buy, I'd suggest using Google to search for other local or online retailers that carry the Eee PC.

Almost a year after the release of the Eee PC, because of their extreme popularity, a fire in a manufacturing facility that makes batteries for ASUS, and a shortage of Atom processors, the diminutive laptops can be scarce in certain markets. Internet retailers frequently sell out quickly and waiting lists are common. With a tight supply and big demand, don't expect to find below-retail bargains. That may be changing in the very near future though. The surprise popularity of the Eee PC has caused just about everyone and their brother to start offering their own mini-laptop models. Competition is already starting to drive prices down and likely will into the future.

Chapter 2

First Steps with the Eee PC

In this chapter, I tell you everything you need to know about getting your Eee PC up and running. I begin with turning on the mini-laptop for the first time, and then I give you some details about using the touchpad — even if you're an experienced laptop user, skim through this section to see how the Eee PC's touchpad may be different from your other laptop.

Eee PCs are available with either Linux or Microsoft Windows XP operating systems installed. Because Windows is much more widely known and used than the version of Linux used on the mini-laptop (a custom version of a product known as Xandros), I spend some time bringing you up to speed on the fundamentals of using a Linux Eee PC. The Linux interface is very easy to use, but it's different enough from Windows to warrant a bit of discussion and explanation.

(If you have an Eee PC that runs Windows XP or are planning to purchase one, feel free to skip the section on Linux. Or better yet skim through it — you may decide you want to install Linux on your mini-laptop to give it a try.)

Because I start with turning on the Eee PC, it makes sense to conclude the chapter with turning off the mini-laptop — specifically the ins and outs of shutting down.

Powering On for the First Time

There's a little more to turning on your Eee PC for the first time than simply pressing the power button. Read on as I explain.

Charging the battery

If you just got a new Eee PC, I'm sure you're eager to use it. But before powering on your Eee PC for the first time, I recommend you fully charge your mini-laptop's battery. That means

1. **Make sure the battery is properly inserted into the mini-laptop.**

2. **Plug the power supply into a wall socket.**

The power supply that comes with the 900, 901, and 1000 models outputs a higher voltage than the 7-inch screen models. Do not use these power supplies with an Eee PC 2G, 4G or 8G. It's easy to tell the power supplies apart because the 900/901/1000 models use a cord that detaches from the power supply.

3. **Plug the power supply adapter into the Eee PC.**

The Eee PC is rated to handle between 100 to 120 and 220 to 240 volts of AC (alternating current). That means you can use the computer almost anywhere in the world where you can get electricity from a wall socket. Depending on where you travel, you may need to purchase an inexpensive adapter so the plug fits the socket-type correctly.

4. **Wait until the orange battery status light goes out.**

No light means the battery is fully charged. Depending on the battery's discharge state, this can take up to two hours (or longer for newer Eee PC models such as the 901 and 1000 which have larger capacity batteries).

Status LED lights

On the right corner of the Eee PC are four LED status lights. Ordered from left to right, they are

- **Power** — When the green light is glowing, the Eee PC is turned on. If the light is blinking, the Eee PC is in standby mode.

- **Battery** — When the Eee PC is turned on, the orange battery status light has three states:

  - **On** — The battery is charging.

  - **Off** — The battery is fully charged.

  - **Flashing** — The battery has less than 10 percent life remaining. Time to find a power outlet!

- **Drive** — Whenever there's drive activity, this light flashes.

- **Wireless** — When the internal wireless card is turned on, so is this blue light.

If you're impatient and can't wait to use your new laptop, you won't hurt your Eee PC if you don't initially top off the battery. It's just good practice to do this with any battery-powered device, however, and it helps prolong overall battery life.

When the Eee PC is plugged into a wall socket, the USB ports are powered even if the computer is turned off. This means you can use the Eee PC to charge your USB devices (such as MP3 players) even when the laptop isn't turned on.

Powering on

After the battery is charged, open up the Eee PC's lid, and press the power button to turn it on.

The first time you run your Eee PC, you are greeted with a series of setup screens. Setup is obviously different depending on whether you're running Linux or Windows, but generally it works the same. You are prompted for information such as which nationality keyboard you'll be using, a user account name and password, your time zone, and other settings. After setup is done, your mini-laptop is ready to use.

Although Linux is a multiuser operating system, the version of Linux that comes installed on the Eee PC only supports creating a single-user account. However, running Windows XP allows you to create multiple user accounts.

Touchpad Basics

Using the touchpad on an Eee PC is just like using any other laptop. In the following section, however, I cover the 900/901/1000 models, which are a bit different.

On the Eee PC 2G, 4G, and 8G, the silver bar directly below the touchpad (the recessed rectangular area below the keyboard) is the mouse button. Although it looks like only a single button, there are actually two.

- ✔ Click the left side of the bar to left-click the mouse button.
- ✔ Click the right side of the bar to right-click the mouse button.

The 900/901/1000 models have two distinct mouse buttons like most laptops.

Multi-touch

The Eee PC 900/901/1000 models have a larger touchpad that supports a feature called *multi-touch*.

Multi-touch lets you use two fingers at the same time to navigate the screen. It's the same technology found in Apple's iPhone, iPod touch, MacBook Air, and Pro products.

Multi-touch is pretty cool state-of-the-art technology. In Linux programs like OpenOffice Writer and Impress (and various Windows applications), you can zoom out by placing two fingers on the touchpad and moving them apart — pinch them together to zoom in. You can also scroll windows by placing both fingers together on the touchpad and then together dragging them up or down.

Most programs support two-finger scrolling, but not all programs support finger zooming.

If the mouse buttons feel a little stiff and clunky, you may prefer to use the touchpad, which supports tapping (a tap on the touchpad is treated as a mouse click). I discuss configuring the touchpad on a Linux Eee PC for tapping in Chapter 9. In Windows, you can change touchpad settings in the Control Panel.

If you've never used a touchpad before, read on. Experienced laptop users, feel free to skip the first part of this section. However, if you have a 900/901/1000 model, read about some important differences in the "Multi-touch" sidebar.

The touchpad is the recessed rectangle below the keyboard. It's the laptop version of a mouse.

Lightly drag your finger (whichever one feels the most natural) across the touchpad surface to move the onscreen cursor. Drag to the right, the cursor moves right. Drag up, the cursor goes up. You get it.

To move the cursor more than a short distance, simply lift your finger when it starts to go off the touchpad, put it back down on the touchpad, and drag again. Repeat until the cursor is where you want it to be.

The touchpad has what looks like a blunt sewing needle printed on its right side. This is a visual clue that the touchpad supports scrolling. That means if you drag in the touchpad scrolling area, you can control programs that display a vertical scrollbar. Drag up to scroll up. Drag down to scroll down.

You can change many touchpad settings, including sensitivity and whether tapping and scrolling are enabled. Check out Chapter 9 if you have a Linux Eee PC or with Windows, use the Control Panel to change settings.

If you're so inclined, you can always plug a USB mouse into the Eee PC (a Bluetooth mouse if the model supports it) and use it instead of the touchpad.

In addition to the touchpad, quite obviously you can use the keyboard. Check out the cheat sheet in the front of the book for a list of all Eee PC function keys and what they do.

Using a Linux Eee PC

When you turn on a Linux Eee PC for the first time, you undoubtedly think, "This sure isn't Windows."

Linux Eee PCs run a customized version of Xandros — which features a tabbed desktop user interface as shown in Figure 2-1. Unlike Windows, where you can copy, paste, and move desktop icons around, the icons in the Linux desktop are fixed.

The Eee PC Linux desktop interface is known as Easy Mode — the interface is built on the IceWM window manager. Technically it's not really a true desktop, since a tab window is always displayed. By default, you don't have much control over customizing the interface as you do with Windows. This really isn't a downside because it makes the Eee PC an easy-to-use computing appliance. If you want to tinker though, I describe some advanced techniques for customizing the interface in Chapter 21.

Figure 2-1:
Linux Eee
PC desktop.

Reviewing the tabs

There are six tabs at the top of the desktop window. When you click a tab, it displays program icons associated with the tab's label. The tabs include the following:

- ✔ **Internet** — Programs for connecting to and accessing the Internet, including applications for Web browsing, e-mail, instant messaging, and making online phone calls.

- ✔ **Work** — Work-related programs including a word processor, spreadsheet, presentation application, PDF reader, file manager, and accessories.

- ✔ **Learn** — A collection of educational applications including several graphics editors.

- ✔ **Play** — This tab contains a media player, music player, photo manager, Web cam and sound-recording utilities, and popular desktop games.

- ✔ **Settings** — The Settings tab has, you guessed it, programs for changing various Eee PC settings.

- ✔ **Favorites** — The last tab is Favorites. Here you add shortcuts to any of the Eee PC programs. It's a convenient place to keep links to all the programs you frequently use.

In Part II, I devote chapters to each of the tabs, describing programs and giving you tips for using them.

Although the Eee PC Linux desktop is easy to use, it's not Windows — which is probably the system you already have experience with. Be patient as you come up to speed. Learning a new operating system and user interface doesn't happen overnight.

Navigating the tabs and running programs

Navigating through the Linux desktop tabs is simple. Click a tab to show the programs associated with it. For example, Figure 2-2 shows programs on the Work tab. The tab that's currently selected is highlighted.

To run a program inside a tab, follow these steps:

1. **Move the cursor over a program icon.**

   A highlighted rectangle appears around the icon.

2. **Left-click the selected icon.**

   Just once, please. You don't double-click as you do in Windows.

You can also press the Enter key to run a highlighted program.

The program window appears on top of the desktop. The program name appears at the bottom of the screen in the taskbar — more about the taskbar coming up.

Hold down Alt+Tab to display all the currently running programs. While continuing to hold the Alt key down, press Tab to scroll through the programs. When you release Alt+Tab, the selected program is brought to the front.

Some icons in the desktop tabs are directories, even though they aren't depicted as folders — for example Accessories in the Work tab. You open a directory just as you run a program, by single-clicking. An open directory is shown in Figure 2-3.

Directories and *folders* are the same thing. Some longtime Linux users will use the term *directories* (since the operating system is command-line based and lacks file system icons). Other users refer to *folders* — popularized by modern graphical user interface operating systems. Either term is acceptable in talking about where you store a group of files.

You can always tell you're inside a directory because, to the right above the program icons, is a button with an arrow. Click the button to go back to the tab you were previously viewing.

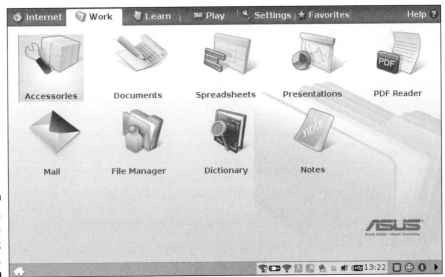

Figure 2-2:
Linux Eee
PC Work
tab.

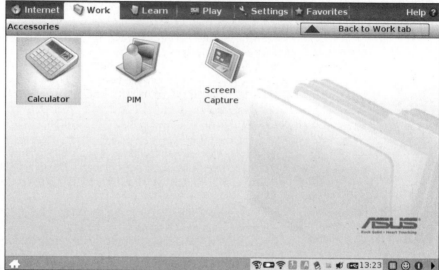

Navigating program windows and menus

After you start running programs, you'll find the Eee PC's Linux user interface is very similar to Microsoft Windows. Generally, here's how things work:

- ✔ Minimize, Maximize, and Close buttons for windows look and function the same way.

- ✔ You can resize some windows by dragging the bottom right-hand corner.

- ✔ Horizontal and vertical scroll bars look and behave the same.

- ✔ Dialog box controls work the same — you can tab through controls and use the spacebar and Enter keys to select and execute controls.

- ✔ Menus appear and work similarly — including keyboard shortcuts such as invoking a menu by holding down the Alt key and typing the underlined letter of a menu item.

Probably the biggest difference is the visual appearance of windows, controls, dialog boxes, fonts, and icons. Although everything looks familiar, it's just different enough to let you know you're not using a Microsoft operating system.

A few Linux programs have quirky user interfaces; but for the most part, if you're comfortable using Windows you shouldn't have any trouble using a Linux Eee PC.

Where's the button?

At times you may encounter a Linux program that displays a window that extends off the screen — usually it's a dialog box. This can be a problem if there are buttons or other controls you need to use but can't see or click them, and there doesn't seem to be any way to move the window up.

There's a little trick you should know. Here's what to do:

1. **Hold down the Alt key and click the left-mouse button. The cursor turns into a cross with four arrows.**

2. **While continuing to hold down Alt and the left-mouse button with one hand, use your other hand use to drag the window up with the touchpad.**

3. **After you get to the bottom of the window, release Alt and the left-mouse button.**

You can now click the button or control that previously appeared offscreen.

Using the taskbar

At the bottom of the Linux desktop is the taskbar (as shown in Figure 2-4).

The taskbar contains information about your Eee PC including running programs, network connections, keyboard caps and number lock status, speaker volume, and time. In addition, you can use the taskbar to switch between open programs.

The taskbar is always shown unless you choose to hide it. I discuss this in a minute.

Move the cursor over a taskbar icon to get to more information about it. For example, if you have a USB thumb drive inserted, placing the cursor over the USB icon displays pop-up information that shows how much free space is on the device.

Figure 2-4:
Linux Eee PC desktop taskbar.

Items that are shown in the task bar include the following:

Home

The icon at the left of taskbar that looks like a house is Home. Click it to show the desktop. (You can also press the key with a house on it to bring the desktop to the front.)

Running programs

Whenever you run a program, its icon and name (or the name in the program's window title) appears in the taskbar. Click a program in the taskbar to bring it to the front.

You can also right-click a program in the taskbar to bring up a pop-up menu and close the program.

Status icons

To the right of any running programs in the taskbar are a series of status icons. Some status icons may be added to the taskbar and the order of icons changes. For example, the SD card icon appears only when you have an SD card inserted.

Status icons include

- ✔ **Wireless** — Click the Wireless icon (it looks like radio waves with a wrench) to display a window with available access points. Access point names, whether or not they use encryption, and signal strength are shown. (I talk more about wireless connections in Chapter 3.)

- ✔ **Power** — When you are running on batteries, a battery icon with white bars is displayed. Four bars indicate a full battery — the number of bars decreases as your battery discharges. When the power supply is plugged in, the icon changes to a power cord.

  Move the cursor over the battery icon to see how much battery life you have left. Numbers are rounded to the nearest 10 percent. The Eee PC provides several warnings before your battery completely discharges.

- ✔ **Network Connection** — There are three network status icons:

  - • If you're connected to a wireless access point, a radio waves icon appears.

  - • If you're connected to the Internet with an Ethernet cable, an icon with two PCs is displayed.

  - • If you're not connected to a network, an icon with two PCs and a red and white X is shown.

  Click the Network icon to display the Network Connections dialog box. I discuss connecting to the Internet in Chapter 3.

✔ **Num Lk** — When you press the Num Lk (Numbers Lock) key, the square icon with a number 1 in the center turns green. When Numbers Lock is turned off, the icon is dimmed to gray.

✔ **Caps Lock** — When you press the Caps Lock key, the square icon with an A in the center turns green. When Caps Lock is off the icon is dimmed.

If you're having problems correctly entering a password, always check whether the Caps Lock is turned on.

✔ **SD card** — If you have an SD or MMC card inserted in the card reader, a blue icon that looks like an SD card displays.

To avoid losing data, whenever you eject an SD or MMC card, right-click this taskbar icon and select the Safely Remove menu item.

✔ **Input method** — This icon is for controlling the Smart Common Input Method (SCIM) — a way to change input for the Eee PC based on different languages. (Depending on the model and the market the Eee PC was sold in, this icon may or may not be present.) Unless you're switching between English and Chinese, you shouldn't need this program.

✔ **Volume** — Single right-click the speaker icon to change speaker and microphone settings including volume, balance, and muting. The icon has a red slash through it when the volume is muted.

✔ **USB device** — When you insert a USB device, such as a thumb drive, a USB icon is displayed. Up to three icons may appear depending on how many devices you have plugged in at once. Move the cursor over an icon to get a short description of the device.

Just as you do with an SD card, whenever you unplug a USB device, right-click the taskbar icon and select Safely Remove.

✔ **Programs** — Some programs may insert an icon in the taskbar when they are running — instead of appearing to right of the Home icon. For example, Notes adds an icon that looks like a sticky note. Right-click a program icon to display a pop-up menu of commands.

✔ **Time** — The current system time is displayed in 24-hour format.

There's not a quick way to change the clock setting to AM/PM. However in Chapter 21, I tell you about techniques for modifying the taskbar — including changing the time format.

Task Manager

The green square icon to the right of the time is the Task Manager — if you move the cursor over it, the letters SOS appear. The Task Manager (shown in Figure 2-5) shows all processes — a process is a program or piece of code that's running.

You can select a process and stop it with the Kill button. This is useful if a program is hung and you can't exit out of it.

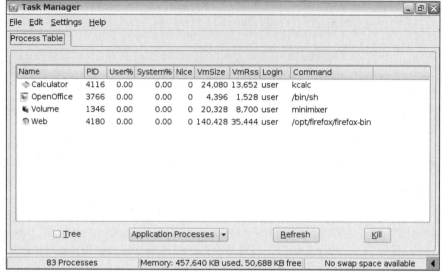

Figure 2-5:
The Task
Manager
displays
running
processes.

Be careful killing processes. If you stop a system process without knowing what you're doing, you may be forced to restart your Eee PC.

Tips

Clicking the yellow smiley face icon opens the Web browser and displays a collection of Eee PC tips and tricks. Although it's a relatively short list, it's worth reading.

Shutting down

Click the taskbar's Shut Down icon (it's a red circle to the right of the smiley face) to shut down your Eee PC. I tell you more about this in the upcoming "Powering Down" section.

Hiding and showing the task bar

The last item on the far-right side of the taskbar is a right-facing arrow icon. This icon lets you hide and show the taskbar — with the Eee PC's small screen, every bit of real estate can count.

- ✔ Click the arrow to hide the taskbar. The arrow icon still appears, but now it points left.
- ✔ Click the arrow again to show the taskbar. The arrow goes back to pointing right.

Powering Down

Using your Eee PC is a lot of fun, but at some point you must turn it off. Here's what you need to know, depending if you're running Linux or Windows.

Linux

If you have a Linux Eee PC, click the Shut Down icon in the taskbar — it's the red circle at the far right. A window is displayed with five options (as shown in Figure 2-6).

Pressing the power button once is the same as clicking the Shut Down icon. However, see the following warning about pressing the button too long.

The options are as follows:

- ✔ **Task Manager** — Runs the Task Manager.
- ✔ **Standby** — Puts the laptop in standby mode — the screen goes black, power is reduced, and memory is written to the drive. Press the power button to come out of standby and resume using the Eee PC.

  When you close your Eee PC's lid and it's powered on, you also put the laptop into standby mode.
- ✔ **Restart** — Shuts the Eee PC down and then restarts it, just as you turned it off and then powered it back up again.
- ✔ **Shut Down** — Turns the Eee PC off.
- ✔ **Cancel** — Click Cancel in case you changed your mind and want to continue using the laptop. The Shut Down window closes.

Windows

If you're running Windows XP, click the Start button and select Turn Off Computer.

On both Linux and Windows Eee PCs, if you press and hold the power button for several seconds, your mini-laptop turns off. I don't recommend this because the system won't have a chance to perform normal housekeeping tasks associated with shutting down. You likely won't hurt your Eee PC, but you may lose data.

Figure 2-6:
Linux
shutdown
options.

Chapter 3

Getting Connected with the Eee PC

· ·

In This Chapter

▶ Connecting to the Internet

▶ Managing wired and wireless connections

▶ Finding your MAC address

▶ Using the Network Connection Wizard

▶ Integrating a Linux Eee PC into a Windows network

· ·

*W*ith a built-in wireless card, wired Ethernet adaptor, and preinstalled networking software, the Eee PC is ready to connect to the Internet and local area networks.

In this chapter I tell you the ins and outs of getting connected with the Eee PC (I focus primarily on Linux models). I show you how to set up wired and wireless Internet connections, how to manage connections to networks, and how to connect to a Windows network so you can share files, folders, and printers.

Connecting to the Internet

Probably, one of the first things you want to do with your Eee PC is connect to the Internet (I discuss Internet-related programs that come bundled with the Linux Eee PC in Chapter 4).

You have two options: Connect wirelessly with the mini-laptop's 802.11 WiFi card; or go the old-fashioned wired way, and plug a cable into the Eee PC's 10/100 Mbps Ethernet adapter.

Wireless connections

Anytime you want to get a wireless Internet connection, the first thing you do is glance down to see if the blue LED light on your powered-on Eee PC is illuminated. If it's not, that means the wireless card is turned off. To turn it on, press Fn+F2.

With that small gotcha out of the way, here is how to find and connect to a wireless access point.

Finding access points

To get a wireless Internet connection, you need to be in range of a wireless access point. To view available access points and networks, click the Wireless Networks icon in the desktop's Internet tab.

You can also click the taskbar icon that looks like a wrench on top of radio waves.

This runs a program that displays visible wireless access points, as shown in Figure 3-1.

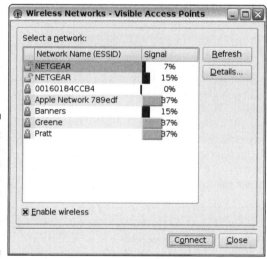

Figure 3-1: The Wireless Networks utility shows visible wireless access points.

For each access point, the following information is provided:

- **Security** — A lock icon indicates whether the access point is secured. An unlocked icon means the network is open and anyone can connect to it. A locked icon indicates the network is encrypted with WEP or WPA (two standard wireless security options) and a password is required to connect.

- **Network Name** — The name of the wireless network (by the way, ESSID stands for Extended Service Set ID, which is what the network name is officially called).

- **Signal** — The strength of the access point signal, shown with a bar and a numeric percentage value. Obviously, the stronger the signal, the better the possible connection.

You can get additional information about an access point by selecting it in the list and clicking the Details button.

Available networks and signal strength don't automatically update if you move your Eee PC. You must click the Refresh button to get the most current information about access points.

Connecting to an access point

To connect to an Internet access point, run the Wireless Networks program, and follow these steps:

1. **Select an available access point from the list.**

2. **Click the Connect button.**

3. **If the access point is secured, specify the encryption type and provide a password.**

A dialog box with status information is displayed while a connection is made. The dialog box closes after successfully connecting.

If the dialog box continues to be displayed (often Pending status is reported), the connection failed. This could result from an incorrect password or occur for other reasons. Click the Details button to view a log of detailed status messages.

The Eee PC can have difficulties connecting to wireless access points secured with WPA encryption if the password includes spaces or special characters. If you have trouble connecting to a WPA-secured access point, try changing the password so only letters and numbers are used.

If you continue to have troubles connecting, refer to Chapter 22 where I present some tips for troubleshooting problematic wireless connections.

Automatically connecting

If you want a wireless connection (let's say, one you frequently use at home) to automatically start when you boot your Eee PC, here's what you need to do:

1. **In the Linux desktop Internet tab, click Network.**

2. **Select the wireless connection in the Network Connections dialog box.**

3. **Click the Properties button below the list of connections.**

4. **In the Connection Properties dialog box, select On Boot in the Start mode drop-down list (as shown later in Figure 3-4).**

5. **Click OK.**

The next time you turn on your Eee PC, it automatically connects to the selected network.

If your connection doesn't automatically start, run the Network program, select the wireless network, and click the Connection button to manually connect. Once connected, click the Properties button and change the Start mode drop-down list item to On Boot. If you're connecting to multiple networks, sometimes the settings confuse the Eee PC, causing this problem. If you continue to have problems, try deleting a connection and creating a new one. I talk about this in the upcoming section "Managing Your Connections."

Ethernet cable connections

The other alternative for connecting your Eee PC to the Net is to use a cable (this method is faster than wireless, if you have a choice). You need an Ethernet cable (look for a Category 5, also known as CAT 5, cable) and a router/switch or network wall outlet to plug into. (I always carry a short length of CAT 5 cable with me while on the road with my Eee PC, just in case I have the option of a wired connection.)

If you have an active wireless connection, I suggest disconnecting before you connect with a cable. Although it's possible to have two simultaneous Internet connections, this can potentially lead to network glitches.

By default, the Eee PC assumes you are connecting to a network that uses dynamically assigned IP addresses (DHCP or Dynamic Host Configuration Protocol). That means you shouldn't have to do anything, just plug the cable in and voilà, an instant, high-speed Internet connection.

If you're connecting to a network that doesn't automatically assign an IP address, read the section "Using the Network Connection Wizard" later in this chapter. It covers connecting to a network that uses static IP addresses.

Managing Your Connections

Information about your connections, both past and present, can be found with the Network Connections utility. You use this program to manage your connections.

To run Network Connections, do the following:

1. **In the desktop Internet tab, click the Network icon.**

   You can also click the Network icon in the Linux desktop taskbar to run the program.

2. **The Network Connections window opens, as shown in Figure 3-2. You can now see information for the following:**

- **Connection Name** — The name you've given a connection, such as the wireless network name.

- **Type** — Whether the connection is wireless, dial-up, or local area network (LAN). An icon representing the network type is also displayed.

- **Status** — The status of the connection, such as enabled disconnected, or pending. (Pending means the Eee PC is waiting for something to complete the connection.)

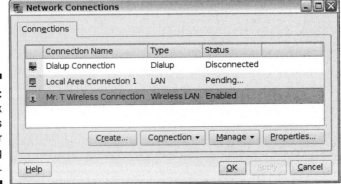

Figure 3-2:
Network
Connections
utility for
managing
connections.

Connecting and disconnecting

To connect, disconnect, or reconnect, follow these steps:

1. **Select the connection (such as a wireless access point).**

2. **Click the Connection button, which displays a drop-down list where you can go to connect, disconnect, or reconnect.**

Certain commands may not be available depending on the connection status. For example if a selected connection is enabled, the Connect item in the drop-down list is dimmed and can't be chosen.

A dialog box displays with status information. Click the Details button as the network connects or disconnects to view detailed messages as shown in Figure 3-3.

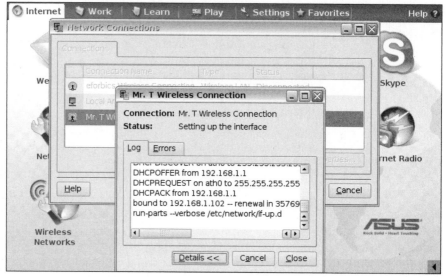

Figure 3-3:
Detailed
status
information
is shown
while a
network
connects.

After you've connected to a wireless access point, instead of using the Wireless Networks program to connect to the access point in the future, use the Network program in the Linux desktop Internet tab. Each time you connect to a network, the settings information is stored in the Network Connections list. Wireless Networks is more of a tool for discovering and initially connecting to access points.

Deleting, renaming, and copying

Clicking the Manage button gives you three options for a selected connection:

✔ **Delete** — Delete removes the connection from the list. If the connection is enabled, you must first disconnect it. Use this button for cleaning up the list by removing connections you previously made — for example, while traveling.

✔ **Rename** — Rename enables you to give the selected connection a new name. Type the name in the Connections list and click Another Connection to save the new name.

✔ **Make Copy** — This option makes a copy of the connection settings under a different name that you provide. The new connection appears in the Connections list. This is handy for duplicating an existing connection for editing, instead of using the Network Connection Wizard (which I discuss later in this chapter).

Getting and setting information

To get information about a connection, as well as to change some of its settings, follow these steps:

1. **Select the connection from the list.**

2. **Click the Properties button.**

   A tabbed, window labeled Connection Properties is displayed as shown in Figure 3-4.

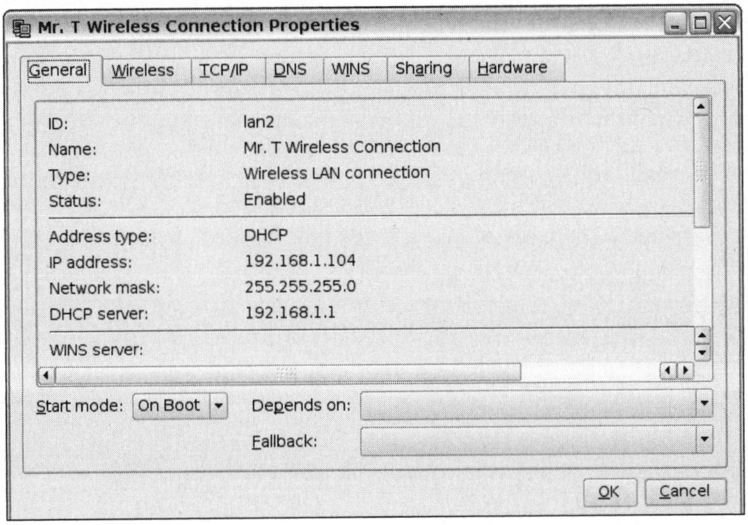

Figure 3-4:
Properties
window of
a wireless
connection.

Here in the Properties window, you get information about a connection and can edit various settings. (Be sure to first disconnect from the connection before making any changes.)

Click the tabs to view and set different types of information. A few of the tabs may be different depending on the type of connection you selected. For example, a wireless connection has a Wireless tab, whereas a LAN connection does not.

Finding Your MAC Address

All network adaptors have a unique identifier called a Media Access Control (MAC) address. The MAC address is composed of six groups of two-digit hexadecimal numbers. An example looks like this: *01-23-45-67-89-ab*.

The first six digits are a vendor code identifying the manufacturer that made the network adaptor. The remaining digits identify the adaptor (no two network adaptors have the same MAC address — although it is possible to temporarily change a MAC address with software so it matches another network adaptor's address). If you know a MAC address and want to look up the manufacturer, check out this Web site: `http://coffer.com/mac_find/`.

When you configure security settings on a wireless access point, it's possible to use something called MAC address authentication. This means you provide a list of MAC addresses for the computers that you want to have access to the wireless network. Computers with MAC addresses not on the list won't be able to get a wireless connection.

This isn't necessarily bulletproof security because anyone who knows the MAC address of one of the trusted computers can change the MAC address of his own laptop to match it (called *spoofing*). With a wireless sniffer, it's easy to view the MAC addresses of computers currently connected to an access point.

If you need to know the MAC address of your Eee PC, follow these steps:

1. **On the Linux desktop Settings tab, click Diagnostic Tools.**

2. **Click the Details button.**

3. **Select Ethernet in System Information.**

The MAC addresses for both the wireless card (*wifi0*) and wired Ethernet adaptor (*eth0*) are displayed as shown in Figure 3-5. Notice there's a device named *ath0* that has the same MAC address as *wifi0*. This is the physical wireless card, which is an Atheros-based card, thus *ath0*.

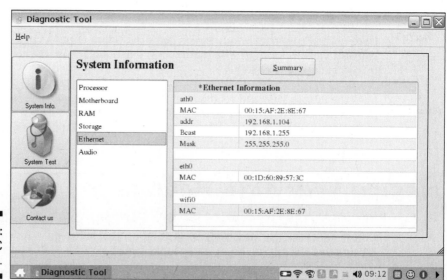

Figure 3-5:
Eee PC MAC addresses.

You can also find out your MAC address using the Linux console (which I thoroughly describe in Chapter 20) and this command: `sudo ifconfig -a`.

Using the Network Connection Wizard

Up until now, I've been discussing how to access networks that are immediately available. But what if you want to set up a connection to a network you currently don't have access to? Or perhaps you have a USB modem and need to set up a connection to a dial-up account? Or you're dealing with a network that doesn't dynamically assign IP addresses?

Your solution is to use the Eee PC's Connection Wizard. Here's how:

1. **On the Linux desktop Internet tab, click the Network icon.**

2. **Click the Create button.**

   This runs the Connection Wizard as shown in Figure 3-6.

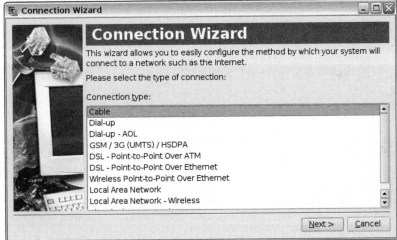

Figure 3-6:
Eee PC
Network
Connection
Wizard.

3. **Select the type of connection you want to make and click Next.**

   Specify which hardware you'll be using to make the connection, whether you'll use a static or dynamic IP address, the phone number and login information (for dialup accounts), a name for the connection, and whether you want to automatically connect when the Eee PC starts up.

4. **Click Finish to save the connection settings.**

   The connection now appears in the Network Connections list. Click the Manage button to delete, rename, or make a copy of the settings.

Connecting to a Windows Network

If you have a Windows network at home (or perhaps work), your Eee PC can connect to it. This means that the Linux mini-laptop can access shared files, folders, and printers on Windows computers in the network.

 Okay, I have to warn you. Theoretically you should be able to connect to a Windows network with no problems. However, sometimes it's a pain to get Windows PCs even to talk to each other on a Windows network, so don't be too shocked if you encounter unexplained difficulties in getting your Linux Eee PC onto the network. I present some troubleshooting advice in the following sections and in Chapter 22. If that doesn't work, I suggest you consult the EeeUser.com forums (http://forums.eeeuser.com). And if you're still tearing your hair out, take the path of least resistance and set up a *sneakernet*. That's where you use a USB thumb drive and walk between computers (using your sneakers, get it) to transfer files.

Accessing shared Windows folders

Let's say you want to copy some files from a Windows PC on a network to your Eee PC. You first need to set up a shared folder on the Windows PC (refer to Windows online help for how to do this). After you have a shared folder and moved the files you'd like to share into it, you access the folder from your Eee PC by doing the following:

Do the Samba

Whenever you connect Linux and Windows computers over a network, you have to deal with Samba. No, I'm not talking about some geeks appearing on *Dancing with the Stars*. I'm referring to an open-source software package that allows penguins (as in Tux) and PCs to talk to each other.

Samba gets its name from SMB (Server Message Block), which is the protocol used by the Microsoft Windows network file system. Linux computers use a different networking protocol, and it's Samba that provides a way for the two operating systems to talk to each other

so you can access shared files, directories, and printers.

ASUS keeps most of the Samba nuts and bolts hidden from you, so you don't need a deep understanding of the software and the protocol. If everything is working correctly, it's just a matter of clicking to access Windows shares from your Linux Eee PC.

If you're interested in learning more about Samba, visit the official project Web site at www.samba.org.

1. **In the Linux desktop Work tab, click File Manager.**

2. **In the left window pane, click Windows Network.**

   The default Windows workgroup name is Workgroup. If you have given your workgroup a different name, it should also appear.

3. **Double-click your workgroup.**

   If your Eee PC successfully connects to the workgroup, a list of computers in the workgroup is displayed as shown in Figure 3-7.

4. **Double-click a computer to display shared resources.**

   Any files, folders, or printers that have been shared on that computer are shown. An example of a connected PC running Windows is shown in Figure 3-8.

If no workgroups are displayed, do the following:

1. **Right-click Windows Network and select Find.**

   This brings up the Find Computers dialog box.

2. **Click Start Search to look for networked computers.**

   Any computers found are displayed in a list.

3. **Choose a computer, right-click, and select Explore.**

   This opens a window that displays any shared folders. (If you can't find any networked computers, you may need to change your workgroup name. I tell you how to do this at the end of this chapter.)

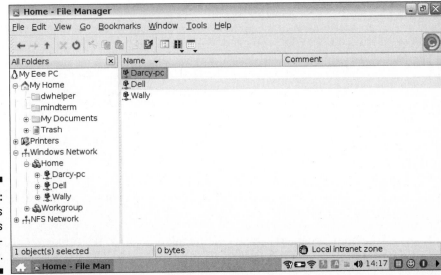

Figure 3-7:
Windows computers in a workgroup.

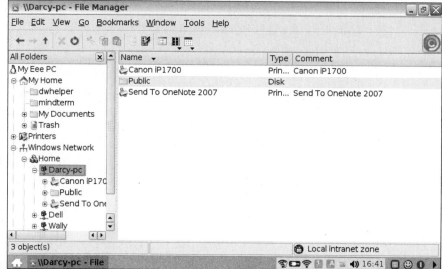

Figure 3-8:
Shared
resources
on a
Windows
Vista PC.

Still having trouble connecting to a shared Windows computer? Check that the Windows PC's firewall settings allow connections from an internal network.

If you're running Vista and want to share resources on a Windows network, be sure to refer to this Microsoft Technet article: `http://technet.` `microsoft.com/en-us/library/bb727037.aspx`.

Sharing a directory

To share the contents of a directory on your Eee PC across a Windows network, here's what you need to do:

1. **On the Linux desktop Work tab, click File Manager.**

2. **Select the folder you want to share and right-click.**

3. **In the pop-up menu, choose Sharing⇨Windows Sharing.**

   This displays the Properties dialog box, as shown in Figure 3-9, where you can set sharing options.

4. **Check Share This Item and Its Contents.**

5. **Click OK to make the folder available to other computers on the network.**

An upturned hand appears on the folder icon in File Manager, indicating that the folder is shared.

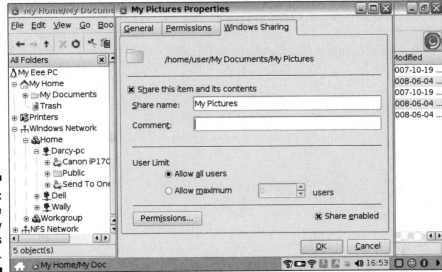

Figure 3-9:
Setting Eee
PC directory
properties
for sharing.

In the Permissions tab of the folder's properties (right-click a folder a select Properties from the pop-up menu), you can password-protect the directory and make it read-only, so no one other than you can make changes to the contents.

To turn off sharing on a folder, select the folder and follow the same steps you used to share it, but this time uncheck Share This Item and Its Contents.

Accessing shared Windows printers

If you're sharing a printer on a Windows network, your Eee PC may be able to use it to print over the network.

Notice I said *may be able to use it*. A shared printer is no guarantee your Eee PC can print. It depends completely on the printer and whether it supports Linux. If a Linux driver is available, you should have no problems. If there's no driver available, you are probably out of luck. I talk about printer issues like this and offer possible solutions in Chapter 9.

Before following the upcoming steps for accessing a shared printer, I recommend you first check whether the printer is Linux compatible by visiting the Linux Foundation's OpenPrinting Database at: http://openprinting.org/printer_list.cgi

If the printer doesn't look like it's supported under Linux and you're the patient type, you may still want to try to get it working. (I, personally, wouldn't hold my breath.)

If the shared Windows printer does get a Linux thumbs-up in the database, perform the following steps:

1. **In the Linux desktop Settings tab, click Printers.**

2. **Click the Add button.**

3. **Select Network printer and click Next.**

4. **Select Windows as the network type.**

5. **Click the Browse button to select a shared Windows printer.**

   Figure 3-10 shows a shared Windows printer being selected.

   Alternatively, you can skip browsing if you know the network path to the printer. In that case, just enter the full network path in the Path text box. For example, \\Wally\Multipass points to a shared printer named Multipass on a computer named Wally in a Windows network.

6. **Select the printer manufacturer and model from the drop-down lists. The correct driver is selected for you.**

   If your printer isn't shown, try a similar model or Generic.

7. **Optionally, print a test page and click Finish.**

If you can't get your printer to work, try not to get too obsessed. Life is too short, and it's easy enough to transfer files on a USB thumb drive from your Eee PC to a computer with a working printer.

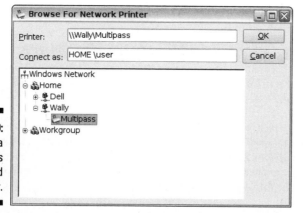

Figure 3-10:
Selecting a
Windows
shared
printer.

Changing your computer's name

On a Windows network, your computer's name appears as *eeepc-something*. The *something* is whatever you named the computer when you ran it for the first time (usually your name, if you followed the instructions).

If you want to change your computer's name, here's how:

1. **Start a Linux console session by pressing Ctrl+Alt+T.**

2. **Enter** sudo kcontrol.

   This runs the KDE Control Center program where you can make various changes to the desktop environment.

3. **Click the plus sign next to Network in the left window.**

4. **Click Network Connections.**

5. **In the Identification tab, enter the new name of the computer.**

   Figure 3-11 shows the Identification tab.

6. **Click Apply and exit the KDE Control Center.**

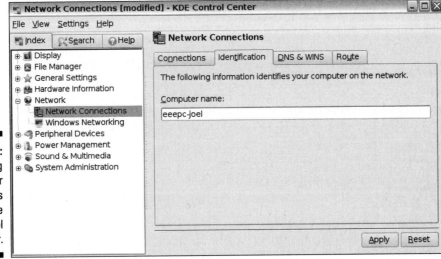

Figure 3-11: Changing your computer's name in the KDE Control Center.

Changing your workgroup name

By default, the Eee PC uses WORKGROUP as its Windows network workgroup name. This is the same default workgroup name that Windows uses when you create a network. If you didn't change the network's name, the Eee PC should happily connect to WORKGROUP.

If you did change the Windows network workgroup name to something other than WORKGROUP (such as HOME, MYNETWORK, and so on) and your Eee PC doesn't display that workgroup in File Manager, here's what you need to do:

1. **Start a Linux console session by pressing Ctrl+Alt+T.**

2. **Enter** sudo kcontrol.

   This is the same KDE Control Center program we just used to change the computer's name.

3. **Click the plus sign next to Network in the left window.**

4. **Click Windows Networking.**

   Windows Networking settings appear as shown in Figure 3-12.

5. **Enter the name of your workgroup in all caps and click Apply.**

With the workgroup name changed, you now should be able to connect to shared Windows network resources in that workgroup.

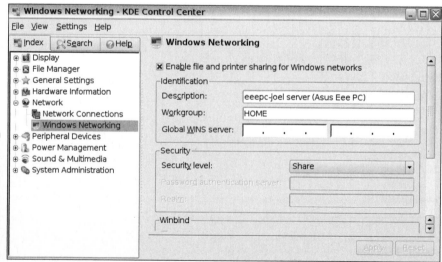

Figure 3-12: Changing your workgroup name in KDE Control Center.

Part II
Day to Day with the Eee PC

The 5th Wave   By Rich Tennant

"Ronnie made the body from what he learned in Metal Shop, Sissie and Darlene's Home Ec. class helped them in fixing up the inside, and then all that anti-gravity stuff we picked up off the Learn tab on our new Eee PC."

In this part . . .

*L*inux Eee PC models come bundled with a large, comprehensive collection of software. Essential Internet programs, work-related applications, games and entertainment programs, a variety of utilities, and even some educational packages for the kids, are all preinstalled. In this part, I describe the software that comes with Linux models (conveniently organized by the Internet, Work, Learn, Play, and Settings tabs in the user interface) and show you how to get started using it.

Microsoft Windows users shouldn't feel left out because I also discuss the differences between Linux and Windows, provide instructions for installing your own copy of Windows on a Linux Eee PC, and tell you how to get the most out of models that come preinstalled with Windows.

Chapter 4

Cruising the Internet

*I*n this chapter, I discuss the programs found on the Internet tab of the Eee PC, as shown in Figure 4-1. As you might have guessed, all the icons in this tab relate to the Internet in one way or another.

The Internet tab offers a Web browser, an instant messaging program, Skype, and other icons for accessing Web e-mail and other services. (ASUS also includes icons for a world clock and e-book reader that, although not directly related to the Net, are still useful.)

Keep in mind that not every icon represents a program. In a number of cases, icons are simply links to Web pages. Think of them as easy-to-find, preset bookmarks. For example when you click Internet Radio, a spiffy radio program doesn't pop up as you might expect. Instead, a Web site with a list of radio shows is loaded (if you're connected to the Internet, that is).

I cover the Network and Wireless Networks icons in Chapter 3. I assume you have an Internet connection, so let's get started.

Basic instructions for all the programs that I describe in this chapter can be found in the Eee PC online help. On the Linux desktop, click the Help menu item and, when you are inside the Help file, click the Internet tab.

901 Eee PC and Beyond

On 901 and later Eee PCs, you might find some additional icons in the desktop Internet tab. These include:

✔ **Google Search** — Displays the search page (www.google.com) in the browser.

✔ **Google Maps** — Displays the street map Web page (http://maps.google.com).

✔ **Video Search** — Loads the YouTube video site (www.youtube.com) in the browser.

✔ **YOStore** — Runs a program for transferring files to and from your Eee PC via the Internet and an online storage site.

✔ **EeeConnect** — Runs a utility that allows Eee PCs to remotely connect over the Internet.

For more information on these icons and programs, refer to your user manual or consult the online help.

Figure 4-1:
The Internet tab.

Browsing the Web

When you click the Web icon, the Eee PC loads the Firefox Web browser (shown in Figure 4-2). Firefox (www.mozilla.com/firefox) is a popular, free, open-source browser with versions that run in Linux, Windows, and Macintosh OS X.

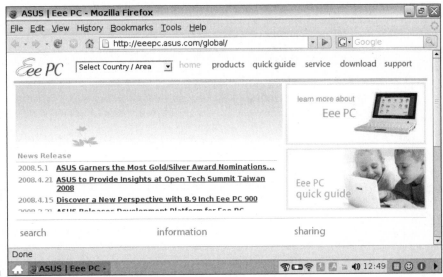

If you've been using Windows and Microsoft's Internet Explorer, Firefox is very similar. A few interface differences are explained on the following site: www. mozilla.com/en-US/firefox/switch.html.

Firefox features

Most browsers share basic functions and generally work the same way, but if you've never used Firefox before, I want to mention a few features that make it my preferred browser on the Eee PC (as well as other computers).

- ✔ **Built-in spell checking** — Words that aren't in the browser's spelling dictionary are underlined in red as you type. This is especially useful for composing Web e-mails.

- ✔ **Enhanced security** — Having done a lot of computer security work over the years, it's my humble opinion that Firefox takes top honors when it comes to browser security. You'll find phishing and spyware protection, easy private data clearing, and prompt update releases when security vulnerabilities are discovered.

- ✔ **Multiple search integration** — Type something in the toolbar and then select where you'd like to search — such as Google, Yahoo, Wikipedia, eBay, or any other.

- ✔ **Pop-up blocking** — Firefox can automatically block annoying (and sometimes malicious) pop-up windows.

- ✔ **RSS reader** — Get RSS (Really Simple Syndication) feeds such as blog entries, news headlines, and Web site updates from within the browser.

✔ **Session restore** — If your computer crashes while Firefox is running (or you shut it down), the browser remembers and loads all the Web sites you had open the next time it runs.

✔ **Speed** — Firefox is quick, even on the Eee PC with its small amount of memory and not exactly blazing-fast processor.

✔ **Tabbed browsing** — Firefox pioneered the use of tabs versus separate windows for browsing, and it has a number of different options for maximizing tabbed Web surfing.

While cruising the Net with your Eee PC, you might sometimes get a "Server Not Found" error after entering a Web site address. Carefully check the link you just typed. With the Eee PC's small keyboard, it's easy to accidentally enter a comma instead of a period in a Web address.

I could go on listing more features, but your best bet is to start using the browser and discover what it has to offer. If you do want to read more about browsing the Firefox way, visit the official Web site at: `http://support.mozilla.com` or check out the forums at `http://forums.mozillazine.org`.

Because of Eee PC's small screen, you may frequently find yourself using the horizontal scrollbar to view content that appears off the screen. This is a Web site formatting issue. Some Web sites dynamically format content based on the PC's screen size so you don't have to scroll to the right. Other sites use fixed length lines of text, assuming the user will be viewing with a normal-sized monitor. There's not much you can do in Firefox (or any other browser) to address this, aside from getting a larger screen Eee PC or connecting an external monitor to your Eee PC.

What's in a name?

Maybe you've noticed the name Mozilla and you're wondering what it has to do with Firefox. Back in the early days of the Web, the first Web browser was called Mosaic. When Marc Andreesen, who co-founded Netscape, developed a browser to compete against Mosaic, it was internally dubbed Mozilla (a play on words with Mosaic and Godzilla, foretelling what was going to happen to the rival browser). Netscape was eventually acquired by AOL, and the Mozilla browser became an open-source project. Along the way some developers thought Mozilla was getting too bloated, and they decided to create a leaner, meaner version. That browser was first called Phoenix (as in rising from Mozilla's ashes), but there were trademark issues with the name. Next it became Firebird, but there was already an open-source database with that name. The developers finally settled on Firefox (it was similar to Firebird, and they liked the sound of it) in 2004, and the name has stuck ever since.

Installing and using Firefox add-ons

One of the advantages Firefox has over other browsers is the large number of add-on programs and themes people have written for it.

Add-ons come in three different types:

- ✔ **Extensions** — Small programs designed to extend the browser's functionality.
- ✔ **Languages** — A feature that changes the language of the user interface.
- ✔ **Themes** — Code that alters the browser's user interface.

Add-ons tend to be relatively small in size and don't take up a lot of disk space — which is important when it comes to the Eee PC.

They are also very easy to install. The Firefox add-ons Web site (`https://addons.mozilla.org`) contains descriptions, links, and reviews of over 1,000 available add-ons. Installation, which I talk about in the next section, is a matter of clicking a few buttons.

Finally, add-ons are platform independent. That means if you run Firefox in Windows and have a favorite add-on, you can also use it with your Eee PC.

Installing an add-on

To download and install a Firefox add-on, follow these steps:

1. **Select an add-on you want to install from the Firefox add-on site.**

2. **Click the Add to Firefox button.**

   A software installation dialog box appears.

3. **Click the Install Now button**.

   A dialog box is displayed that provides status information about the download and install process. Wait until the install is successfully completed.

4. **Click the Restart Firefox button.**

   Firefox must restart before you can use the newly installed add-on.

After Firefox has restarted, the add-on is now available to use.

Running and setting preferences

Once you've got the add-on installed, it's time to take it for a spin. To run an add-on or set its preferences, follow these steps:

1. **From the Tools menu, select Add-ons.**

   A dialog box is shown with the add-ons and themes that are currently installed in the browser.

2. **You have two options at this point:**

   - By selecting an add-on extension, you can click the Preferences button to set preferences, the Disable or Enable button to control whether the add-on is running, or the Uninstall button to remove it.

   - By selecting a theme, you can choose to use that theme or uninstall it. When you change themes, you restart Firefox for the theme to take effect.

For setting preferences and issuing commands, depending on the add-on, you might see an icon placed on the toolbar or a menu item added to the Tools menu.

To get you started with add-ons, here are a few of my favorites that you may want to try:

- ✔ **Adblock Plus** — Blocks Web site advertisements, which is especially useful for the Eee PC with its small screen: `https://addons.mozilla.org/firefox/addon/1865`.

- ✔ **Forecastfox** — A slick little weather add-on that gets forecasts from Accuweather.com and displays them in the status bar: `https://addons.mozilla.org/en-US/firefox/addon/398`.

- ✔ **NoScript** — If you're concerned about Java and JavaScript security, use this add-on to execute scripts from only the sites you trust: `https://addons.mozilla.org/en-US/firefox/addon/722`.

- ✔ **Video DownloadHelper** — Saves YouTube and other online videos to your drive: `https://addons.mozilla.org/en-US/firefox/addon/3006`.

Have fun with add-ons. With the large number of available titles, you can spend hours browsing through the add-on database, reading reviews and descriptions, and downloading different versions.

If you've installed an add-on and no longer use it, be sure to uninstall it to save space. Owning an Eee PC means paying attention to drive space.

Add-ons take up memory and processor cycles, so if you go crazy installing a lot of them, Firefox's performance will begin to suffer. If this happens, just start removing add-ons as I described in the preceding section.

Maximizing screen space for the Eee PC

Although screen space is at a premium on the Eee PC, you can maximize the viewing area in Foxfire in several ways. Try some of the following:

- ✔ **Hide the Eee PC taskbar** — Click the arrow on the far-right side of the desktop taskbar to hide it. (Clicking the arrow again shows the taskbar.)

- ✔ **Hide Firefox toolbars** — In Firefox's View menu, select Toolbars. Then uncheck Navigation Toolbar and Bookmarks Toolbar.

- ✔ **Hide the Firefox status bar** — In the View menu, uncheck Status Bar.

- ✔ **Use a Firefox add-on** — Several add-on themes can help you maximize screen space. They include

  - • **miniFox** — Maximizes space between interface elements: https://addons.mozilla.org/en-US/firefox/addon/607.

  - • **Tiny Menu** — Replaces the default menu with a reduced size version: https://addons.mozilla.org/en-US/firefox/addon/1455.

  - • **Compact Menu** — Provides several ways of compressing the menu: https://addons.mozilla.org/en-US/firefox/addon/4550.

  - • **Full Fullscreen** — Starts up Firefox in full-screen mode, and hides the toolbars: https://addons.mozilla.org/en-US/firefox/addon/1568.

There are other add-on themes for small laptop screens besides the ones I just mentioned. Visit the Firefox add-ons site (https://addons.mozilla.org/firefox/) and do a search for *compact*.

Accessing Your Web Mail

I'm a big fan of using Web mail accounts on the Eee PC. They're convenient, you don't need to worry about running out of disk space on the Eee PC's small drive, and you don't have e-mails scattered between your primary computer and the mini-laptop.

Figure 4-3: Web mail options.

When you click the Web Mail icon, it opens a new window with four icons (as shown in Figure 4-3). The icons are links to popular Web mail services, and include

- ✔ **Gmail** — Google's e-mail service
- ✔ **Hotmail** — Microsoft's e-mail service
- ✔ **Yahoo** — Yahoo's e-mail service
- ✔ **AOL** — America Online's e-mail service

When you click an icon, the Web browser loads the e-mail service you selected. (If Firefox is already running, the Web mail service is loaded into a new tab.)

If you don't have a free account with one of these services, you can create one on the login Web page that is displayed.

For a great comparison of features that the different Web e-mail services offer, visit: `http://blogs.swebee.com/e-mail-service/free-webmail-services-comparison/2008-05-01_69-1.html`.

When the browser is running, you can click the Home icon in the taskbar to return to the desktop. To return the Internet tab, click the arrow above the Web mail icons.

For some reason ASUS decided to put the e-mail client icon in the Work tab instead of the Internet tab. I discuss Thunderbird, the preinstalled e-mail client, in Chapter 6.

Making Calls with Skype

If you've never heard of Skype, it's a program and service that allows you to make free-of-charge telephone calls to other Skype users over the Internet (the technical term for this is *Voice over Internet Protocol* or *VoIP*). With a subscription fee, you can also make phone calls to cell phones and landlines (cutting down on your long distance bills). In addition to phone calls, Skype supports instant messaging features and file transfer.

After you have an Internet connection, plug a speaker/microphone headset into your Eee PC, click the Skype icon, log in, and you're ready to use the program.

Skype is very popular. (At the beginning of 2008, over 300 million accounts were in use with the service.) Free versions of the program are available for Linux, Windows, and Mac OS X; these all have the same basic features and work similarly. (Setting Skype preferences on the Eee PC is shown in Figure 4-4).

If you've used Skype on a PC or laptop before, you'll find it functions the same way when you run it on an Eee PC — with two exceptions:

✔ When you run Skype, it adds an icon to the Linux desktop taskbar. Right-click the icon to display a pop-up menu with program commands.

✔ When the Eee PC was first released, it shipped with a version of Skype that didn't support videoconferencing (Web cam support for the Linux version was in beta test at the time). If you're using a version of Skype that's less than 2.0, you can download a newer version that supports Web cams. I discuss how to download software updates in Chapter 12.

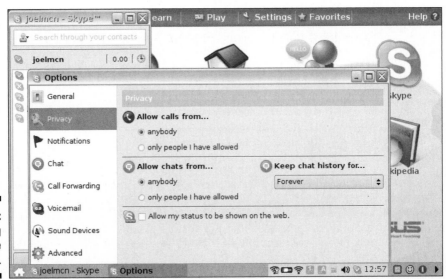

Figure 4-4:
Setting
Skype
preferences.

If you haven't used Skype and want to give it a try, you need to sign up for a free account (there is a link for creating one when you run the program).

Before doing that, I suggest you visit the Skype Web site at www.skype.com to learn more about the service.

To get help on using Skype, check out the Skype Community site at http://forum.skype.com/.

Instant Messaging

If you want to use your Eee PC for instant messaging (IM), click the Messenger icon on the Internet tab. This runs a popular open-source IM client named Pidgin (in the old days, the program was known as GAIM). Pidgin works with most popular instant messaging networks including AIM, Google Talk, ICQ, IRC, MSN, MySpaceIM, Yahoo!, and others.

The first time you run Pidgin, you're asked to add account information for any IM accounts you already have (as shown in Figure 4-5).

Adding an existing account is simple. You specify an IM service from a drop-down list box and provide your user ID, password, and nickname.

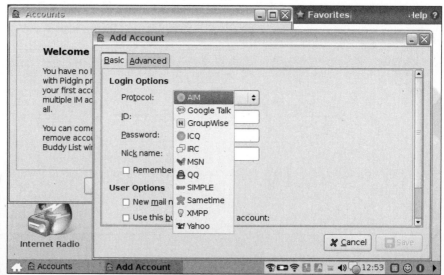

Figure 4-5:
Setting up Pidgin for instant messaging.

Making the connection

If you don't have an instant messaging account, here are some Web links to Pidgin-compatible services where you can register for one:

- ✔ **AIM:** www.aim.com
- ✔ **Google:** http://mail.google.com/mail/signup
- ✔ **ICQ:** http://web.icq.com/register

- ✔ **MSN** (if you have Hotmail email): http://registernet.passport.com/
- ✔ **MSN** (to use a non-Hotmail email address): http://register.passport.net/
- ✔ **Yahoo:** http://edit.yahoo.com/config/eval_register

Fill in the requested information to create a free account, which you can then add to Pidgin.

After you've successfully logged onto an IM network (remember, you need an Internet connection), your Buddy List (personal instant messaging phonebook) appears, and you're ready to start chatting.

Pidgin supports simultaneously logging into multiple IM networks. That means you can be talking with buddies on AIM and Yahoo at the same time. This is a great feature if you have multiple personalities.

Pidgin has most of the same features as other IM clients, such as file transfers, away messages, and notifications, as well as an extensive collection of add-on programs that extend its functionality.

Pidgin adds an icon to the Eee PC's taskbar. Right-click the icon to display a pop-up menu with commands.

You can learn more about Pidgin by selecting Online Help in the program's Help menu. Or, you can visit the Pidgin project Web site at: www.pidgin.im.

Getting the Facts with Wikipedia

When you click the Wikipedia icon, the Web browser opens and loads the Wikipedia home page (http://wikipedia.org/). If the browser is already running, Wikipedia opens in a new tab.

If you've never used Wiki before (most users drop the *–pedia* when they refer to it), the Web site is a multilingual, free encyclopedia. The Wiki home page is shown in Figure 4-6. Select which language version of the encyclopedia you'd like to view to get started.

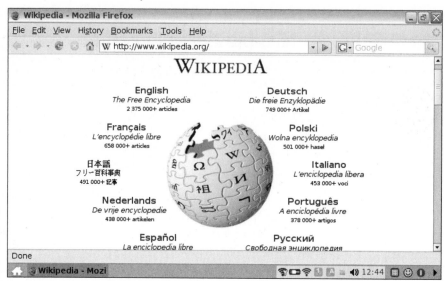

What makes Wiki unique is that all the content (including text and images) has been added to the site by its users. People from all over the world contribute information about topics they know (and/or are passionate about). Other users have the ability to add to the content or edit it to enhance accuracy and increase comprehensiveness.

User-created and -edited content has generated controversy for Wiki over the years, especially as there have been cases where incorrect information was purposely submitted. Despite this, Wiki still remains an excellent general, one-stop-shopping, information resource for a wide variety of subjects. However, if you are researching something of importance, always check multiple sources. Don't put all your eggs in the Wiki basket.

After you get inside Wiki, on the right side of the page is a search text box. Type in whatever you are interested in looking for and click the Go button. Wiki searches its database and displays a matching article. (If there are multiple articles, you can select the one that most closely matches what you are seeking.)

Wiki is easy to use and has online help to assist you with searching and using the encyclopedia.

Using Google Docs

Clicking the Google Docs icon loads the Google Docs (http://docs. google.com) Web site into the Eee PC's Firefox browser.

Google Docs is a free, online suite of office programs, including a word processor, spreadsheet, and presentation application. Instead of the conventional approach of using standalone programs installed on your PC, Google Docs lets you create, edit, and store documents online, using a Web browser and an Internet connection. The Google Docs interface is shown in Figure 4-7.

You need a free Google account to use Google Docs. Either sign in with your existing account information or create a new account.

Some of Google Docs' features include

- ✔ A simple, easy-to-use interface
- ✔ The capability to save documents in PDF and other common formats
- ✔ The capability to import Microsoft Office and OpenOffice (which is preinstalled on the Linux Eee PC and which I talk about in Chapter 5) documents
- ✔ Collaboration options that allow documents to be shared, opened, and edited by multiple users at the same time
- ✔ The capability to publish documents as Web pages

New features are regularly added to Google Docs. To keep up with the latest, check out the Google Docs development team's blog at: `http://google docs.blogspot.com/`.

Figure 4-7:
The Google Docs desktop interface.

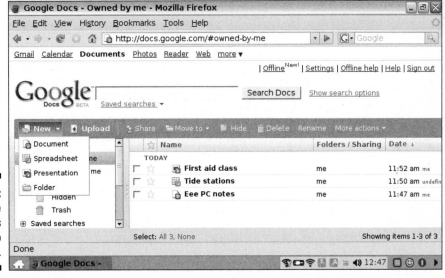

Being able to store your documents online and work on them from anywhere there's an Internet connection is pretty appealing. However, before you start relying completely on Google Docs, you should be aware of a few limitations.

- ✔ **Internet connection required** — It goes without saying, "No Net, no access to documents." Google Docs does, however, allow you to save documents to your own drive.

- ✔ **Basic features** — The word processor, spreadsheet, and presentation programs have basic features. If you need advanced functions and features, you should turn to a conventional office program.

- ✔ **Document size and total storage space** — There are limitations on how large a single document can be as well as the total number of documents that can be stored online.

- ✔ **Theoretical security issues** — There are some theoretical security and privacy issues with using Google Docs. Not to be overly paranoid, but I wouldn't use it to work on a document that contains sensitive information.

I've just scratched the surface on Google Docs, and there's a lot more to learn, so pay a visit to `http://documents.google.com/support/`.

Custom Start Pages with iGoogle

Clicking the iGoogle icon on the Internet tab takes you to Google's service for creating a customizable start page (`www.google.com/ig`, as shown in Figure 4-8).

iGoogle allows you to easily build your own personalized home or start page. You have a choice of a number of different themes as well as gadgets that display RSS feeds, weather, YouTube videos, and more. If you use other Google services such as Gmail, Google Docs, or Google Calendar, the page provides a quick, centralized way to access them.

You need a Google account to set up an iGoogle page. Either sign in with your account information or create a new account.

After you've created an iGoogle page, you can set it as your Firefox home page, so the page is displayed when you start the browser. With the iGoogle page displayed follow these steps:

1. **In the Firefox Edit menu, select Preferences.**

2. **Click the Main tab and set the iGoogle page as your home page with the Use Current Page button.**

3. **Click Close.**

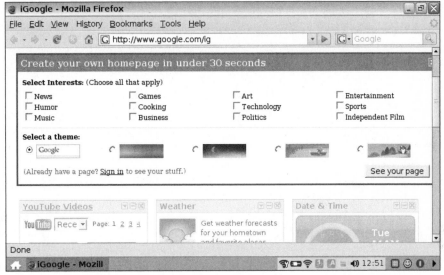

Figure 4-8:
The iGoogle custom home page.

Listening to Internet Radio

When you click the Internet Radio icon, your Web browser goes to the mediaU home page (www.mediayou.net), as shown in Figure 4-9. This is a Taiwanese site that allows you to use your browser to listen to music and radio programs from all over the world. The interface is a bit busy, but it gives you some decent media selections.

If you're learning a foreign language, international Internet radio stations are a great resource for practicing your listening skills.

Listen to the music

Lots of other Web sites provide free Internet radio or directories of online stations. Some popular radio sites to consider dialing in on your Eee PC include:

✔ **Live365:** www.live365.com

✔ **Radio Tower:** www.radiotower.com

✔ **SHOUTCast:** www.shoutcast.com

✔ **Radio Locator:** www.radio-locator.com

✔ **BBC Radio:** www.bbc.co.uk/radio

✔ **National Public Radio (NPR):** www.npr.org

Figure 4-9:
MediaU
offers
Internet
radio from
all over the
world.

Keeping Track of World Time

Clicking on the World Clock icon displays a nifty map of the globe, showing where it's day and where it's night (as seen in Figure 4-10). You'll have to ask ASUS what this program has to do with the Internet, because I sure don't know. Maybe because the Internet spans the globe? But I digress, so back to the clock.

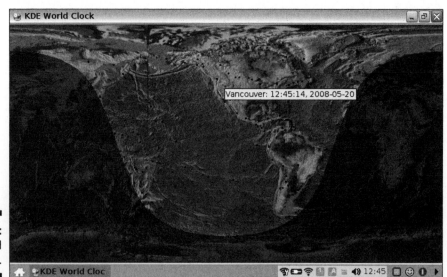

Figure 4-10:
The World
Clock.

In Eee PC 901 and later models, the World Clock appears in the desktop Work tab.

Move the cursor anywhere on the map to display time zone information, including nearby cities and the current date and time.

If you right-click the map, a pop-up menu is displayed that allows you to change program settings. Options include the following:

- **Flags** — You can select different color flags and place them on the map.

- **Clocks** — This command lets you add clocks below the map that show the current time in a selected time zone. Right-click a clock to remove it.

- **Map Theme** — This command displays a flat or physical relief map.

- **Show Daylight** — This command toggles day and night display on and off.

- **Show Cities** — This option controls whether time zone information is shown when you move the cursor on the map.

- **Show Flags** — This command displays or hides flags.

- **Save Settings** — This command saves any changed settings.

To learn more about using the World Clock, check out the KDE World Clock documentation at `http://docs.kde.org/stable/en/kdetoys/kworld clock/index.html`.

Reading e-Books

The Eee PC comes with an e-book (electronic book) reader called FBReader (as shown in Figure 4-11). Click the e-Book icon to run the program.

In case you don't see it, the e-book reader icon has a habit of disappearing on some Eee PCs. (I discuss disappearing desktop icons and remedies in Chapter 22.)

Whether the icon is present or not, the open-source FBReader is still there, allowing you to read your favorite e-books on your Eee PC. Some of its features include

- Support for multiple e-book formats, including
  - HTML (Web page formatting)
  - CHM (Microsoft Compiled HTML; frequently used for Windows help files and technical e-books)

- RTF (Rich Text Format)

- Plain text

- Other common formats, including plucker, PalmDoc, and ZTxt

FBReader doesn't support Digital Rights Management (DRM) formatted books (e-books you purchase that have some form of copy protection). Also, to read an e-book saved in the PDF format, use the PDF Reader in the Eee PC's desktop Work tab.

✔ Rotating text so the Eee PC can be held like an open book

✔ Selectable fonts and sizes

✔ Searchable text

✔ Keyboard and button navigation

In 901 and later Eee PC models, ASUS also includes an e-Book program called MeReader. Run the program by clicking the Mebook icon in the Eee PC's desktop Learn tab.

Figure 4-11:
FBReader
in action.

Using the eBook icon

When you click the eBook icon, it runs the File Manager (which I discuss in Chapter 6) and displays the contents of My EBooks in the My Documents folder directory. The idea is for you to store all your ebooks in this directory; whether you do is completely up to you.

When you're in the File Manager, follow these steps:

- ✔ **Double-click an e-book to display it**. For example, in the My EBooks folder there is a file named *manual.chm* (which happens to be an Eee PC user manual for all the installed Linux programs). FBReader displays the user manual when you double-click the file.

- ✔ **Use the File Manager *Open with* command**. Select the e-book file you'd like to read, right-click it, and then choose *E-book reader* from the *Open With…* menu item.

When there's no eBook icon

If there's no eBook icon, you can always use the File Manager to open an e-book by double-clicking on the e-book's file icon. But there's also an advanced method to run FBReader:

1. **Press Ctl+Alt+T.**

   This brings up a Linux command-line console window. I tell you much more about this in Chapter 20.

2. **Type** FBReader.

   Make sure to capitalize exactly as you see it here, and then press the Enter key after you're done.

This runs the FBReader program. Congratulations! You just successfully used command-line Linux. If you know the names of other programs, you can use these same steps to run them, too. Because you're done with the console, you can close its window to tidy up.

To learn more about FBReader, visit the project's Web site at www. fbreader.org.

No library card needed

If you want to use your Eee PC as a portable library, here are a few of my favorite links to Web sites where you can download free e-books to view with FBReader.

✔ **Project Gutenberg** (www.gutenberg. org/wiki/Main_Page) — The grand-daddy of free book sites includes thousands of titles, including many classics.

✔ **MemoWare** (www.memoware.com) — Originally started for PDAs (Palms and Pocket PCs), but now equally applicable for mini-laptops.

✔ **Many Books** (http://manybooks. net) — Books from the Gutenberg collection and others, but in more formats.

✔ **University of Virginia Electronic Text Center** (http://etext.lib. virginia.edu/ebooks) — The University of Virginia Library houses an extensive collection of fiction, literature, history, and children's books.

✔ **Munsey's** (www.munseys.com/) — A great collection of old, pulp-fiction novels (adult themes and racy covers, so for mature audiences only please).

There are lots of other sites with free e-books. If you exhaust these sources, Google is your friend.

Chapter 5

Getting Down to Work I: OpenOffice

Considering its small size, the Eee PC is a surprising little workhorse. The Linux version of the mini-laptop comes preinstalled with virtually everything you need for word processing, spreadsheet calculations, creating and giving presentations, and performing other work-related activities. All these programs are conveniently located in the Linux desktop's Work tab.

There are lots of programs in the Work tab, so I use two chapters to tell you all about them. In this chapter, I discuss the Documents, Spreadsheets, and Presentations programs, which are actually part of a nifty, free, open-source application suite similar to Microsoft Office called OpenOffice. I continue getting down to work in Chapter 6, presenting the remaining programs found in the Work tab.

Before I get started, keep in mind that I only have a limited amount of space to give you a general overview of OpenOffice and its features. But don't fear. I list lots of Internet resources for you to find out more about using and getting the most from the application suite.

Basic instructions for all of the programs I describe in this chapter can be found in the Eee PC online help. On the desktop, click the Help menu item and then, at the top of the help page, select the Work tab.

Some Linux Eee PC models come installed with StarOffice, a variation of OpenOffice. The programs and commands are generally the same, and aside from some minor differences in dialog boxes and other user interface elements, everything I discuss in this chapter applies to both office suites.

Opening Up OpenOffice

OpenOffice is an office application suite of programs. Think of it as a free, open-source Microsoft Office alternative (with a few more features, actually).

Just so you know, the trademark to the *OpenOffice* name is held by someone other than the OpenOffice, open-source project. To resolve this sticky legal situation, the project trademarked the name *OpenOffice.org* (abbreviated *OOo*); which is now the official name for the program suite. Everyone still seems to call it OpenOffice though, so whenever you see *OpenOffice* in the upcoming pages, I'm really talking about *OpenOffice.org*. And that statement should keep all the lawyers in the house happy, I hope.

OpenOffice started life in the late 1990s as StarOffice, a commercial office application suite. Sun Microsystems (which was in a pitched battle with Microsoft at the time) purchased the software from a German company and then made it available for free. In 2000, Sun released the source code and OpenOffice became an open-source project. Over the years it has evolved from a slightly clunky collection of programs to a full-featured, viable alternative to Microsoft Office.

StarOffice, which comes preinstalled with Windows XP Eee PCs and some Linux models, has most of the same programs and interfaces as OpenOffice.

Getting back to the Linux Eee PC again, it has three icons in the Work tab (as shown in Figure 5-1) for running OpenOffice programs. They include

- **Documents** — OpenOffice Writer: A word processor that has a similar set of features (and a similar look and feel) as Microsoft Word.
- **Spreadsheets** — OpenOffice Calc: A spreadsheet program similar to Microsoft Excel.
- **Presentations** — OpenOffice Impress: A presentation program similar to Microsoft PowerPoint.

In addition to these programs, OpenOffice also includes

- **OpenOffice Draw** — A vector graphics program with features comparable to early versions of CorelDRAW.
- **OpenOffice Base** — A database application similar to Microsoft Access.
- **OpenOffice Math** — A utility for creating and editing mathematical equations (similar to Microsoft Equation Editor if you're a math/science type).

Figure 5-1:
The
OpenOffice
icons in the
Work tab.

Depending on the Eee PC model, Draw and Math might not have icons in the Work tab. However, you can access them, and Base, from the other three OpenOffice programs (I show you how coming up).

Now I don't want you to think I'm one of those pushy, high-pressure open-source salesmen. I'm not going to say you should get rid of all your Microsoft software and only use Linux and open-source programs. That choice is up to you.

What I do want to sell you on is this. For the most part OpenOffice is compatible with Microsoft Office format files. That means you can copy a Word file from your PC onto a USB thumb drive, plug it into the Eee PC, and work on the document with OpenOffice. And when you get back to your main PC, Word will happily read all the edits you made on your Eee PC.

You will likely run into compatibility troubles if your Microsoft Office documents have complex graphics, fancy fonts and formatting, nested tables, complicated macros, and embedded OLE objects. Also, new Microsoft Office file formats such as DOCX and XLSX are not supported. (There are conversion utilities so you can use these files, and they will be supported in OpenOffice 3.0.)

And speaking of file types, OpenOffice programs can save files in Adobe Acrobat PDF format so there's no need for commercial or free conversion applications. Now that's what I call a feature.

Versions of OpenOffice are available for Linux (obviously), Windows, and Mac. To learn more about OpenOffice or to download a version for your primary computer (hint, hint) visit: www.openoffice.org.

If you want to give OpenOffice a try in Windows without installing it on your hard drive, check out this portable version: `http://portableapps.com/apps/office/openoffice_portable`. It runs on a USB thumb drive or SD card with about 250 MB of free space available. After you've installed it, just plug in the drive or card and run OpenOffice on any Windows PC.

Shared OpenOffice Commands

Before I talk about the OpenOffice suite of programs, I want to give you a quick overview of how to perform some common tasks. The OpenOffice applications conveniently share ways of doing certain things (such as opening and saving documents). For example, you use the same steps to create a new document in Writer as you would in Calc.

But before we get to those steps, here's the scoop on OpenOffice's extensive online help system. It's indispensable for learning how to use and take advantage of all the suite's features (although OpenOffice is similar to Microsoft Office, the menus, commands and dialog boxes are somewhat different). If you've never used OpenOffice before, I suggest you get started with the following.

Getting help

Two types of help are available inside OpenOffice programs, *What's This?* and a traditional online help system. Here are the basics for using both.

What's This?

What's This? provides summarized information about the command icons and other OpenOffice elements you see on the screen. To use the *What's This?* Feature, follow these steps:

1. **In the Help menu, select *What's This?***

   The cursor turns into a question mark.

2. **Move the cursor over toolbar items and buttons to learn more about them.**

   A pop-up box provides information about the command (as shown in Figure 5-2).

Click the mouse (the cursor can be anywhere on the screen) to turn off help and return the cursor to normal.

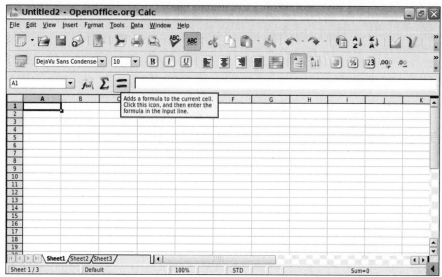

Figure 5-2:
The *What's This?* pop-up box.

Online Help

OpenOffice programs also feature a built-in online help system. To view the online help, follow these steps:

1. In the Help menu, select OpenOffice.org Help.

The help system is loaded as shown in Figure 5-3. You can also press F1.

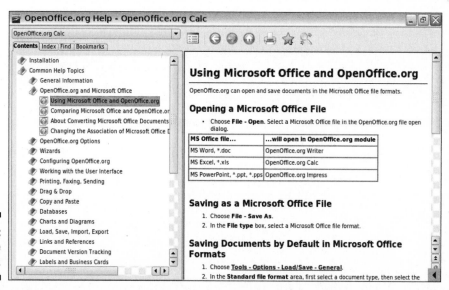

Figure 5-3:
OpenOffice online help.

2. Use the left pane to select what information you want to view.

The right window pane is where detailed help content is shown.

There are four, tabbed options at the top of the left pane for displaying information:

- ✔ **Contents** — This tab shows a table of contents with available help topics. Double-click a book icon to expand it. Double-clicking a question mark icon displays help for that particular topic in the right window pane.

- ✔ **Index** — An alphabetical list of subjects. Double-click a subject to display information about it.

- ✔ **Find** — This tab allows you to search for words in the help database. Enter a word and click Find. Matches are shown, and you can double-click each one to display the associated help information.

- ✔ **Bookmarks** — You can assign bookmarks to help topics by clicking the star icon in the toolbar. Bookmarks are displayed in this tab.

The drop-down list box above the tabs allows you to display help for other OpenOffice programs.

Internet help resources

If you can't find an answer to your question in OpenOffice's online help, then consult these indispensable Internet resources

- ✔ **OpenOffice main support page** — `http://support.openoffice.org/`

- ✔ **OpenOffice Wiki** — `http://wiki.services.openoffice.org/wiki/Main_Page`

- ✔ **OpenOffice User Guides: Authors documentation project** — `http://documentation.openoffice.org/manuals/oooauthors2/index.html`

- ✔ **Tutorials for OpenOffice** — `www.tutorialsforopenoffice.org`

- ✔ **OpenOffice community forums** — `www.oooforum.org`

Creating a new document

By default, when you run an OpenOffice program it starts with an empty document that you can immediately start working on.

If you're editing a file you've previously saved and want to create a new document, simply select New from the File menu. However, because OpenOffice is an integrated program suite, when you create a new document, you first need to specify the type (as shown in Figure 5-4).

This means if you are in a Calc spreadsheet and you decide you need a new word-processing document, you don't need to go back to the desktop and click the Documents icon. In Calc's File menu, just select the file type in the New menu item.

The following file types are available:

- **Text document** — A word processing file.
- **Spreadsheet** — A spreadsheet document.
- **Presentation** — A PowerPoint-like presentation document.
- **Drawing** — A graphics file.
- **Database** — A database file.
- **HTML Document** — A Web page (Writer also serves as an HTML editor).
- **XML Form Document** — An Xform document (Web page that contains forms).

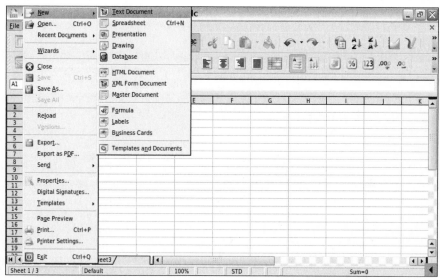

Figure 5-4: Select from different types of new documents.

✔ **Master Document** — An index file for organizing other documents (for example a Master Document could contain chapters, an index, and a table of contents for a book).

✔ **Formula** — A mathematical equation (you can format the equation with math symbols).

✔ **Labels** — Labels for printing.

✔ **Business Cards** — You guessed it, business cards.

✔ **Templates and Documents** — A collection of templates (resumes, letters, and so on).

The OpenOffice program associated with a file type runs (if it's not already running), and a new window is opened. You can now start working on the document.

If you're new to OpenOffice, experiment by opening different file types to see what happens. You won't break anything, trust me.

Saving a document

After you've worked on a document, you undoubtedly want to save it.

With a new document, use the Save or Save As command in the File menu. A Save As dialog box appears as shown in Figure 5-5.

If you are editing a document you previously created (either with an OpenOffice or Microsoft Office program), use the Save command in the File menu. The format the file was originally saved in is retained. Use the Save As command in the File menu to save the file in a different format or give the file a new name.

By default, all OpenOffice documents are saved to the /My Documents/My Office directory. However, you can save the file anywhere you like.

You can specify the file format of a document with the Filter drop-down list box in the Save As dialog box. If you plan to edit the document with a Microsoft Office program, be sure to select a compatible file type, such as `.doc`, `.xls`, or `.ppt`.

To save a file to a USB thumb drive you have plugged into your Eee PC, follow these steps:

1. **In the File menu, select Save As.**

2. **Click the My Eee PC icon.**

    The My Eee PC icon has a penguin, whose name is Tux by the way.

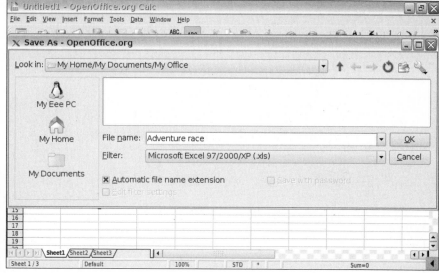

Figure 5-5:
The
OpenOffice
Save As
dialog box.

3. Double-click All File Systems.

4. Double-click the name of the USB drive.

It should look something like this: */media/Cruzer Mini/partition1* or */media/D:*.

5. Type a name for your file and click OK.

Instead of associating letters with mounted volumes as you do in Windows (for example D:), older Eee PC models use a Linux file system convention with volume names and partition numbers (such as */Cruzer/partition1*). Newer Eee PC models incorporate the more user-friendly letters (such as *D:*).

Opening a document

To open a previously saved document (either created with OpenOffice or a compatible Microsoft Office program), do the following:

1. In the File menu, select Open.

An example Open dialog box is shown in Figure 5-6.

2. Navigate through directories, select a file, and click OK.

By default, the /My Documents/My Office directory is opened first.

You can open all compatible OpenOffice documents. For example if you are in Writer, you can select a spreadsheet and Calc runs and loads the file.

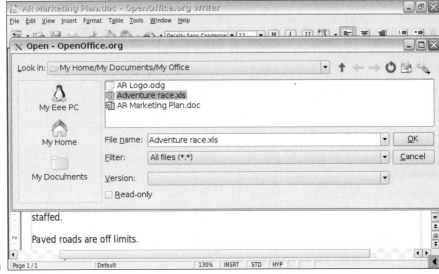

Figure 5-6:
The
OpenOffice
Open dialog
box . . .
opens
documents.

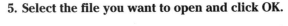

Opening a document on a USB drive

To open a document that is on a USB thumb drive you have plugged into your Eee PC, follow these steps:

1. **In the File menu, select Open.**

2. **Click the My Eee PC icon.**

3. **Double-click All File Systems.**

4. **Double-click the name of the USB drive**.

   It will look something like this: */media/Cruzer Mini/partition1* or */media/D:*.

5. **Select the file you want to open and click OK.**

Open documents appear on the Linux desktop taskbar. If you have multiple documents open, click a document in the taskbar to bring it to the front.

Writing and Editing

Writer is similar to Microsoft Word. Run the program by clicking the Documents icon in the Work tab.

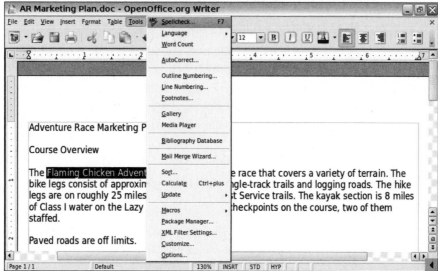

Figure 5-7:
The
OpenOffice
Writer word
processor.

You'll find that using OpenOffice Writer (shown in Figure 5-7) is pretty much like working with any other word processor. It's a snap to create new documents as well as edit existing ones (remember, OpenOffice is compatible with most Microsoft Word formatted files). The Eee PC in combination with Writer is ideal for taking notes and editing documents on the road.

The tiny screen on the Eee PC can be challenging for older eyes; especially when doing a lot of writing. Here's a tip that will help. In the View menu, select Zoom. You can zoom to 130% and see the entire page without needing to horizontally scroll (after you center the scrollbar). The larger page size is a blessing for the eyes.

To learn more about how to use Writer's features, check out the OpenOffice Writer FAQ at `http://documentation.openoffice.org/faqs/word_processing/index.html`.

Installing a dictionary

Because the Eee PC is sold all over the world, a spelling dictionary doesn't come installed with OpenOffice. (You'd run out of drive space pretty quick if you included all the available language dictionaries.)

The Dictionary icon found in the desktop Work tab is a separate program that doesn't work with OpenOffice. I discuss this dictionary in Chapter 6.

However it's easy to install an English or other language dictionary, as well as thesaurus and hyphenation files. Here's how:

1. **In the File menu, select Wizards⇨Install new dictionaries....**

2. **The DicOOo window is shown. Click the English link.**

3. **Click the Start DicOOo button and then follow the steps in the Wizard dialog box.**

   You are prompted to retrieve dictionary, hyphenation, and thesaurus files. Specify English (United States) for each.

4. **After the files have successfully downloaded, quit and then restart OpenOffice Writer.**

5. **In the Tools menu, choose Options⇨Language Settings⇨Writing Aids**

6. **Check each of the Available language modules.**

7. **Click OK.**

You can now spell check your documents. You can also use these same steps to add other language dictionaries to OpenOffice.

Using the standard OpenOffice toolbar

If you're getting to know OpenOffice using some of the Internet resources I previously mentioned, you may find that some tutorials refer to icons and commands that don't appear in the toolbar. Here's why.

The version of Writer that comes with the Eee PC doesn't display the default, standard OpenOffice toolbar that many tutorials reference. Instead, ASUS uses a simplified toolbar named *eeePC* that contains a limited number of command icons.

To display Writer's default toolbar, follow these steps:

1. **In the View menu, select Toolbars.**

2. **Uncheck eeePC.**

3. **Check Standard.**

The Standard toolbar, with a full collection of tools, is now shown.

Spreadsheet Calculations

Calc is the OpenOffice cousin of Microsoft Excel. Run the program by clicking on the Spreadsheets icon in the Work tab. You find an example spreadsheet, showing the interface, in Figure 5-8.

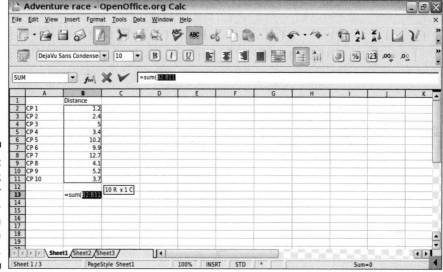

Figure 5-8:
Keep track
of your
spread-
sheets with
OpenOffice
Calc.

If you've used Excel before, aside from a few differences in the user interface, you should have no trouble working with Calc. Calc is compatible with .XLS files, and unless your spreadsheet has some advanced calculations, macros or Visual Basic scripts, you should be able to open and edit files you've created on your primary desktop or laptop PC.

To read the FAQ for OpenOffice Calc, go to `http://documentation.openoffice.org/faqs/spreadsheet/index.html`.

Making Presentations

Impress is the OpenOffice equivalent of Microsoft PowerPoint. Click the Presentations icon in the Work tab to run the program. An example presentation, showing the Impress interface, is shown in Figure 5-9.

Presentations are one of the areas where the Eee PC really shines. With its small size and VGA port, the Eee PC is the ultimate portable presentation machine. (I discuss changing desktop settings for presentations in Chapter 9.) Even when not connected to a projector, the Eee PC is still great for making up-close presentations for one or two people sitting around the mini-laptop.

Figure 5-9:
Create
presenta-
tions with
OpenOffice
Impress.

Impress enables you to load, edit and run PowerPoint presentations (basic ones, that is — complex presentations with sound, animation and other multimedia elements can be problematic). You can also create presentations with Impress and save them in a number of different formats — including Flash, which makes it easy to add a presentation to a Web page.

While you can create presentations with Impress on your Eee PC, it's much easier to build a presentation on your primary desktop or laptop using PowerPoint (or Impress), copy the file to a USB thumb drive or SD card, and then move the presentation to the Eee PC for display. A larger screen makes a big difference when creating and formatting a presentation.

It takes a while for Impress to load a PowerPoint format presentation. To speed things, after the presentation is loaded, save it as an OpenDocument Presentation (ODP) file. This is Impress' internal file format which makes loading and editing quicker. PowerPoint isn't compatible with ODP files, so you need to save the presentation as a PPT file before transferring it back to your primary PC.

Sometimes when you open a PowerPoint presentation in Impress, the transitions don't work correctly. Here's a link to a tutorial that shows you how to fix the problem: www.tutorialsforopenoffice.org/tutorial/Convert_ PowerPoint_To_Impress_Presentation.html.

I suggest visiting the official Impress FAQ to learn more about the program's features and how to use it: http://documentation.openoffice.org/ faqs/word_processing/index.html.

Working with Databases

Base is similar to Microsoft's Access database. Although there isn't an Eee PC desktop icon for the application, you can run the program by opening Writer, Calc or Impress, selecting New from the File menu, and specifying a database file. A wizard guides you through the initial steps of creating a new database or you can open an existing one.

OpenOffice Base is SQL-compatible and like other databases has easy-to-use tools for creating Tables, Queries, Forms, and Reports (the form design tool is shown in Figure 5-10).

You might find the Eee PC's small screen a challenge when creating databases. If you need a database, I recommend building at least the forms interface with OpenOffice on your primary PC and then copying it to the Eee PC's drive or loading the database file from a USB thumb drive. If you need a simple, list-oriented database, consider using Calc instead of Base.

Unlike other OpenOffice applications that are compatible with their Microsoft counterparts, you cannot directly open Access .MDB files.

To read more about Base's features, point your browser to the OpenOffice wiki at `http://wiki.services.openoffice.org/wiki/Database`.

To learn how to use Base, I suggest this tutorial: `http://sheepdogguides.com/fdb/fdb1main.htm`.

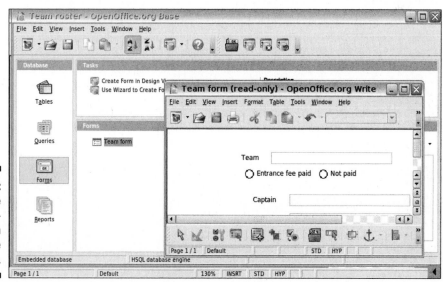

Figure 5-10: Manage your databases with OpenOffice Base.

Creating Graphics

OpenOffice comes with a graphics program named Draw (shown in Figure 5-11). To run the program, while in Writer, Calc or Impress, select New from the File menu and then choose the Drawing menu item.

Draw is a vector graphics program. That means it uses objects such as points, lines, and shapes to create images. A raster graphics program (such as Paint) uses individual bits to create an image. Vector graphics programs are primarily used for commercial art, drawing floor plans or schematics, and creating organizational charts. Raster graphics programs are for editing digital photos or scanned images.

Considering the Eee PC's small screen and touchpad and its relatively underpowered processor, the laptop isn't really suited for doing graphics work. Draw is fine for working on simple graphics or sketching out ideas during a meeting, but leave everything else for your primary PC.

To get the lowdown on common questions about OpenOffice Draw, check out `http://documentation.openoffice.org/faqs/drawing_graphics/index.html`.

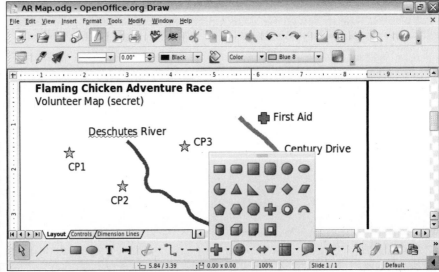

Figure 5-11: Make some pictures with OpenOffice Draw.

Chapter 6

Getting Down to Work II: Other Programs

*T*he Linux Eee PC's Work tab is where you go to get things done. In Chapter 5, I bring you up to speed on OpenOffice applications that come with the mini-laptop. In this chapter, I continue with the productivity theme by presenting the other programs located in the Work tab (as shown in Figure 6-1).

In this tab you find a PDF viewer, e-mail client, file manager, calculator, Personal Information Manager, and other useful productivity applications.

So let's get down to work and investigate them.

You can find basic instructions for all the programs I describe in this chapter in the Eee PC's online help. At the Linux desktop, click the Help menu item and then select the Work tab.

Figure 6-1:
Linux Eee
PC Work tab
programs.

Viewing PDF Documents

PDF files (Portable Document Format files), more commonly known as Adobe Acrobat files, are just about everywhere you look. Recognizing this, ASUS included a program to view them on the Eee PC.

When you click the PDF Reader icon in the Work tab, Adobe Reader runs as shown in Figure 6-2.

This is a full version of Adobe Reader for Linux, with the same basic user interface and features found in Windows releases of the program. Because Adobe Reader is so widely known, I won't take up space describing how to use it.

If you need more information on the program, consult the online help or visit www.adobe.com/products/reader/.

 The bottom of the Print dialog box in Adobe Reader appears off the screen on Eee PCs with smaller monitors. This means you can't click the Print button. Press the Alt key, hold down the left mouse button, and then drag up the dialog box with the touchpad to get to the button.

 If your Eee PC came with version 7.0 of Adobe Reader, you might be wondering whether you should upgrade to the latest version (8.0 at the time of this writing). My recommendation for upgrading any software that comes pre-installed on the Eee PC is this: If you don't have a compelling reason, don't upgrade. I discuss the reasons for this seemingly controversial approach in Chapter 12.

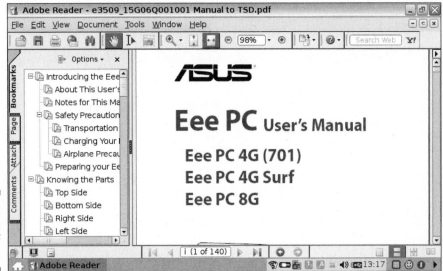

Figure 6-2:
Adobe
Reader PDF
viewer.

E-mail with Thunderbird

When you click the Mail icon in the Work tab, it loads a popular open-source e-mail client called Thunderbird, as shown in Figure 6-3. This program is from the same folks that bring you the Firefox Web browser. (Note: If you have a 2G Eee PC, Thunderbird doesn't come preinstalled.)

Figure 6-3:
Thunderbird
e-mail
client.

Some of Thunderbird's features include the following:

- ✔ Outstanding spam filtering
- ✔ Easy access to Gmail and .Mac/MobileMe Web mail accounts
- ✔ Built-in spell checking
- ✔ Customizable themes and user interface
- ✔ Integrated newsreader
- ✔ Phishing (scam Web site) protection

An alternative to Thunderbird and other traditional e-mail clients is to use a Web-based e-mail account, such as Hotmail, Gmail, or Yahoo Mail. Advantages include no synchronization issues with e-mail messages spread across differ-ent computers and no need to worry about large volumes of e-mail taking up precious drive space.

To learn more about Thunderbird (or to download a Windows or Mac ver-sion) visit `http://www.mozilla.com/en-US/thunderbird/`.

If you have a support question, check out the forums at `http://forums.mozillazine.org`.

Importing and exporting data

You can import and export data between Thunderbird and many e-mail and PIM programs as well as Web mail services. The following is a link to step-by-step instructions on importing and exporting e-mail data for a variety of popular programs and services:

`http://kb.mozillazine.org/Importing_and_exporting_your_mail`

If you want to import data to your Eee PC running Thunderbird, follow the directions and save the data from the other e-mail program or service to a USB thumb drive.

After you have done so, follow the instructions for importing, using the USB thumb drive plugged into the Eee PC as the data source.

Enhancing Thunderbird with add-ons

Thunderbird has a number of free add-ons to expand its functionality and usefulness.

Add-ons come in three different forms:

- ✔ **Extensions** — Small programs designed to extend Thunderbird's features.
- ✔ **Languages** — Changes the user interface language (for example, the Eee PC comes with several Chinese-language packs installed so localized programs can be used in Chinese markets).
- ✔ **Themes** — Code that changes Thunderbird's appearance.

Add-ons tend to be relatively small in size and typically don't take up a lot of drive space.

They are also very easy to install. The Thunderbird add-ons Web site (`https://addons.mozilla.org/en-US/thunderbird/`) contains descriptions, links, and reviews of available add-ons. Installation is a matter of clicking a few buttons as I describe in the following section.

Finally, add-ons are platform independent. That means if you run Thunderbird in Windows and have a favorite add-on, you can also use it with your Eee PC.

Installing a Thunderbird add-on

To download and install a Thunderbird add-on, follow these steps:

1. **Select an add-on that you want to install from the Thunderbird add-on Web site.**
2. **Right-click the add-on link and choose Save Link As to download and save the file to your Eee PC's drive.**
3. **In the Thunderbird Tools menu, select Add-ons.**
4. **At the bottom of the dialog box, click the Install button.**
5. **Select the file you downloaded and click Open.**
6. **Click the Install Now button in the Software Installation dialog box.**
7. **Click the Restart Thunderbird button.**

After Thunderbird restarts, the add-on is available to use.

Setting preferences

You can set preferences for an add-on you just installed. In the Tools menu, select Add-ons. A dialog box is shown with add-ons that are currently installed in Thunderbird. You can use it to make modifications to the following:

✔ **An add-on extension** — You can click a button to set preferences, disable or enable the add-on, or uninstall it.

✔ **A theme** — You can choose to use that theme or uninstall it. When you change themes, you need to restart Thunderbird for the theme to take effect.

✔ **A language** — You can enable or disable a language pack.

To set preferences, an add-on may install an icon in the toolbar or add a menu item to the Tools menu.

If you've installed an add-on and no longer use it, be sure to uninstall to save drive space.

To get you started with add-ons, here are a few of my favorites that you may want to try and where you can find them:

✔ **Lightning** — Adds a calendar features to Thunderbird (`https://addons.mozilla.org/en-US/thunderbird/addon/2313`).

✔ **miniBird** — A theme well-suited for the Eee PC that shrinks Thunderbird's interface (`https://addons.mozilla.org/en-US/thunderbird/addon/1064`).

✔ **Signature Switch** — Changes your e-mail signature (great if you're using multiple accounts) (`https://addons.mozilla.org/en-US/thunderbird/addon/611`).

✔ **Contacts Sidebar** — Displays an address books in a sidebar (`https://addons.mozilla.org/en-US/thunderbird/addon/70`).

Managing Files

When you click File Manager in the Work tab, it loads the Xandros File Manager (as shown in Figure 6-4). With the File Manager you can do the following:

✔ Access and display files on the internal drive and external storage devices (SD cards, USB thumb and hard drives, and CD/DVD drives)

✔ Copy, delete, and rename files

✔ Search for files

✔ Access shared network resources

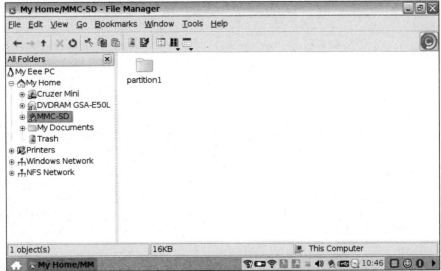

If you have experience using Windows Explorer, the Eee PC's File Manager generally works the same. Here are a few tips to get you started:

- ✔ Double-click a folder to open it.
- ✔ Select a file by single-clicking. You can then copy it to a folder by dragging.
- ✔ Double-click a file to load it and run the associated program (if the Eee PC doesn't know which program to use, it asks you).
- ✔ Right-click a file to display properties.
- ✔ Use the View menu to change how files are displayed (icons, thumbnails, detailed listings, and so on).
- ✔ Use the Window menu to change how windows and files are displayed.

To learn more about the File Manager and how to use all its features, go to the Help menu and select File Manager Handbook.

By default, the File Manager only allows you to access files and directories in your Home directory and on external devices. To view all files and directories, including hidden ones, in the File Manager's View menu select Show Hidden Files and Show All File Systems.

Accessing external storage

Whenever you insert an SD card or a USB device (thumb drive, hard drive, or CD/DVD drive) into the Eee PC, a dialog box is displayed that asks if you want to view the contents in the File Manager. If you click OK, the File Manager runs, and directories and files on the card or drive are displayed.

External storage devices are shown in the left window below the My Home icon (as shown in Figure 6-4). On older Eee PC models that don't have the latest operating system updates, note the following:

- ✔ USB devices are labeled with the name of the device.
- ✔ SD cards are labeled MMC-SD.

Click the plus sign to the left of the device icon to display the contents in the right window.

With SD cards and USB drives, on older Eee PC models a folder named *partition1* is shown. Click the *partition1* folder to display files and directories on the card or USB drive.

Newer models and older Eee PCs that have the latest system updates display devices and drives with letters (such as D:), just like you're used to with Windows. Click the device letter to show files and directories.

Accessing network resources

If you are connected to a network, you can use the File Manager to access other computers on the network.

At the bottom of the left window are two icons, labeled as follows:

- ✔ Windows Network
- ✔ NFS Network (Network File System — widely used with UNIX-type computers)

You may want to connect to a Windows network (such as a workgroup you've created at home, so multiple computers can share files). I discuss Eee PC networking in Chapter 3, but here are some quick steps on how to access a network with the File Manager:

1. **Double-click the Windows Network icon.**

   A list of available workgroups is displayed in the right window. (The Eee PC lists the default named Workgroup and any other workgroups that are available.)

2. **Double-click the name of your workgroup.**

   Computers that have been set up to share files and printers are shown.

3. **Double-click the computer you want to connect to.**

   If a password is required, enter the password. Shared folders and printers associated with the computer are shown.

4. **Double-click a folder to access files stored inside.**

 The File Manager also can serve as a Web browser. In the View menu, select Toolbars⇨Address Bar. If you have an Internet connection, you can now enter a Web site address, and it will be displayed in the right window. Although this is a browsing option, I still recommend using Firefox as your primary browser.

Helpful Accessories

Clicking the Accessories icon in the Work tab displays the three icons shown in Figure 6-5:

- ✔ **Calculator** is, drum roll please, a calculator program.

- ✔ **PIM** is a Personal Information Manager.

- ✔ **Screen Capture** allows you to take a picture of whatever is on your Eee PC's screen.

Read on for more information about these programs.

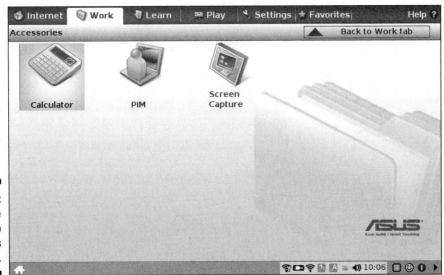

Figure 6-5:
Linux Eee PC Work tab Accessories programs.

Adding things up with Calculator

Clicking Calculator runs a program called KCalc. KCalc (shown in Figure 6-6) is a scientific calculator. To use it, click a number or symbol button or type with the Eee PC keyboard. You can add different types of function buttons (such as statistics, logic, and trigonometric) in the Settings menu.

Figure 6-6:
KCalc
calculator.

To learn more about the calculator, in the Help menu select KCalc Handbook or read the user manual on the Web at `http://docs.kde.org/kde3/en/kdeutils/kcalc/index.html`.

Managing personal information

When you click the PIM (Personal Information Manager) icon, an open-source program named Kontact runs. Kontact (its interface is shown in Figure 6-7) brings together several KDE applications that are installed on your Eee PC but aren't readily available through desktop icons. These programs include

- ✔ E-mail client
- ✔ Contact list

- ✔ Calendar
- ✔ To-do list
- ✔ Journal
- ✔ Pop-up notes

Other components including RSS feeds, news, and synchronization, are also available. In the Settings menu, choose Select Components to add these other programs to the PIM.

If you're using another program or Web service to manage contact, calendar, and e-mail information, you may want to share the data with Kontact. Here's how:

- ✔ **Microsoft Outlook** — Use the free, open-source Outport utility, which exports Outlook data in a variety of formats. You can then import the data into Kontact. Visit `http://outport.sourceforge.net/` to learn more.

- ✔ **Google Apps** — You can easily sync data from Google Apps (such as Gmail and Google Calendar) with Kontact. Here's a link to a step-by-step tutorial: `www.linux.com/feature/122054`.

To find out more about Kontact, in the Help menu select Personal Information Manager Handbook or visit the project Web site at: `www.kontact.org/`.

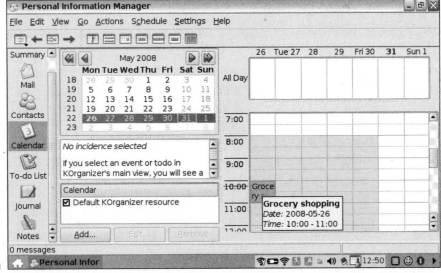

Figure 6-7:
The Kontact Personal Information Manager (PIM) with calendar.

Capturing screens

Clicking the Screen Capture icon runs a program called KSnapshot (as shown in Figure 6-8). KSnapshot is a screen-grabber utility. It's similar to the Windows Prnt Screen function in that it takes a snapshot of the Eee PC's screen. KSnapshot offers additional capabilities such as

- ✔ Capture the full screen, a window, or a region.
- ✔ Display a preview of the captured image.
- ✔ Save, the screen directly to a named file.
- ✔ Support multiple graphics formats (BMP, JPG, and PNG to name a few).
- ✔ Delay taking a snapshot (in seconds).

Instead of running KSnapshot by using the Screen Capture icon, press Fn+Ins — the Ins key is also labeled Prt Sc.

If you're using the Advanced Desktop mode that I describe in Chapter 19, press Ctrl+Fn+PrtSc to save the screen to the clipboard. Alt+Fn+PrtSc saves the currently selected window to the clipboard. You can then paste the clipboard contents into a graphics program and save the screen image to a file.

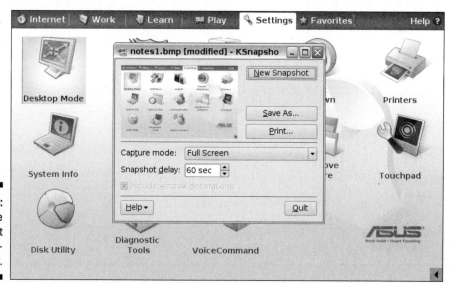

Figure 6-8:
The KSnapshot screen capture utility.

To learn more about the screen capture utility, click the Help button in the dialog box and then select Ksnapshot Handbook in the pop-up menu. You can also read the user manual on the Web at `http://docs.kde.org/stable/en/kdegraphics/ksnapshot/`.

Using the Dictionary

When you click the Dictionary icon, as you might have guessed, a dictionary is displayed. (Note that depending on the model and the country the Eee PC was destined for, the dictionary program may not be installed.)

On older Eee PC models, users were greeted with a Mandarin Chinese interface that can't easily be switched to English (as shown in Figure 6-9). Ah, mysteries of the East. If you have this version of the dictionary, you can still look up English words. Click the Eng-Eng icon (that's English to English) and then select a word in the left window pane. Its definition appears to the right.

ASUS does have an updated version of Longman Dictionary that has a configurable English interface that's easier to use (see the difference in Figure 6-10). If you have an older version of the dictionary, you can download and install the new version with the Add/Remove Software program in the desktop Settings tab. (I tell you about adding and removing software in Chapter 12.)

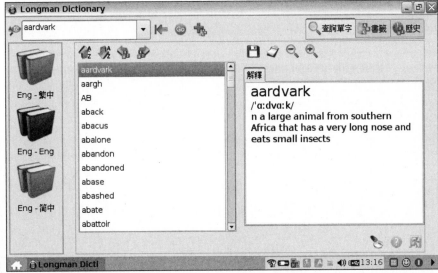

Figure 6-9: The Longman Dictionary with Chinese interface.

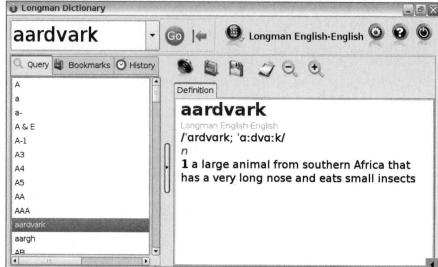

Figure 6-10:
The updated
Longman
Dictionary
with English
interface.

Updating to the newer version of the dictionary can potentially remove or change desktop icons. Before you update, I recommend backing up the *simpleui.rc* file. I show you how to do this in Chapter 21.

The quality of the definitions in this dictionary (at least, in English) isn't that great and, if you have kids in the house, be forewarned. It contains a fair number of X-rated words with some rather interesting definitions.

If you're looking for a better dictionary, I'd recommend using *Stardict* (`http://stardict.sourceforge.net/`). Refer to this post from the EeeUser Forum site for information on installing `http://forum.eeeuser.com/viewtopic.php?id=6198`.

The alternative is to use a Web dictionary, such as

- `http://dictionary.reference.com/`
- `www.merriam-webster.com/`
- `www.thefreedictionary.com/`
- `www.websters-online-dictionary.org/`

Posting Notes

The Eee PC comes with a program called KNotes for adding pop-up notes to the Linux desktop (a sample note is shown in Figure 6-11). These resemble the common, yellow paper sticky notes that seem to be magnetically attracted to computer monitors.

KNotes is a part of the Kontact personal information manager (PIM) that I described earlier in the chapter. You can also access the notes program from within the PIM.

KNotes installs an icon in the taskbar — the icon resembles a pad of yellow sticky notes. Right-click the taskbar icon to display a pop-up menu with commands and settings.

Right-click the title of a note on the desktop to display a pop-up menu with commands.

To learn more about KNotes, in the Help menu, select Popup Notes Handbook or read the user manual on the Web at `http://docs.kde.org/kde3/en/kdeutils/kcalc/index.html`.

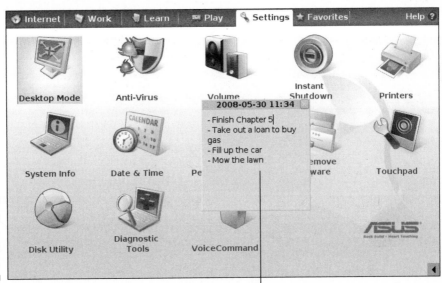

Figure 6-11: KNotes pop-up note on the desktop.

A pop-up note

901 Eee PC and Beyond

On the 901 and later model Eee PCs you might find some additional icons in the desktop Work tab. These include:

✔ **Draw** — OpenOffice Draw graphics editor.

✔ **Math** — OpenOffice Math equation editor. (Keep in mind that you can still run both of these OpenOffice programs even if the icons aren't present. I briefly discuss them in Chapter 5.)

✔ **Freemind** — An open-source mind-mapping program written in Java. For more information see `http://freemind.source`

`forge.net/wiki/index.php/Main_Page`.

✔ **World Clock** — A clock that displays international time. On older Eee PC models, the program was included in the Internet tab. I describe World Clock in Chapter 3.

For more information on these programs, refer to your user manual or consult the online help.

Chapter 7

Eee PC for Kids

● ●

In This Chapter

▶ Studying science

▶ Learning about language

▶ Majoring in math

▶ Getting an A in Art

▶ Using education resources on the Web

● ●

*O*ne of the Es in Eee PC is *easy to learn*. Now obviously, *easy to learn* can mean *easy to figure out*. But in this case, I think *learn* has more of an educational connotation.

The Eee PC, particularly models running Linux, serves as a great computer for education and kids. Why you ask?

✔ It's affordable.

✔ Smaller fingers like smaller keyboards.

✔ It can survive an occasional bump and drop (within reason).

✔ The operating system is stable and easy-to-use.

✔ Lots of productivity and educational software comes with it. (Children can start with kids programs and then move on to Internet and office applications as they progress.)

✔ Basic computing concepts and skills carry over to other PCs operating systems, and programs.

ASUS obviously views kids as potential Eee PC users, considering there's a tab named Learn in the Linux desktop. The tab contains icons for all sorts of educational software (as shown in Figure 7-1).

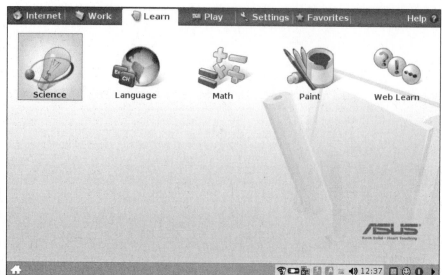

Figure 7-1:
The Eee
PC desktop
Learn tab.

I describe these programs in the upcoming pages as well as list other helpful resources for using the Eee PC as a learning tool.

If you're a parent or grandparent considering purchasing an Eee PC for your child (or thinking about sharing yours with him or her every now and then,) read on.

Basic instructions for all the programs I describe in this chapter can be found in the Eee PC's online help. At the Linux desktop, click the Help menu item and then select the Learn tab in the online help file.

Studying Science

I always liked science classes in school, so that's where I'll start. Clicking the Science icon in the Learn tab, displays two icons (as shown in Figure 7-2):

- ✔ **Periodic Table** is a program for learning about chemical elements.
- ✔ **Planetarium** is an astronomy program for viewing stars and planets.

In this section, I give you an overview of these two science programs.

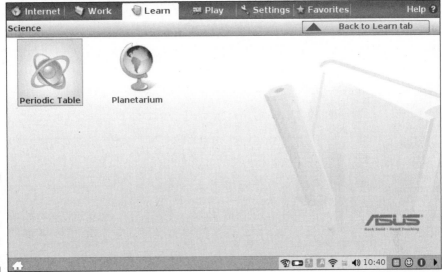

Figure 7-2:
The science
programs
in the
Learn tab.

It's elementary: The Periodic Table

Unless you're a scientist or a teacher, you've probably forgotten all about the Periodic Table. To refresh your memory, it's a table that contains information about all the known chemical elements (remember, everything on the planet is made up from some combination or another of these elements).

Get some bonus points with your kids when you tell them that Dmitri Ivanovich Mendeleev is credited with creating the first Periodic Table in 1869 and that *periodic* means *recurring*, as in recurring trends of the elements' properties.

When I was in school, Periodic Tables were rather boring posters filled with little colored squares, element symbols, and other arcane information you had to memorize.

Times have changed, and the Periodic Table that comes with the Eee PC is actually kind of fun and interesting. The program (shown in Figure 7-3) is an open-source application called Kalzium (that's German for *Calcium* in case you're wondering).

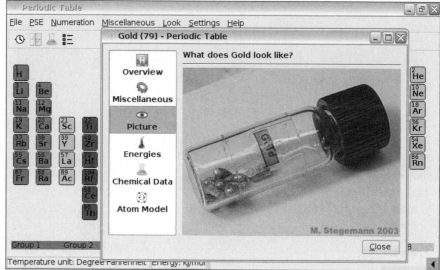

Figure 7-3:
The Kalzium
Periodic
Table
brings the
elements
to life.

It has all the same information that appeared on those old classroom posters, but is designed to be highly interactive. You can click an element and see a picture of what it looks like and different element groupings. You can move a control to see if an element is liquid, solid, or gas at different temperatures, and much more.

For more on using the Periodic Table, go to the Help menu and select Periodic Table Handbook. You can also visit the program's Web site at http://edu.kde.org/kalzium/.

Stargazing with Planetarium

If you or your child has ever looked up in the night sky and wondered about the stars and planets, the Eee PC comes with the perfect program for you.

Clicking the Planetarium icon runs an open-source application called KStars (see Figure 7-4). The stargazing program displays a simulation of the night sky from anywhere on Earth (for any given date and time). The extensive database charts over 130,000 stars, 13,000 deep-sky objects (that's anything outside our solar system), constellations, the Sun, the Moon, all the planets, and thousands of comets and asteroids. You can zoom in, zoom out, and move around. It's like having NASA inside your mini-laptop.

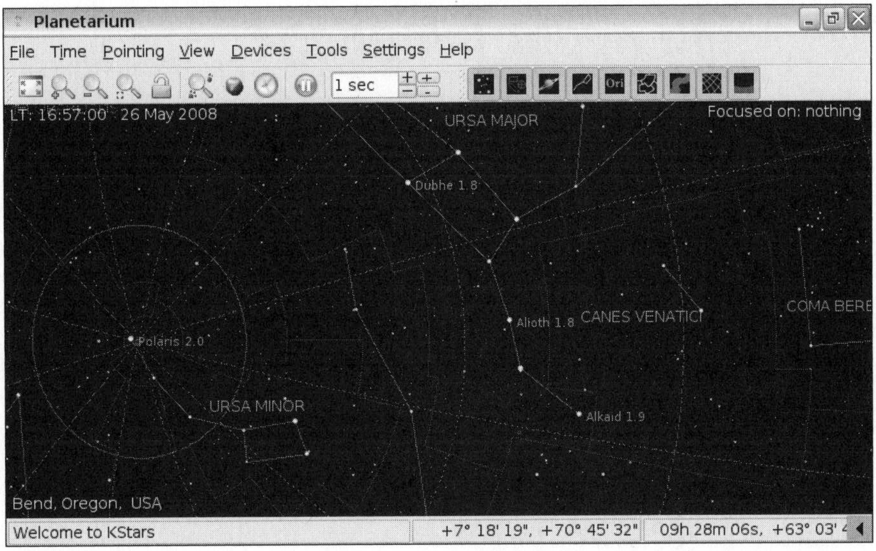

Figure 7-4: KStars desktop planetarium program.

The Eee PC is so light and portable, you can grab it at a moment's notice and head outside on a clear night to see what's out shining above. By default, KStars is synched to the laptop's clock, so what you see on the screen is what's in the sky at that time (stars and planets move in real time). The Eee PC with KStars is the perfect companion for the novice or experienced astronomer.

TIP

In the Settings menu, select Color Schemes⇨Night Vision to display the stars and labels in a subdued red. This helps you maintain your night vision when you're looking at the screen.

KStars isn't just for kids. It's actually a sophisticated astronomy program that can control telescopes and cameras, calculate celestial coordinates, show fields of view (it displays a circle that matches what you'd see from a pair of binoculars or a telescope), and more.

I recommend spending some time reading the extensive online help by selecting Desktop Planetarium Handbook in the Help menu. Or visit the KStars Web site at `http://edu.kde.org/kstars/`.

901 AND BEYOND

In later Eee PC models, ASUS includes a program called Stellarium in the Science tab. Stellarium is similar to KStars but includes photo-realistic images of the sky. If your Eee PC doesn't have Stellarium preinstalled, I tell you how to download and install the program in Chapter 13. To learn more about Stellarium, visit `www.stellarium.org`.

Learning about Language

As you probably guessed, the Language tab (inside the Learn tab) relates to learning about letters and words (English in this case, no foreign language lessons here). Three programs are contained in the Language directory (as shown in Figure 7-5).

- ✔ **Typing** is a typing tutor program.
- ✔ **Letter Game** displays jumbled words that you need to unscramble.
- ✔ **Hangman Game** is an electronic version of the old kid's game where you need to guess letters in a word and eventually the whole word.

Read on for more about each of these programs.

Teaching typing

When you click the Typing icon, it starts an open-source typing tutor program called Tux Typing 2 (Figure 7-6 shows the main screen).

Tux Typing 2 (or TuxType for short), helps kids learn how to type. It three components are

Figure 7-5:
Language
programs
in the
Learn tab.

- **Fish Cascade** — Fish with letters or words drop out of the sky, and you must type the correct letter or word to help feed a hungry penguin.

- **Comet Zap** — Comets from outer space, again with letters or words on them, threaten cities; and only a penguin and you can save the day by typing letters and words that match.

- **Lessons** — In addition to the two games, you can write scripts to create more conventional typing lessons.

Figure 7-6:
Learn
to type
with Tux
Typing 2.

Just who is Tux?

If you're running Linux on your Eee PC, you may have noticed lots of references to penguins. You might wonder or your kids may ask, "What's the deal with the cute, little penguin?"

That's just Tux, the official mascot of Linux. Here's his story.

In 1996, developers were trying to think up a mascot for Linux. Sharks and eagles were considered, but Linus Torvalds (the father of Linux, as in LInus uNIX) mentioned he was fond of penguins. That sealed it. A contest was then proposed to come up with a suitable-looking bird, but when Larry Ewing showed his version of a cuddly penguin, everyone agreed it was the one. Because penguins appear to be wearing tuxedos, someone suggested the name Tux, and the rest is history.

That's the Reader's Digest version. If you want the full, illustrated history of Tux, head over to: `www.sjbaker.org/wiki/index.php?title=The_History_of_Tux_the_Linux_Penguin`.

The games have lots of sounds with colorful animations and get high marks from young children in the fun department. You can set a number of different options, including difficulty, to make things more challenging and interesting as a child masters different levels.

The program has online help or, if you want to explore more, visit the project Web site at `http://tuxtype.sourceforge.net/`.

Rearrange the letters

Clicking the Letter Game icon runs a program called KMessedWords (many KDE programs start with the letter K, if you haven't noticed). This is a game where a scrambled up word appears on the screen, and you have to successfully enter the correct unjumbled word. The program screen is shown in Figure 7-7.

Three levels of difficulty make the game suitable for all ages. That includes adults, too. Commercial *brain fitness* software products often have similar programs for giving your mind a workout.

A bug sometimes causes the Letter Game icon to disappear from the Eee PC desktop. (I discuss the problem of vanishing icons in Chapter 22.) You can still run the program by pressing Ctrl+Alt+T (which brings up the Linux terminal), typing **kmessedwords**, and pressing the Enter key.

Figure 7-7:
The
KMessed-
Words
game.

To learn more about playing the game, in the Help menu select Letter Order Game Handbook. You can also visit the program's home page at `http://edu.kde.org/old/kmessedwords/`.

Learning words with Hangman

The last program in the Language directory is Hangman Game. It's actually an open-source program called KHangMan that's based on the pencil and paper game where you have to figure out which letters are in a word. For each wrong guess, a part to the hangman is added (the game is rated G, as the default hangman is holding onto the rope instead of it being wrapped around his neck). Figure 7-8 shows a sample screen.

There are different levels of difficulty, and you can change the appearance of the game.

As with the other programs, Hangman offers online help (in the Help menu select KHangMan Handbook) or visit the game's Web site at `http://edu.kde.org/old/khangman/`.

Figure 7-8: The KHangMan word game.

Sugar, Sugar

The One Laptop Per Child (OLPC) XO laptop has a unique user interface and set of programs that were designed from the ground up for education. Known as Sugar, the interface abandons the familiar desktop metaphor found in Windows, OS X, and KDE (Linux) for a unique, activity- and group-based approach to computing. (Sugar is a bit hard to describe in words alone so point your browser at `wiki.sugarlabs.org` to get a better idea of what it's all about.)

With the OLPC project drifting away from Linux and towards the Windows operating system, Walter Bender, Sugar's developer and former OLPC president of software and content established Sugar Labs, a non-profit organization that works on new versions of Sugar.

When he began Sugar Labs, Bender stated he would like to bring Sugar to low-cost laptops such as the Eee PC. This would provide yet another option for using the Eee PC for education. Because it's possible to boot another operating system off of a USB thumb drive or SD card, you can conceivably run Sugar for your kids while keeping the installed version of Linux or Windows intact. Stay tuned to the Sugar Labs wiki mentioned above for more information.

Boning Up on Math

When you click the Math directory icon (in the Learn tab), the following four math-related learning programs are displayed, as shown in Figure 7-9:

- **Fraction Tutorial** — Test your knowledge of fractions with this drill program.
- **TuxMath** — Help Tux the Linux penguin save the world by solving math problems.
- **Geometry** — Explore the fundamentals of geometry with this interactive program.
- **Function Plotter** — Plot mathematical functions that you enter.

Here is a brief overview of each of the math programs.

Figuring out fractions

When you click Fraction Tutorial, the KBruch program runs (in German, Bruch means *fraction* — a number of developers from Germany have been involved in creating educational programs for KDE).

KBruch is a skill-and-drill program (a sample screen is shown in Figure 7-10) where you're presented with different problems to solve, including

✔ Adding, subtracting, multiplying, and dividing fractions

✔ Determining if fractions are larger, smaller, or equal

✔ Converting fractions

✔ Factorization

Figure 7-9:
The Math
programs
in the
Learn tab.

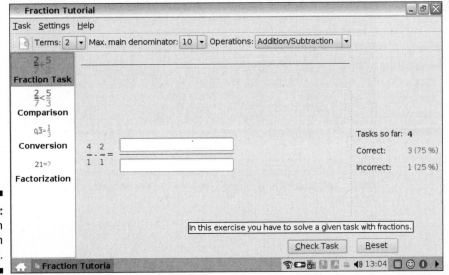

Figure 7-10:
KBruch
Fraction
Tutorial.

The program keeps track of right and wrong answers, and you can change various options to make things easier or harder. (As an adult, this application kind of makes my brain hurt — I'm glad I'm not in school anymore.)

In the Help menu, select KBruch Handbook to get extensive information about using the program or visit `http://edu.kde.org/kbruch/`.

Tux the math tutor

When you click TuxMath, the Tux of Math Command game runs. (It's a lot like the old arcade game Missile Command; see Figure 7-11.)

Falling fireballs threaten cities, and you and Tux have to save the world by entering answers to math equations. Type the correct answer and a laser beam blasts the fireball. The primary audience is children ages 4 to 10.

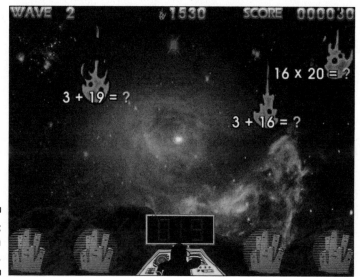

Figure 7-11:
Tux of Math
Command.

Lots of sound effects, color, and animation make this a fun, but educational game. You can change speed and the types of math problems to increase the difficulty.

It's easy to figure out the game instructions, but a help option is available when you start the game in case you need it. (There's more about TuxMath at http://tux4kids.alioth.debian.org/.)

Getting in line with geometry

Clicking on the Geometry icon runs an open-source program called Kig (as in KDE Interactive Geometry) — a sample screen is shown in Figure 7-12. Kig is designed for high school (or beyond) geometry students and teachers.

Instead of using a classroom blackboard to work through geometry concepts and problems, Kig allows you to interactively explore geometric figures — you can move components to see how other parts change as a result. In addition, you can create mathematical figures with Kig to insert as illustrations in other documents.

Kig is a fairly advanced program that doesn't have much use outside of geometry. You can get thorough online help by selecting Kig Handbook in the Help menu. Or visit the Kig Web site at http://edu.kde.org/kig/.

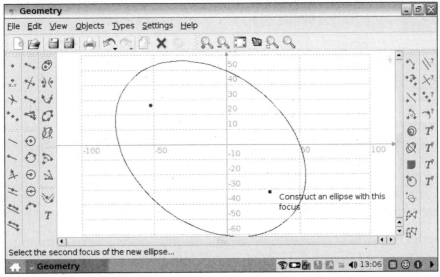

Figure 7-12:
The Kig geometry program.

KDE Education Project

The KDE Education Project is an initiative to create and distribute free Linux educational software that uses the KDE interface. Its focus is developing software for children ages 3 to 18. Many of the educational programs included with the Eee PC are part of this project.

ASUS elected not to bundle a number of titles with the Eee PC, including programs for language, math, science, and geography. (In addition,

the KDE Education Project is an ongoing effort, and new programs are occasionally added to the collection.)

Visit the project Web site at `http://edu.kde.org` to see what programs are available. If you're interested in a program that doesn't come preinstalled on the Eee PC, in Chapter 12, I describe how to install Linux software.

Plotting functions

The last icon, Function Plotter, runs a program called KmPlot (as shown in Figure 7-13). KmPlot is an application for learning about relationships between mathematical functions and their graphical representation in a coordinate system. As with Kig, this is an advanced program suited for high school or college use.

An online manual is available in the Help menu, or you can visit the KmPlot home page at `http://edu.kde.org/kmplot/`.

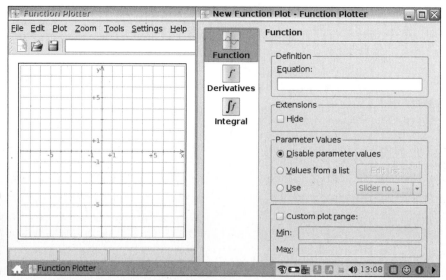

Figure 7-13: The KmPlot plotting program.

The Next DaVinci

The Eee PC comes with several art programs. These aren't art history or fine art applications, but graphics, paint-type programs. The Paint icon is actually a directory; and when you click it, the following two icons appear as shown in Figure 7-14:

- ✔ **Tux Paint** — A graphics application with a kids-oriented user interface.
- ✔ **Paint** — A traditional paint program, similar to Paint that comes with Microsoft Windows but with more features.

Here is more about each program.

Tux Paint for kids

Tux Paint (as shown in Figure 7-15) is designed for kids between 3 and 12 years old. It's a fun, easy-to-use graphics application with a surprising number of features (versions of Tux Paint are also available for Windows and the Mac). You can learn more about Tux Paint by visiting www.tuxpaint.org.

If you turn a kid loose with the program, he or she will soon figure it all out by experimentation and trial and error. (Consider turning the speaker volume down if you're in the room because the sounds can get a little annoying.)

Figure 7-14: Linux paint programs.

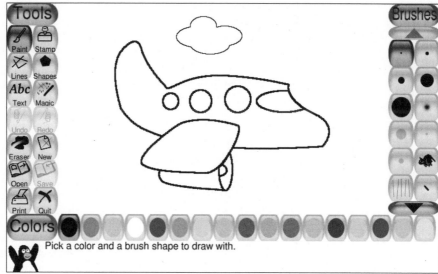

Figure 7-15: Tux Paint for kids.

However if you're not a kid, here are a few tips on getting started using the program — just in case junior has a question or two.

Tools

On the left side of the window (see Figure 7-15) are a series of tools — each icon has a symbol and a name so you have a general idea of what it does. Click an icon to select the tool. Tux the penguin gives you some additional guidance at the bottom of the screen.

On the right side of the window are more icons. These icons change depending on the tool you select. For example, when you click the Paint tool, different brushes appear. Or if you click the Text tool, a choice of fonts is displayed.

The Magic tool in the toolbar has lots of special effects, including darkening, lightening, blurring, and paint fill.

Below the drawing area is a line of color icons. Click an icon to select its associated color for drawing.

Opening and Saving

Files are stored in an easy-to-use thumbnail directory (a number of coloring-book style, line drawings are included to get a child started). The directory is displayed when you click the Open tool. Select a picture you want to edit and then click the Open button.

When you save a picture, you're not prompted for a name. The file is saved to the drive, and the picture appears in the directory when you use the Open tool. If you make changes to an existing picture, the program asks if you want to replace the old picture or save a new one.

That's enough with the tips. You'll need to play with the program to learn more. And be sure not to have too much fun.

Mastering mtPaint

If you're looking for a graphics program that's more suited for older kids and adults, click the Paint icon. This runs an open-source program called mtPaint (the mt stands for Mark Tyler by the way, the developer, as in Mark Tyler's Painting Program).A sample screen is shown in Figure 7-16.

mtPaint is a raster graphics program, which means it's designed to work with individual pixels. It supports BMP, GIF, JPEG, and PNG file formats and has a number of advanced features.

I find mtPaint especially useful for reducing the size of digital photos for e-mail or blogs and doing quick edits. The Eee PC's portability makes it easy to carry around with a digital camera. Shoot some photos, insert the camera's SD card into the Eee PC, and you're ready to go. When you're done with your edits, find a wireless connection, and share your photos with the world.

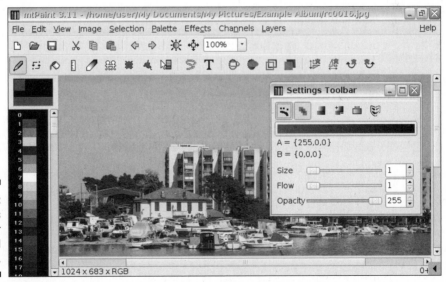

Figure 7-16: mtPaint is for older kids and adults.

Edubuntu

Edubuntu (www.edubuntu.org) is an educational version of the popular Ubuntu Linux distribution. It comes with a large number of education-related programs for kids as well as the usual Internet and office applications. Edubuntu has most of the same learning programs that come with the Eee PC plus some different ones. (Check the Web site for details.)

It's possible to install Edubuntu on an Eee PC — either on a bootable USB drive or by reformatting the drive and replacing Xandros. However, the full versions of Edubuntu and Ubuntu are both rather resource intensive and can tax the Eee PCs memory and processor (especially the 2G and 4G models).

Instead, use a *light* version of Ubuntu (such as eeeXbuntu) and then install any of education programs you're interested in. Or see if any of the programs are available in the repositories I discuss in Chapter 12.

In the Load Image File dialog box, if you can't traverse folders by clicking, select the folder you want to open and then press Enter.

The mtPaint online manual doesn't come installed; so if you want to learn more about the program, go to http://mtpaint.sourceforge.net/.

Learning on the Web

When you click the Web Learn icon (on the Learn tab), it opens the browser and, if you have an Internet connection, loads a site called Skoool (www.skoool.ie). This is an interactive education project designed to serve Ireland's secondary and high school students. The online program debuted in 2002, and has won many awards. Its model is being adopted in other countries around the world with sponsorship from Intel. To visit other Skoool projects and to find out more, go to www.skoool.com.

I want to mention a few other education-related sites that the Eee PC doesn't reference. Parents and teachers may find these useful.

Internet4Classrooms

Internet4Classrooms (alias I4C) is an amazing collection of links, tutorials, and other resources for K-12 teachers. Even if you're not a teacher, this is a great place to find educational activities for your kids to supplement their school curriculums. The site is located at www.internet4classrooms.com.

Curriki

Curriki (as in Curriculum Wiki) is where teachers share curriculum and resources. You can find lesson plans, lectures in PowerPoint, and all manner of classroom-proven material. Visit the site at `www.curriki.org`.

Ed Tech Review

If you want to keep up with technology in education (including software, Web sites, and hardware), Ed Tech Review (`www.edtechreview.net`) is a great blog to consult. Besides the new content, it's worthwhile spending some time going through the archives and reading older posts.

AOL Kids Homework Help

Whereas the other sites I've just mentioned have been for grown-ups, this one is for children. America Online (AOL) developed a kid-friendly (and safe) Web site called KOL (Kids Online). One of the featured sections is called Homework Help, which has a number of educational resources and links for kids. You can check out the site at `http://kids.aol.com/KOL/1/HomeworkHelp`.

AOL ran a pretty good educational Web site called AOL@SCHOOL (`www.aolatschool.com`) with content for both students and teachers. The educator tools and resources are now housed at the National Education Association's (NEA) Academy Web site (`www.nea.org/classroom/aol.html`).

More Learn icons

On the 901 and later model Eee PCs you might find some additional icons in the desktop Learn tab. These include:

- ✔ **Mebook** — The MeReader e-book viewer

- ✔ **Go Chinese** — A program that teaches you the basics of Chinese languages

- ✔ **Kids Game** — A collection of children's educational games

- ✔ **Star Map** — The Stellarium star program that I describe in the Studying Science section of this chapter

For more information on these programs, refer to your user manual or consult the online help.

Chapter 8

Eee PC at Play

· ·

In This Chapter

▶ Playing Eee PC games

▶ Watching videos

▶ Listening to music

▶ Working with digital photos

▶ Using the Web cam

▶ Recording sound

· ·

All work and no play makes the Eee PC a dull computer (or something like that). ASUS recognized this universal truth, and decided to include a variety of programs on the mini-laptop that are expressly designed for your enjoyment and entertainment.

In this chapter, I look at programs found in the Linux desktop Play tab (as shown in Figure 8-1). These include a collection of games (some new ones and a few familiar old favorites), a media player for watching videos, a music manager for playing tunes, a digital photo manager, a Web cam utility, and a sound recorder.

So kick back and relax, and let's get down to the serious business of play.

You can find basic instructions for all the programs I describe in this chapter in the Eee PC's online help. At the Linux desktop, click the Help menu item and then in the browser window, select the Play tab.

Figure 8-1:
Programs
in the
Play tab.

Playing Games

You can't have a computer without games, so it should be no surprise that lots of games come installed on the Eee PC.

Clicking the Games icon in the Play tab displays seven program icons shown in Figure 8-2. These icons include

- **Solitaire** is the ever-popular, time-wasting card game.
- **Frozen Bubble** is a game where you shoot colored bubbles to form groups of the same color.
- **Crack Attack** is a variation of the popular Tetris Attack, a Super Nintendo game.
- **Penguin Racer** turns Tux the penguin into a bobsled that you guide down snowy mountains.
- **Sudoku** is an electronic version of the popular number-based, logic puzzle.
- **Potato Guy** is the game where you dress up a potato (and other characters).
- **LTris** is a Linux version of the classic Tetris game.

Read on for more information about all these games.

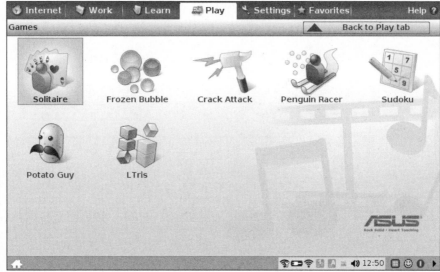

Solitaire

When you click the Solitaire icon, you're rewarded with the card game
that bosses love to hate, as shown in Figure 8-3. It's a Linux version named
KPatience. (Americans call the game Solitaire, whereas Europeans call it
Patience — the developers who wrote this program were Europeans.)

More games

In addition to the games I just listed, if you have
a 901 or later model Eee PC you'll find several
more games preinstalled. These include

✔ **TuxPuck** is a virtual air hockey game (see
`http://home.no.net/munsuun/`
`tuxpuck/`).

✔ **Supertux** is a Linux version of the popular
SuperMario arcade games (see `http://`
`supertux.lethargik.org/`).

✔ **BOS Wars** is a real-time strategy war
game — with an economic twist (see
`www.boswars.org/`).

✔ **Mahjongg** is the classic Chinese board
game where you match tiles (see `www.`
`lcdf.org/xmahjongg/`).

✔ **Enigma** is a puzzle game where you
uncover pairs of colored stones (see `www.`
`nongnu.org/enigma/`).

For more information on these programs, refer
to your user manual or consult the online help.
If you don't have these games installed but are
interested in them, I tell you how to download
and install Linux software in Chapter 12.

Figure 8-3:
The
KPatience
solitaire
card game.

If you like playing Solitaire on Windows, you'll love KPatience. Some of its features include

- Seventeen different types of games (rules for each of the games are found in the online help)
- Customizable graphics (with a large number of backgrounds and cards)
- Animation
- Statistics
- Hints

To learn more about this version of solitaire, in the game's Help menu select KPatience Handbook. You can also read the user manual on the Web at http://docs.kde.org/development/en/kdegames/kpat/.

Frozen Bubble

Frozen Bubble (as shown in Figure 8-4) is one of more popular Linux arcade-style games. You control a small cannon that dispenses colored bubbles (you aim with right- and left-arrow keys and the up-arrow key fires). You shoot at bubbles at the top of the screen, trying to group three or more bubbles of the same color. When you match a group, the bubbles come falling down. The goal is to get all the bubbles to fall.

Figure 8-4:
The Frozen
Bubble
game.

Use the arrow keys and Enter to select options when you first start the game. Press the Esc key to end the game.

You can play the game solo or with others (including over the Net), at different difficulty levels. Read the basic instructions when you start Frozen Bubble, or visit the game's home page at www.frozen-bubble.org.

Crack Attack

Crack Attack (as shown in Figure 8-5) is based on the Tetris Attack game for Super Nintendo. Crack Attack gets its name from its fiendishly addictive nature.

The goal of the game is to keep a rising stacks of blocks from reaching the top of the screen (as time goes on, the speed of the rising blocks increases). Get rid of blocks by lining up three or more blocks of the same color. You do this using a set of brackets controlled by the arrow keys. Press the spacebar to switch the positions of two blocks between the brackets or to move a single block. Use the brackets to line up same colored blocks or make them drop.

Press P to pause. Press P again to resume.

If you get addicted to the game on your Eee PC, versions are available for Windows and Mac and can be downloaded at: www.nongnu.org/crack-attack.

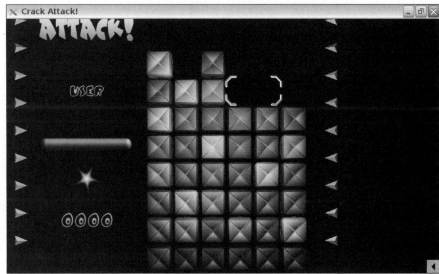

Figure 8-5:
The Crack
Attack
game.

Penguin Racer

When you click Penguin Racer, a game called PlanetPenguin Racer loads. This is a version of the popular Tux Racer game. Tux is Linux's penguin mascot, who in this case is sliding down a mountain on his front side like an avian bobsled (see what I mean in Figure 8-6).

Figure 8-6:
The Planet-
Penguin
Racer game.

You control Tux with the right- and left-arrow keys. The down arrow slows him down and the up arrow paddles his flippers, which makes him go faster at low speeds. (Use the cursor to click Configuration when the game first loads to see other keyboard commands.)

Keep the penguin on course between the race flags and score extra points by collecting fish on the way down the hill. Press Esc when you're done playing.

For more on the game, check out the Wiki entry at `http://en.wikipedia.org/wiki/Tux_Racer`.

Sudoku

Sudoku (as shown in Figure 8-7) is the digital version of the internationally popular number puzzle that appears in newspapers, magazines, and books. The game features nine large squares (blocks), with each block composed of nine smaller squares. The goal is to fill the squares so each column, row, and each of the blocks contains the numbers 1 to 9 only one time each.

Click a square, and then enter a number. If that number is already in a column, row, or block, it turns red. If you need a little assistance, click the Hint icon in the toolbar (it looks like a lifesaving ring) to show what possible values can fit in the currently selected square.

This is a great "brain training" game for improving your observation, logic, and reasoning skills.

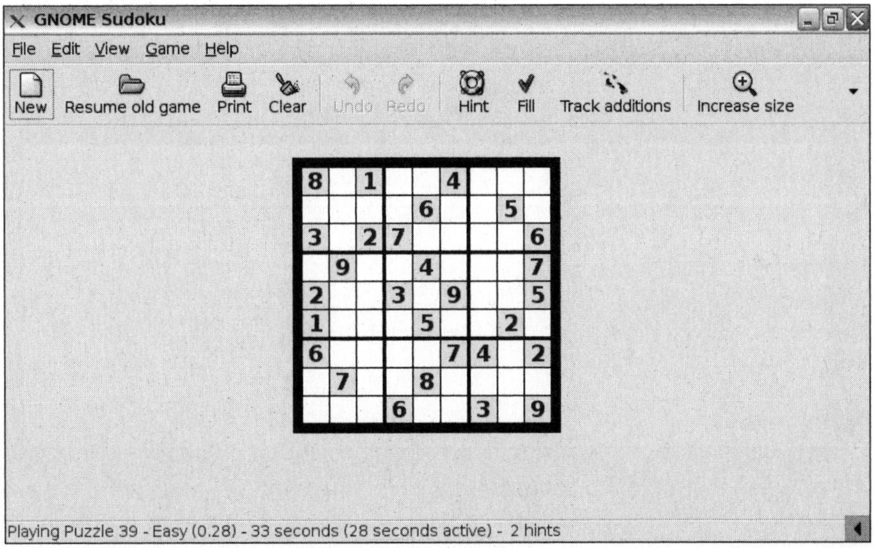

Figure 8-7:
A Sudoku
puzzle.

Get more information about this version of Sudoku by visiting the game's Web site at http://gnome-sudoku.sourceforge.net/.

There are a number of well-established strategies for successfully completing a Sudoku puzzle in the shortest possible amount of time. If you're new to the game, to learn some strategies you can visit www.sudokudragon.com/sudokustrategy.htm.

Potato Guy

Click the Potato Guy icon to play a kids game called KTuberling (you may have noticed some of the KDE programs have rather unique K names; in this case, a potato is also known as a tuber). This is a digital version of the old Mr. Potato Head game, where you stick eyes, a nose, a mouth, and other decorative ornaments on a spud (as shown in Figure 8-8). You can also dress up Tux the penguin and create a deep sea aquarium scene. When you're finished with your masterpiece you can print or save the picture.

Potato Guy is pretty straightforward to play, but if you need documentation, in the Help menu, select KTuberling Handbook or read the user manual on the Web at http://docs.kde.org/development/en/kdegames/ktuberling.

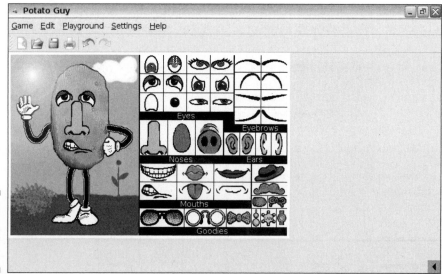

Figure 8-8:
The Potato Guy program.

More Linux games

Looking for other Linux games to play? Check out the Linux Game Tome at http://happypenguin.org. This site lists and describes games, including screen shots, features, and user reviews. Find the name of a game that looks interesting, and then see if it's available in one of the repositories I list in Chapter 12.

LTris

LTris is a clone of the classic 1980s computer game Tetris. If you wonder where the name Tetris came from, it's a mix of *tetra* (all the pieces contain four segments) and *tennis*, the author's favorite sport.

The goal of the game is to, well, keep playing. Prevent the falling pieces from stacking up and reaching the top of the screen by arranging the blocks so they form an unbroken horizontal line across the playing area. This eliminates that row of blocks. An example screen is shown in Figure 8-9.

Figure 8-9:
The LTris game.

Move a falling piece to the right or left with the right- and left-arrow keys. Rotate a piece with the up arrow. Cause the piece to drop quickly with the down arrow. Use the Esc key to end a game and exit the program.

At the opening screen, leave the cursor on a command or option to display pop-up information.

Watching Videos

When you click the Media Player icon, an open-source program named SMPlayer runs, as shown in Figure 8-10. (SMPlayer is an improved user interface version of a popular program called MPlayer.)

You can right-click anywhere in the main window to display a pop-up command menu. This is handy if you're in the middle of watching a video and want to pause it.

As you probably guessed, SMPlayer is for playing audio and video media. Here are some of its features:

- ✔ Support for common file formats including MPEG, DivX, Windows Media, RealAudio/Video, and QuickTime
- ✔ DVD playback
- ✔ Extensive subtitle support
- ✔ Internet audio and video streaming support
- ✔ User-created playlists
- ✔ Multiple playback speeds

Figure 8-10: The SMPlayer media player.

Many Eee PC users run a DVD-ripping program on their primary computer, and then save the DVD movie to an SD card. This makes it easy to watch movies on the Eee PC without an attached DVD player. If you've never ripped a DVD before (converted a DVD to a file that can be played on a computer using SMPlayer or another media player), a number of free programs make the process easy. For more information on the programs and the process, visit www.doom9.org/.

The version of MPlayer that comes with the Eee PC does not support h.264 format QuickTime videos. This means you won't be able to play videos created for the Apple iPod. You can convert the videos to another format or do a bit of hacking and install an older version of MPlayer that supports h.264 videos. Here's a tutorial on installing the older version: http://wiki.eeeuser.com/downgradingmplayer.

SMPlayer doesn't come with online help, so to learn more about the program, visit the project Web site at: http://smplayer.sourceforge.net/.

Adding additional codecs

If you have a video that SMPlayer won't play, it's probably because an associated codec isn't present. A codec (which stands for coder-decoder or compressor-decompressor) is a program (or file with instructions for a program) to compress or decompress audio and video. Depending on how the video was encoded, you may need to install another codec to view it.

For example, if you save a YouTube video (in FLV, Flash Video format) to your Eee PC, SMPlayer plays the video with no audio. However, after you install additional codes, as I describe in the following section, the video plays with sound.

A program called Codec Pack is compatible with SMPlayer. It contains a number of different codecs. Here's how to install the Pack:

1. **Connect to the Internet.**

2. **Open a Linux console window by pressing Ctrl+Alt+T.**

3. **Enter the following:** sudo /usr/share/mplayer/scripts/binary_codecs.sh install.

This runs a shell script that installs the codecs. Status messages are displayed during the installation. After the Codec Pack is successfully installed you should be able to play the video you initially had troubles with.

If running the shell script doesn't work, check out this link for the tried and true method of manually downloading and installing codecs: http://news. softpedia.com/news/How-to-Install-Multimedia-Codecs-in- Linux-39555.shtml.

Watching DVDs

If you have a USB DVD player and want to use SMPlayer to watch DVD movies on your Eee PC, you first download and install some additional files.

The files needed to view DVDs are in a library called *libdvdcss*. This library contains code for accessing and unscrambling DVDs encrypted with the Content Scramble System (CSS) protection scheme.

To download and install the files required to watch a DVD, follow these steps:

1. **On your Eee PC, go to this Web site at http://download.videolan. org/pub/libdvdcss/1.2.9/.**

2. **Click the deb/ directory.**

3. **Click libdvdcss2_1.2.9-1_i386.deb.**

4. **Select Save to Disk and click OK**

5. **Click the Save button to save the file to My Documents.**

6. **With the File Manager, go to the My Documents directory.**

7. **Right-click libdvdcss2_1.2.9-1_i386.deb, and from the pop-up menu select Install DEB File....**

   You must provide the password you set the first time you ran your Eee PC. A dialog box tells you when the installation is complete.

After the files are installed (and the DVD player is connected to your Eee PC with a DVD inserted), run SMPlayer. From the Open menu, select DVD from drive to watch your movie.

If the audio and video don't synch, in the SMPlayer Options menu select Preferences. Check Allow frame drop and click OK.

On 901 and later model Eee PCs, ASUS includes a standalone, commercial DVD program in the desktop Play tab called LinDVD. The program is easy to use and doesn't require all the tweaking that SMPlayer does in order to watch DVDs.

Managing and Playing Music

Clicking the Music Manager icon runs an open-source program called Amarok (as shown in Figure 8-11). As the icon name suggests, Amarok is a digital music player and organizer. You can listen to music stored on

- The Eee PC's drive
- An inserted SD card
- An inserted USB thumb or hard drive
- A commercial music CD using an external USB CD/DVD player
- The Internet

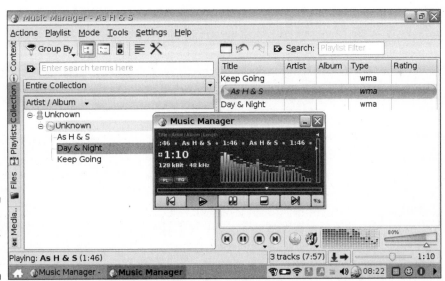

Figure 8-11:
The Amarok music player.

Some of Amarok's features include

- ✔ Compatibility with common media formats such as MP3, WMA, FLAC, WAV and others. (However, Amarok doesn't play files with Digital Rights Management protection, such as music downloaded from iTunes or other commercial sources.)

- ✔ Internet audio streaming and podcast support.

- ✔ MP3 player synchronization.

- ✔ Cover art display.

- ✔ File tagging including MusicBrainz searches. (`MusicBrainz.org` is a free online database that supplies artist and recording information.)

- ✔ The capability to look up and attach lyrics to songs.

- ✔ Visual effects.

- ✔ User-created playlists.

When you run Amarok, it adds an icon to the taskbar. Right-click the icon to Quit. If only the small, *play* window is displayed, click the PL button to show the main playlist window.

To learn more about using Amarok, in the Help menu select Music Manager Handbook or visit the project Web site at `http://amarok.kde.org/`.

---

iPod info

If you have an Apple iPod (and who doesn't these days?), here's the lowdown on using it with the Eee PC.

First off, currently no iTunes compatible programs run on Linux. So don't expect to be able to use iTunes on your Eee PC (unless it's running Windows XP).

Amarok will synch up music with your iPod just like iTunes. But, there's a big catch, so pay close attention. If you have version 1.4.3 of Amarok (select About Music Manager in the Help menu to see) and an iPod that's newer than June 2007, **do not** try to synch your iPod with Amarok. A problem with this release of Amarok can corrupt the iPod's song database. You may be forced to reload all your songs on the iPod (always a good idea to have them synched on another computer, just in case) or perform a system reset. This problem doesn't seem to be present with older iPods. If you have a newer iPod, either update Amarok or use a Linux iPod program called gtkPod (`www.gtkpod.org`). A tutorial for installing gtkPod on the Eee PC can be found at `http://wiki.eeeuser.com/gtkpod`.

You can charge your iPod on the Eee PC without running Amarok. In fact, the Eee PC even provides power from its USB ports even if it's turned off (as long as it's plugged into a wall socket).

Viewing Photos and Graphics Files

The Eee PC comes with a great image viewer named *Gwenview*. When you click the Photo Manager icon, the image viewer loads and displays thumbnails of graphics files in the My Pictures folder of your My Documents directory (if image files are in a subfolder, you open the folder first). Figure 8-12 show Gwenview in action, displaying the contents of the sample Album folder that comes with the Eee PC.

Right-click a thumbnail to copy, rename, move, or delete an image file. You can also edit a file by selecting a graphics program called *KolourPaint* from the *External Tools* pop-up menu.

Some of Gwenview's features include

✔ Browse, view, and open graphics files (including BMP, EPS, JPEG, PNG, and other common formats)

✔ Resize and rotate images

✔ Play a slide show

✔ Display images in full screen mode

✔ Use KIPI add-ons (KDE Image Plugin Interface — small add-on programs for manipulating images)

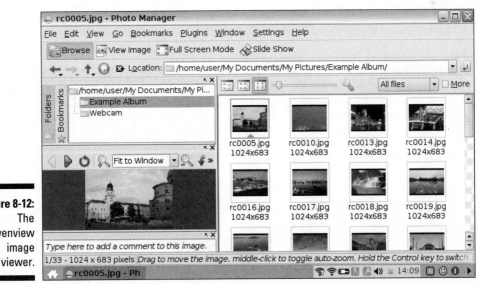

Figure 8-12: The Gwenview image viewer.

Viewing digital camera photos

Instead of looking at the photos you just took on your digital camera's small screen, put Gwenview and your Eee PC to work. You can view individual photos or use Gwenview's slide-show feature to automatically display a series of images.

The two ways to view digital photos are

- ✔ Insert the camera's SD card into the Eee PC and select the folder you want to display with Gwenview.

- ✔ If your digital camera comes with a USB cable, connect the camera to the Eee PC.

Then turn on the camera, select the camera, and choose the camera folder you want to display within Gwenview.

To connect your camera to an Eee PC, the camera must be able to function as a USB storage device; often called UMS (Universal Mass Storage) or MSC (Mass Storage Class). Read your camera user manual to see if it has this feature and how to turn it on. If your camera can serve as a USB device, you can also view and access photos with File Manager.

To learn more about using Gwenview, in the Help menu select Photo Manager Handbook or visit the project Web site at `http://gwenview.source forge.net/`.

If you upgrade to a newer version of Photo Manager and the Plugins menu is no longer displayed, check out this fix courtesy of the EeeUser.com Wiki at `http://wiki.eeeuser.com/gwenviewui-rc_file_fix`.

Organizing Video Files

Don't expect a video-related program with this icon! When you click Video Manager, the File Manager runs and opens the My Videos folder in your My Documents folder of your Home directory. Otherwise, Video Manager isn't an application, but just a quick way to view any videos you have stored in the My Videos folder.

You can copy, delete, and rename files as well as use any of the other File Manager commands.

Smiling for the Web Camera

When you click the Web Cam icon a program called *ucview* runs. Ucview works with the Eee PC's built-in Web cam and allows you to record videos and still images. The program's main window displays what the camera sees, as shown in Figure 8-13.

When the Web cam is turned on, a green light next to the camera lens is lit up.

You control the program with the following command icons in the toolbar:

✔ **Pause** pauses recording. Click Pause again to resume.

✔ **Save Image** saves a JPEG file of the current Web cam image.

✔ **Record Video** starts recording video (and sound). Click Record Video again to stop recording. The video is processed and saved to the My Videos folder in My Documents. Double-click a video in File Manager to play the file with an SMPlayer.

Videos are saved in OGG Theora file format (see http://theora.org for additional information). Ogg Theora is an open-source alternative to the MPEG format. If you want to play an OGG video on another computer, you may need to install a codec for your media player or install VLC (www.videolan.org/vlc/), a multi-platform media play that can play OGG files as well as most other video formats.

✔ **Adjustments** lets you change brightness, contrast, and other color settings.

✔ **Preferences** controls the video quality and specifies where the video and still images are saved to.

Figure 8-13:
The ucview
Web cam
program.

Web cam wizardry

You can manually turn the Web cam on and off with the following console commands. First press Ctrl+Alt+T to display a console window.

To turn the camera on, type

```
sudo echo 1 > /proc/acpi/
   asus/camera
```

To turn the camera off, type

```
sudo echo 0 > /proc/acpi/
   asus/camera
```

If you're going to be shooting a lot of video, especially if you have an Eee PC with a small amount of drive space, set the file save path to an SD card instead of to the internal drive.

There's not much online documentation available for ucview, so if you run into a question or problem, I suggest posting a message to the EeeUser.com forums that I discuss in Chapter 10.

Recording Voice and Sounds

You can take advantage of the Eee PC's soundcard, built-in microphone (or use an external one), and preinstalled software to record voice, music, and sounds. When you click the Sound Recorder icon, a program named krecord runs (as shown in Figure 8-14).

Some of krecord's features include

- ✔ Easy-to-use interface
- ✔ The capability to record and play WAV files
- ✔ Variable recording options including sample rate, number of channels, and 8- or 16-bit PCM
- ✔ Multiple file support
- ✔ Input level and frequency spectrum displays

WAV files are uncompressed and can take up a fair amount of memory and drive space. For example, with default settings, 30 seconds of recording is over 5MB. You can reduce size of a recorded sound by changing the audio format to 8-bit, using mono instead of stereo, and lowering the sampling rate.

For more on using krecord, in the Help menu select Sound Recorder Handbook.

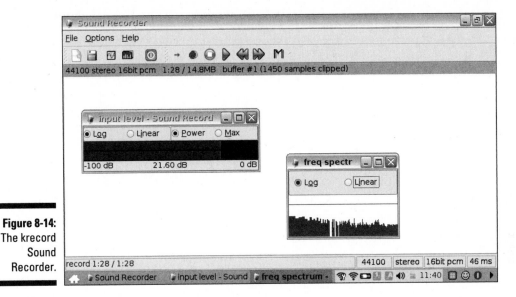

Figure 8-14:
The krecord
Sound
Recorder.

krecord is a great basic sound recording program, but if you're looking for something a little more advanced, check out Audacity (`http://audacity.sourceforge.net/`). If it looks like Audacity is for you, here's a link to a tutorial that shows you how to install the program on an Eee PC: `http://asuseeehacks.blogspot.com/2007/11/installing-audacity-on-eee-pc.html`.

More Play icons

On the 901 and later model Eee PCs you might find some additional icons in the desktop Play tab. Besides the new games I mention in the "Playing Games" section at the start of the chapter, added programs include

✔ **DVD Player** — A standalone, commercial DVD player called LinDVD. Remember, you'll need an external DVD player to watch movies on your Eee PC.

✔ **Picasa** — The popular program for managing, editing, and sharing digital photos (see `http://picasa.google.com`).

For more information on these programs, refer to your user manual or consult the online help.

Chapter 9

Configuring the Eee PC

- -

In This Chapter

▶ Getting system information and running diagnostics

▶ Personalizing your Eee PC

▶ Changing monitor, touchpad, time, and volume settings

▶ Installing and configuring printers

▶ Checking for viruses

▶ Adding software updates

▶ Using VoiceCommand

▶ Shutting down

- -

*I*nside the Eee PC's Linux desktop Settings tab (shown in Figure 9-1) you find a number of programs for changing system settings and handling administrative tasks. Think of the Settings tab as the Eee PC's control center.

Figure 9-1:
The Eee PC
Settings tab.

There are utilities for setting personalization options, speaker and microphone volume, touchpad preferences, time and date, and external display device parameters. You can install printers, check for viruses, get system information (as well as run diagnostic tests), and update software. There's even a program for starting up programs with voice commands.

In this chapter, I discuss these programs and describe how to use them.

Viewing System Info

Click the System Info icon to display system information about your Eee PC. A dialog box is displayed (like the one shown in Figure 9-2), that lists specifics such as the BIOS version, operating system version, CPU, and memory. If you ever need to get support for your Eee PC, it's good to have this information handy.

Figure 9-2:
You'll find important info in the System Info dialog box.

System Info	
BIOS version:	0401
BIOS date:	10/17/2007
Software version:	Eee PC 1.0.1
Build info:	2007-10-19 13:03
CPU type:	Intel (R) Mobile Processor
Memory size:	512 MB
Motherboard version:	x.xx
Battery status:	on AC power

Personalizing Your Eee PC

The Eee PC comes with several programs that allow you to personalize your mini-laptop. You can change the desktop theme and add frequently used programs to the Favorites tab, as well as change your account name and password. Here's the lowdown on doing these tasks and more.

Using Personalization

Click the Personalization icon in the Settings tab to configure account name, password, desktop appearance, and other settings. You can see the Personalization program window in Figure 9-3.

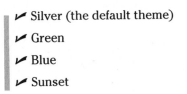

Figure 9-3:
Personal-
ization
program
setting
options.

Editing your account name and password

When you run your Eee PC for the first time, you are prompted to provide an account name and a password. Use the personalization program to change these two settings.

Changing the account name is simply a matter of typing in something new.

To change your password, enter the current one and then type in the new password twice; just to make sure you got it right. Passwords are displayed in asterisks, so if you make a typo, you won't know what you did. If the two passwords don't match, try again.

Setting the desktop theme

The Personalization program also allows you to change the desktop's theme. You don't have a lot of options for customizing the appearance as you do on many other computers. In fact you're limited to choosing from the following four desktop color schemes:

- Silver (the default theme)
- Green
- Blue
- Sunset

Give each one a try, and see which one you like best.

If you want to go beyond these simple themes, check out Chapter 21 where I describe some advanced techniques for customizing the desktop.

Other personalization options

Other settings in the Personalization program, include

✔ **The Keyboard Layout drop-down menu** — This lets you change your keyboard to one of several preinstalled settings. You're best to leave this one alone unless you have a good reason.

✔ **The Log Me In Automatically control** — If this is checked, you won't be prompted for a password each time the Eee PC starts up. If you keep sensitive information on your mini-laptop, I recommend leaving this option unchecked.

✔ **The Turn Off Display After 5 Minutes of Inactivity check box** — If you haven't used the keyboard or touchpad for five minutes, the screen goes black. Brush the touchpad or press any key (Esc is always a good one), to turn the monitor back on.

Adding favorites

I'm going to jump out of the desktop Settings tab for a moment and talk about the Favorites tab, because it also has to do with personalizing your Eee PC (plus there's not enough in this tab to devote an entire chapter to it).

The default content of the Favorites tab has two icons (as shown in Figure 9-4). The icons include

✔ **ASUS.com** — Runs the browser and takes you to the ASUS Web site (if you're connected to the Net).

✔ **Customize** — Runs a program that allows you to copy icons from other preinstalled programs to the Favorites tab.

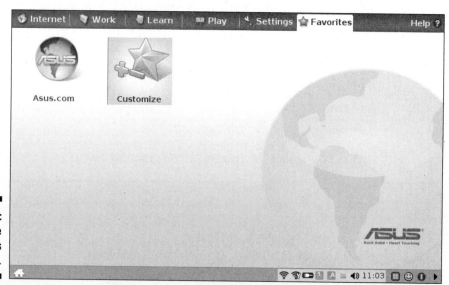

Figure 9-4:
The
Favorites
tab.

On 901 and later model Eee PCs, ASUS also includes a Suggestion Box icon you can click to provide online feedback about your mini-laptop.

The idea is you can keep a collection of commonly used programs in a single handy location. For example, if you often find yourself using Documents (word processor), File Manager, Web (browser), and Solitaire, add them to Favorites so you don't need to jump between desktop tabs. (The program icons still remain in their original tabs; a copy of the icon is just added to Favorites.)

The Customize program displays a list of preinstalled program icons (see what I mean in Figure 9-5). Several commands are available.

- ✔ Select a program name in the Available Favorites list and then click Add to move the program to the Current Favorites list. The program then appears in the Favorites tab.

- ✔ Select a program name in Current Favorites and click the Up or Down buttons to change the order of appearance in the Favorites tab.

- ✔ Use the Remove button to remove a selected Current Favorites file from the Favorites tab.

The Remove button does not uninstall the program. It only removes the icon from the Favorites tab.

Click OK to save your changes. The Favorites tab is now updated with the program icons you added or removed.

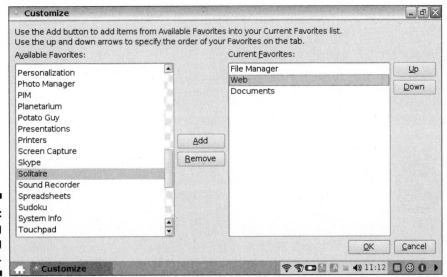

Figure 9-5: Adding and editing Favorites.

Changing the Date & Time

If you travel with your Eee PC, you may want to update the current time (and possibly date) before or after you reach your destination.

Click the Date & Time icon in the Settings tab to set the current day and time. A window is displayed with a calendar, clock, and command buttons (as shown in Figure 9-6).

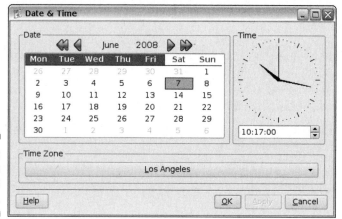

Figure 9-6:
Setting the
date and
time.

To set the current date

Follow these steps to set the date on your Eee PC:

1. **Use the blue arrows above the calendar to scroll through the months and years.**

   Single arrows move forward or backward a month; double arrows move forward or backward a year.

2. **Click the current day.**

3. **Click the Apply button to save the changed date.**

You can use the Date & Time program to scroll through the calendar to find what day of the week a date falls on. Find the month and year you're interested in and then click Cancel instead of OK.

To set the current time

Click the digital clock beneath the analog clock hands to set the current time. You can either type in a number or use the up and down arrows to increment or decrement the current time value (the up arrow advances; the down arrow goes back).

1. **Click hours and enter the current time.**

2. **Click minutes and enter the current time.**

3. **Click seconds and enter the current time.**

4. **Click the Time Zone button and select the current time zone (if it's changed).**

5. **Click the Apply button to save the time change.**

Setting the time and date is pretty straightforward, but if you need additional assistance, click the Help button to display online help.

Setting Speaker and Microphone Volume

The Volume icon in the Settings tab controls the speaker and microphone volume. Normally this program automatically runs when you start your Eee PC, and nothing happens when you click it. (You'll know if the program is running if a speaker icon appears in the taskbar.)

Click the speaker icon in the taskbar to display volume controls as shown in Figure 9-7.

Use the vertical sliders to set speaker (labeled Volume) and microphone (labeled Mic) volume levels. Move the slider up to increase the volume. Move the slider down to decrease the volume.

Figure 9-7: Speaker and microphone volume controls.

Linux and printers

Not all printers will work with Linux. Because Microsoft has been the dominant provider of operating systems over the years, a number of printer manufacturers have elected only to provide Windows drivers (the software that interfaces a printer with a computer). That's changing with the growing popularity of Linux and Macs, but there are many printers out there that you won't be able to use with your Eee PC.

The best Web site to see if your printer is compatible with Linux is the Linux Foundation's

OpenPrinting Database at `http://open printing.org/printer_list.cgi`.

Enter a manufacturer and model number to find out about compatibility.

You can also check the back of your Eee PC user manual, which contains a list of compatible printers or the EeeUser.com Wiki (`http://wiki.eeeuser.com`), which maintains a hardware compatibility list.

Moving the cursor over the speaker icon in the taskbar shows the current volume level setting.

✔ Click the Mute checkboxes to turn the speaker or microphone off.

✔ Use the horizontal slider to control speaker balance. The default setting provides an equal amount of sound to each speaker, but you can change the value to add more to the left or right.

If the speaker icon doesn't appear in the taskbar, click the Volume icon in the Settings tab.

Configuring Printers

Clicking the Printers icon runs a program that enables you to add and configure printers to use with your Eee PC. (If you're interested in connecting to a shared Windows printer, I talk more about this is Chapter 3.)

In this section, I give you a quick overview on how to install and configure printers. For more information, refer to the online help by clicking the Help button at the bottom of the Printers window (as shown in Figure 9-8). Also, be sure to read the "Linux and printers" sidebar.

Adding and configuring printers

To install a printer to use with your Eee PC, follow these steps:

1. **Click the Add... button.**

   This launches the Add Printer Wizard, which steps you through the process.

2. **Select Local printer or Network printer and click Next.**

Adding a local printer

If you decide to add a local printer (which you can connect to the Eee PC with a USB cable), follow these steps:

1. **Give the printer a name and choose which port to use (USB Printer is selected by default).**

2. **Choose the printer manufacturer and model from the drop-down lists. The correct driver is selected for you.**

   The Eee PC has a built-in database of compatible printers and drivers. If your printer isn't shown, you can try a similar model or Generic.

3. **Optionally print a test page and click Finish.**

Adding a network printer

If you elected to add a network printer, follow these steps:

1. **Select a network type (Windows, Unix, or other), provide a printer name, and specify a printer path (use the Browse button).**

2. **Choose the printer manufacturer and model from the drop-down lists. The correct driver is selected for you.**

   If your printer isn't shown, try a similar model or Generic.

3. **Optionally, print a test page and click Finish.**

Figure 9-8:
Use the
Printers
program to
install and
configure
printers.

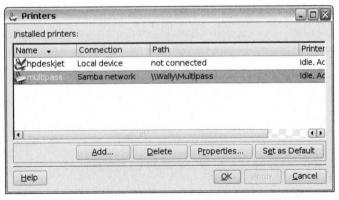

Configuring a printer

After you have added a printer, it appears in the list of installed printers (as shown in Figure 9-8). Four buttons under the list enable you to configure the printers.

- ✔ **Add** — Adds a printer, as I just described.
- ✔ **Delete** — Uninstalls the selected printer and removes it from the list.
- ✔ **Properties** — Displays a dialog box with settings for the selected printer, including name, paper size, ink color, and other printer-specific options.
- ✔ **Set as Default** — If you have multiple printers installed, this option sets the selected printer as default when you print. The default printer has a checkmark on its icon.

If your printer doesn't work

If you can't get a printer to work with your Eee PC (because of compatibility or other issues), here are my suggestions:

- ✔ **Ask for help on the EeeUser.com forums** (`http://forum.eeeuser.com`) — Mention the printer model and what type of problems you're having. Before posting the query, be sure to do a quick search for mention of your printer in the forums — to see if anyone has already asked the same question and had it answered.

- ✔ **Print on another computer** — Copy the file you want to print onto a USB thumb drive or SD card and print it on another computer with a printer that works. This is a low-tech, but effective solution.

 Honestly, getting certain printers to work on the Eee PC can be a time-consuming challenge, even for a Linux guru. Sometimes it's best to go with the path of least resistance.

- ✔ **Purchase a compatible printer** — Check the back of your Eee PC user manual for a list of compatible printers (unfortunately, many of these printers are fairly old, so a number of them are discontinued). Also check the EeeUser.com Wiki for a hardware compatibility list, based on user experiences (`http://wiki.eeeuser.com/#compatibility_information`).

Changing Touchpad Settings

Clicking the Touchpad icon runs a program for changing touchpad settings. The Touchpad Preferences window, as shown in Figure 9-9, has four tabs. The following sections explain what each tab contains.

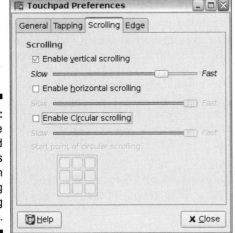

Figure 9-9:
The
Touchpad
Preferences
program
showing
scrolling
options.

General

The General tab contains two controls:

- ✓ **Enable Touchpad** — Make sure this is checked. If it's not, you won't be able to use your touchpad.

- ✓ **Sensitivity** — Set's how much pressure the touchpad requires to work. High means lightly touching the surface moves the cursor. Low means you must press down harder on the surface.

If your cursor doesn't seem to be responsive, always try changing the sensitivity setting.

Tapping

The Tapping tab has three controls that, you guessed it, allow the touchpad to support tapping. When tapping is enabled, the touchpad serves as a mouse button. Tap once to single-click. Tap twice to double-click.

- ✓ **Enable Tapping** — When checked, this option allows you to tap the touchpad to emulate mouse clicks.

- ✓ **Tapping Time** — This option sets the time duration for a recognized mouse click. Short is a fast tap. Long is a slow tap.

- ✓ **Enable Faster Tapping** — Check this box if you tap really fast, and your taps aren't being recognized.

Scrolling

Normally, to scroll in a window, you move the cursor on a scrollbar and click. The Eee PC also supports using the touchpad to scroll. Just place your finger on the edge of the touchpad and drag up or down. Three types of scrolling are available on the touchpad, vertical, horizontal, and circular.

Although most programs support vertical scrolling, not all programs support horizontal and circular scrolling.

Vertical scrolling

When Enable Vertical Scrolling is checked, you can drag up or down in the right corner of the track pad to scroll a window. A slider control enables you to specify drag speed.

Horizontal scrolling

Enable Horizontal Scrolling is turned off by default, but if you check this option, you can horizontally scroll a window by dragging on the bottom edge of the touchpad. You can also control drag speed.

Circular scrolling

Circular scrolling allows you to scroll long distances with fewer motions. You scroll in a circular motion around the touchpad edges. For example, to scroll up, start dragging at the bottom of the touchpad and continue around the edges in a counter-clockwise motion. (If you have an iPod, circular scrolling is like using the click wheel.) Set where on the touchpad you want to start your circular scrolls.

Although it's possible to enable all three types of scrolling at once in the Preferences window, that doesn't mean they will all work at the same time. For example if circular scrolling is checked, horizontal scrolling won't work even though it is enabled.

Edge

These options tell the touchpad how to behave when you drag along the edges. You can specify to scroll or treat dragging along the edge as cursor movements. (Some Eee PC models also don't include the Edge tab, incorporating these options into other tabs.)

On Eee PC models that have multi-touch touchpads, an additional tab named *Two Finger* appears. Here you can change multi-touch settings.

Using the Disk Utility

The Disk Utility isn't really a disk utility in the true sense of the word. When you click this icon, a window is displayed that shows how much space is available on your drive (as shown in Figure 9-10). System, Used, and Available space are the options presented in several different ways.

On Eee PCs with a single internal drive, the Extra Drive tab doesn't provide any information; even if you have an SD card inserted or a USB thumb or hard drive connected. This is normal behavior.

Figure 9-10:
Disk Utility showing used and available drive space.

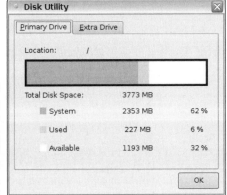

Running Diagnostic Tools

The Diagnostic Tools program provides detailed information about your Eee PC and has a series of hardware tests to ensure everything is working properly.

The three options in the program are System Info, System Test, and Contact Us. Click an associated icon (as shown in Figure 9-11) to run that option. Here is a brief description of each option.

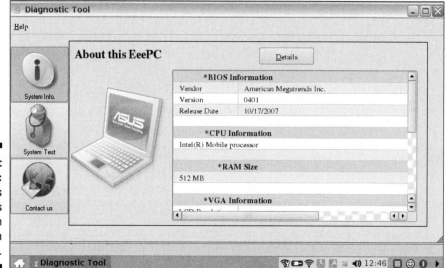

Figure 9-11:
Diagnostic
Tools
provides
system
information
and tests.

TIP

In the Help menu, select Help for detailed, online information about using Diagnostic Tools.

System Info

System Info (which is displayed by default), contains all sorts of information about your Eee PC. A general summary is shown, but you can also click the Details button to get more in-depth information on various system hardware components.

System Test

System Test (as shown in Figure 9-12) offers a variety of hardware tests. If you think something is wrong with a hardware component, click its icon to run the test. You can also click the Test All button to run the entire series of hardware tests.

Each of the tests gives you instructions before running and provides feedback with test results.

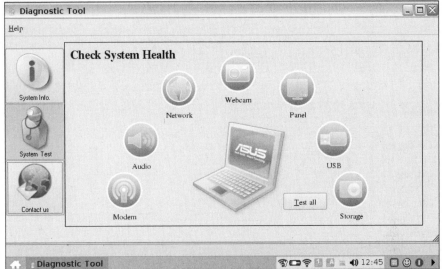

Figure 9-12:
System Test
options.

Contact Us

The last Diagnostic Tools option is Contact Us. Two choices are available:

- ✔ **View Support Website** — Click this button to load the browser and visit the ASUS support site. You need to be connected to the Internet. This may give you a solution to your problem.

- ✔ **Send Feedback with System Log** — If you're still having problems, click this button to send an e-mail to ASUS support. This launches Thunderbird, where you can compose a message describing your issue. A log file is attached to the message with system details that can help support staff diagnose your problem. (If you haven't used Thunderbird, the first time you use it, a wizard steps you through setting up the program.)

Changing Settings for Presentations

The Desktop Mode icon's name and appearance are a little deceiving. This program has nothing to do with the Linux desktop, but instead relates to using the Eee PC with an external monitor that's connected to the VGA port. Click this icon to configure settings when you're giving presentations and using a projector or monitor. The External Display program is shown in Figure 9-13.

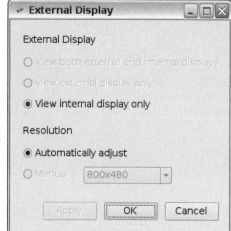

If your Eee PC isn't hooked up to an external monitor, a number of options are grayed out.

Always connect the external monitor or projector first, turn the power on, and then boot the Eee PC.

Three self-explanatory External Device radio buttons control what gets displayed where:

  ✓ **View both external and internal displays.**

  ✓ **View external display only.**

  ✓ **View internal display only.**

Select which you prefer and click Apply.

You can rotate through these display settings by pressing Fn+F5 (there's a picture of a monitor on the F5 key as a reminder). This key combination can be used at any time even if the External Display program isn't running.

In addition to the display settings, there are two radio buttons for Resolution:

  ✓ **Automatically adjust** — The default setting. Use this unless you're having problems with the screen resolution on the external display device.

  ✓ **Manual** — Allows you to manually set one of several predefined monitor sizes.

Click the Apply button to change the settings and then OK to exit the program.

Adding and Removing Software

Add/Remove Software is ASUS's program for providing Eee PC software updates. When you run the program, it connects to an ASUS server over the Internet, checks which versions of software you currently have installed, and sees if any new versions are available. It also displays any new ASUS software that's available for the Eee PC.

This process can take awhile, depending on the current ASUS server load.

After the program is done checking, it displays a tabbed window similar to the Linux desktop. Click a tab to display updated programs that are available. For example, clicking the Internet tab (as shown in Figure 9-14) displays a list of updated Internet programs that you can download and install.

The Remove button doesn't allow you to remove preinstalled software. It only removes the update and then rolls back to the original version. You cannot use the program to remove preinstalled software.

So far, so good. But pay attention now please. Some users report that after running the program to update their software, desktop icons have disappeared and some programs no longer work correctly.

If you're going to use the Add/Remove Software program, please read Chapter 12 where I discuss this issue in depth and offer solutions for getting around potential installation and upgrade woes.

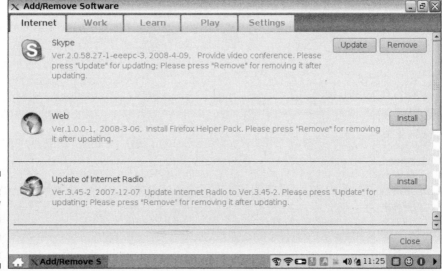

Figure 9-14: The Add/ Remove Software program.

Using VoiceCommand

If you're a fan of Star Trek and always wanted to tell your computer what to do, the Eee PC can fulfill your fantasies of sitting in the captain's chair on the Enterprise, barking out orders.

When you click the VoiceCommand icon in the Settings tab, it installs a small icon in the taskbar (it's a little hard to make out what it is, perhaps a tiny speaker). Right-click the icon to display a pop-up menu as shown in Figure 9-15.

Select Enable to turn on a feature called VoiceCommand. VoiceCommand runs certain programs when you speak out loud. For example if you say, "Computer Clock," the Eee PC replies "Clock" and then runs the world time clock program. All the voice commands are shown in the pop-up menu.

Make sure the microphone is enabled. You also may need to adjust the mic volume depending on how loud you speak and how far away you are from the mini-laptop.

Select Disable in the pop-up menu to turn off VoiceCommand or select Quit to exit the program.

VoiceCommand leans more toward geeky fun than a productivity tool, and is great to impress your friends with (especially fans of Kirk and Spock).

Figure 9-15:
The Voice-
Command
pop-up
menu shows
available
voice
commands.

For 901 and later model Eee PCs, ASUS uses a different voice recognition program called Dr. Eee. It serves the same purpose as the earlier VoiceCommand, but has a different interface. Check the online help for more information on using the program.

Keeping the Viruses Out

When you click the Anti-Virus icon (don't you just love those little bugs and the shield), a program called Clam AntiVirus runs. Popularly known as ClamAV, this is an open-source, anti-virus utility (you can learn more about the program at: www.clamav.net/).

But I thought Linux didn't get viruses?

So what's the deal with including an anti-virus program with the Eee PC? You may have heard you don't need to worry about viruses and malicious software if you're running Linux. Only Windows users require protection software.

This is true to an extent; at present, there are only a few known Linux viruses compared to an estimated several hundred thousand or more viruses that plague Windows users. But here are two good reasons why the Eee PC has an anti-virus utility:

- **Insurance for the future** — As Linux becomes more popular, there's a possibility the platform could be targeted by malicious programmers. ClamAV adds a level of security insurance for the future.

- **Windows** — Because many people use SD cards and USB thumb drives to exchange files between their Eee PC and primary Windows computer, there's always a chance of an infected file. Although a Windows virus shouldn't affect a Linux computer (there are a handful of cross-platform viruses out there, but not enough to worry about), it's nice for the Eee PC to be able to catch a problem file and let you know about it.

Performing a scan

To check for viruses, while in the Scan tab (as shown in Figure 9-16), follow these steps:

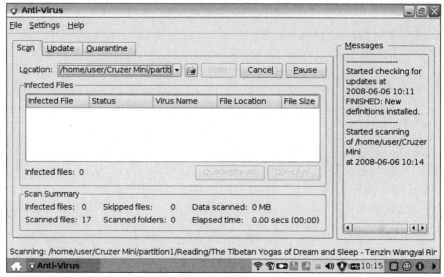

Figure 9-16:
ClamAV
anti-virus
utility.

1. **Click the blue folder button to the left of the Scan button to select a location to scan.**

   This opens a dialog box where you can select a file, directory, or a device to scan. USB drives and SD cards should appear in the User directory.

2. **Select the location and click OK.**

3. **Click the Scan button to search for viruses.**

   After a scan starts, you can Pause or Cancel.

Before you perform a scan, click the Update tab and download the latest version of the virus database.

ClamAV then starts scanning. At the bottom of the window, the name of the file currently being scanned is shown. Above that is the Scan Summary, with information about the number of files that have been scanned and how many (if any) were infected.

Complete online help is available for ClamAV. To view it, select Anti-Virus Handbook in the Help menu.

For 901 and later model Eee PCs, instead of ClamAV, ASUS uses a commercial anti-virus program called NOD32 (see: www.eset.com). NOD32 is more of a full-featured anti-virus utility compared to ClamAV. Check the online help for more information on using this program.

More Settings icons

On the 901 and later model Eee PCs you might find some additional icons in the desktop Settings tab. Added programs include:

✔ **Bluetooth** — On models with built-in Bluetooth, this utility makes Bluetooth connections, transfers files, and configures the wireless card.

✔ **EeeAP** — ASUS makes an 802.11 wireless access point, and if you have one, this is the configuration program to use with it.

✔ **Instant Key** — On models that have configurable *Instant Keys*, use this program to associate a program with a key. When you press the key, the program runs.

For more information on these programs, refer to your user manual or consult the online help.

Shutting Down

The Instant Shutdown icon sounds like it's something special, but in reality it just launches the shutdown program (as shown in Figure 9-17). This is identical to clicking the Shut Down icon (red circle at the far right) in the Linux taskbar. (I tell you everything you need to know about shutting down in Chapter 2.)

Figure 9-17: Shut Down options.

Chapter 10

Getting Help

- -

In This Chapter

▶ Using Eee PC online help

▶ Navigating the ASUS support Web site

▶ Joining the EeeUser.com community

- -

The Eee PC is pretty easy to use, but sooner or later you're going to have a question about one thing or another. You'll likely consult the user manual first (as well as this book, I hope), but what if you can't find what you're looking for? Where do you turn next?

That's what this chapter is all about. I list and describe various Eee PC help and support resources.

I start by covering how to use Help tools that come installed on the Eee PC — actually there are more than meet the eye. My primary focus is on Linux models, but I also briefly touch on Eee PCs running Windows XP.

I then continue by telling you where to go on the Internet to get answers to all of your Eee PC questions. I describe what the ASUS support site has to offer (including how to use it), and then I steer you toward a Web-based community that is the best and most comprehensive source of Eee PC information on the planet (covering all models of Eee PCs, including those running default Xandros Linux, Windows XP, and even other versions of Linux).

So if you have a burning Eee PC question right now, or want to know where to turn in the future, follow me to the answers.

Using Eee PC Online Help

You can get help on Eee PCs in a number of ways, many of which come installed with Xandros Linux. Help is scattered throughout the user interface in some obvious and not so obvious places. Here is where to look.

If you lost your printed user manual, read the upcoming section on using the ASUS support site, where I tell you how to download Eee PC manuals in PDF format. You can then keep a copy on your mini-laptop for handy reference.

Desktop online help

The most obvious source of help is the Help command at the top of the Linux desktop (it's to the far right of the program category tabs). When you click Help, the Web browser is loaded with a file that contains basic instructions for using the desktop and preinstalled programs.

At the top of the Help page (as shown in Figure 10-1) are a series of tabs, just like those that appear on the desktop.

Click a tab to get information about programs that are associated with the tab. A general description and brief instructions for using the program are included. A fair amount of information is included in each tab, so you'll need to scroll down to view it all.

The desktop online Help covers a lot of material that isn't discussed in the printed user manual. You may want to print the pages. If your Eee PC isn't connected to a printer, use the Save Page As... command in the browser File menu and save the Help file to a USB thumb drive or SD card. You can then open the file with the Web browser on your desktop PC and print the page. When you print or save, remember that a separate help page is associated with each desktop tab.

Figure 10-1: Linux Eee PC desktop Help.

E-book online help

An identical version of the desktop Help is also available as an e-book. To view it, follow these steps:

1. **In the Work tab, run the File Manager.**

2. **Open the My Documents folder.**

3. **Open the My Ebooks folder.**

4. **Double-click the manual.CHM file to start the e-book reader and view the file (as shown in Figure 10-2).**

If the .CHM file isn't in the EBooks folder, you can download it from `http://support.asus.com/download`.

There are several advantages to accessing desktop Help as an e-book:

✔ The text appears in a larger font than in the browser and is easier to read.

✔ The e-book reader offers options for configuring viewing preferences.

✔ The e-book reader remembers what you were viewing when you close the program and displays that text when you run the program the next time.

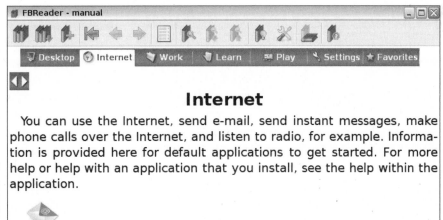

Figure 10-2: The e-book version of Linux Eee PC desktop Help.

There is no vertical scroll bar in the e-book reader. Use the up and down arrow keys to move up and down through the text.

Eee PC Tips

On the far right side of the taskbar is the Eee PC Tips icon which looks like a yellow smiley face — check out Chapter 2 for more on what the taskbar icons look like and do. When you click this icon, a series of tips are displayed in the Web browser (as shown in Figure 10-3). These are common ASUS support questions with brief answers.

Online program help

Always check to see if there is a Help menu in the program you're using. The amount and quality of online help varies from one program to another. Additionally, an Internet connection may be required to use this help because selecting a Help menu item might load a support Web site.

In this book, I mention additional information sources for many of the preinstalled Linux programs. Read the appropriate chapter where I discuss a program to see if any Web-based references may be of help. (For example if you want to learn more about the games that come with the Eee PC, check out Chapter 8, which has lots of Web links relating to the games.)

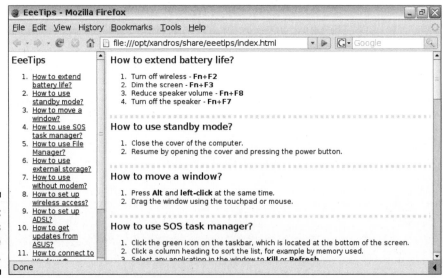

Figure 10-3:
Eee PC Tips
from the
taskbar.

KDE and Linux help

The Eee PC uses a version of Linux with the KDE user interface. The default Linux desktop is a very simplified user interface and doesn't offer the full power of KDE. (In Chapter 19, I describe how you can enable Advanced Mode, which makes the complete KDE user interface, desktop, and programs available.)

If you're new to Linux and want to learn more about the operating system itself and KDE, you can run a program called Help Center. This is a complete online help system for the KDE interface, KDE programs, and UNIX commands. This is a great way to see what KDE and Linux are all about. Here's how to run the program:

1. **Press Ctl+Alt+T.**

   This brings up a Linux command-line console. I tell you everything you need to know about using the console in Chapter 20.

2. **Type** khelpcenter.

   Since Linux is case sensitive, make sure to capitalize the word exactly as you see it here and then press Enter after you're done typing. (If you enter a command and get a *command not found* error message, you've either made a typo or a letter is incorrectly capitalized. Try again.)

3. **Search for the help topic you're interested in.**

The Help Center is shown in Figure 10-4. It's intuitive to use, but here are a few general instructions:

- ✔ The panel on the left is an index of help information, Click categories and topics to display them in the right panel.

- ✔ Use the Search icon (the magnifying glass) in the toolbar to search for text.

- ✔ Click the Glossary tab to display a complete glossary of KDE and Linux terms.

When you're done browsing through the help pages, in the Help Center File menu, select Quit and then close the Linux console window.

Help Center is also displayed when you use the Help menu in some preinstalled Linux programs, such as File Manager.

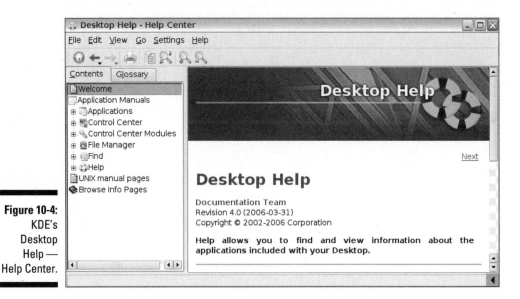

Figure 10-4:
KDE's
Desktop
Help —
Help Center.

Using the Internet to Get Help

If the user manual, online help, or even this book (perish the thought)
doesn't answer your burning Eee PC question, then it's time to fire up your
browser and head to the Internet. I recommend two sites for all Eee PC
models, regardless of the operating system they run.

Eee PC Windows online help

Compared to the Linux models, ASUS doesn't
add much Eee PC–specific online help to its
mini-laptops that come with Windows XP. That
makes sense, because Windows is so widely
used, and people are more familiar with it than
they are with Linux. The printed manual that
comes with Windows models gives you enough
information to get started using your Eee PC.
From there, you can access the online help that
comes with programs as well as Windows'
built-in help system (click the Start button and
then select Help and Support).

If your user manual doesn't answer a Windows-
related Eee PC question, I'd recommend not
bothering to look in online help, but proceeding
directly to the EeeUser.com Web site which I
describe later in this chapter. Here you will find
forums that deal specifically with Windows
issues and knowledgeable users willing to help
answer your questions.

Don't feel obligated to use your Eee PC to access these sites. In fact, if I'm troubleshooting my Eee PC, I'll use a desktop or laptop PC to browse for support information. A larger screen is nice when searching for help, plus I can put the mini-laptop next to the bigger computer, which makes it easy to follow instructions as I read them.

 Web sites are always changing; keep that in mind just in case something I describe doesn't match a Web site when you visit. Even if a Web site's appearance is different, you still should have a good idea of how to access the information I discuss.

Navigating the ASUS support site

Our first stop is ASUS's support site at `http://support.asus.com/`. As shown in Figure 10-5, the site has six main sections. To start finding your way around, click a section link. Sections include

- ✔ **Download** — Download file utilities, drivers, software updates, and user manuals.
- ✔ **FAQ** — View frequently asked questions organized by product.
- ✔ **Forum** — Participate in a support forum for various ASUS products.
- ✔ **Member** — Join a free membership program for ASUS customers.
- ✔ **Registration** — Register your product online.
- ✔ **Troubleshooting** — Look at product troubleshooting information.

You should be primarily interested in the Download, FAQ, and Forum sections. After you click one of these section links, specify some product information to get to the good stuff. All these sections use the same interface to get to the Eee PC department, so . . .

- ✔ In the Select Product drop-down list, choose EeePC.
- ✔ In the Select Series drop-down list, choose Eee PC Series.
- ✔ In the Select Models drop-down list, choose your model (such as Eee PC 4G/Linux).

A dialog box opens, and asks what operating system you're running.

Click the Search button to continue and go to the section you're interested in. Here is what's inside each one.

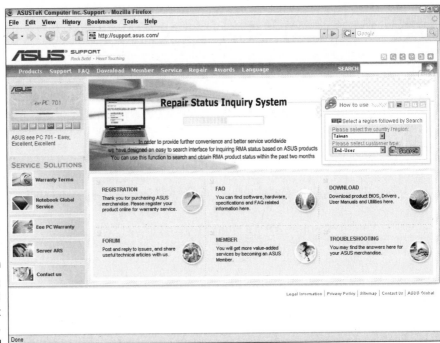

Figure 10-5:
The ASUS
support
Web site.

Download

A new Web page opens with a series of tabs across the top. Click the tab to display files in that category. For example the Manual tab displays different language user manuals for your Eee PC.

Use the Operating System drop-down list box (located above the tabs) to display only those files that relate to Linux or Windows XP. This saves you the time of going through a long list of all files.

The file list includes the filename, version, date posted, operating system, and a description (usually quite terse and often not too helpful).

Beneath each file, different server locations around the world are shown. To download a file, select the nearest server, right-click, and then use the pop-up menu command to save the link to disk. (If a server is slow or doesn't respond, try another one.)

FAQ

In this section, a list of frequently asked questions about your Eee PC model is displayed. When you click a question, a new page opens with the question and the reply from ASUS. Use your browser's Back button to return to the FAQ list.

E-mail support from ASUS

If you can't find an answer to your question after consulting the ASUS support site's references, try the company's e-mail support service. At the top of the main Web page, click Support in the menu bar and then choose Technical Inquiries.

A new page is displayed, where you enter which model of Eee PC you own. You are nicely reminded to first check the Download, FAQ, and Forum sections to see if your question has already been answered. If not, at the bottom of the page is a link named Technical Inquiry Form. Click it, fill in the form describing your support issue, and click Submit.

ASUS support staff will be in touch with an e-mail reply.

You can specify the number of questions to appear on the page as well as display questions posted within a certain timeframe; such as from the last seven days.

Just to prepare you, some of the questions and answers aren't in the most fluent English, and you may need to ponder both the question and answer a bit to grasp the actual meaning.

Forum

Click the Eee PC forum to view questions and replies users have posted. Although this is the official ASUS support forum, if you have a question I recommend you post it instead to the unofficial forums at EeeUser.com — which is a perfect introduction to the next section.

Community-based help from EeeUser.com

In my humble opinion, the best place to go for Eee PC help is a Web site appropriately named EeeUser.com (www.eeeuser.com). This definitive site opened for business several months before the Eee PC first hit the store shelves and has turned into the destination of choice for Eee PC users all over the world.

This is very much an unofficial site. ASUS doesn't run it, and its users don't pull any punches when discussing Eee PC pros and cons. Opinions are loudly voiced, but practical information and sage wisdom are also gladly shared; including an expansive collection of tips, tricks, and techniques.

Two parts of the site are oriented toward support and help: the wiki (http://wiki.eeeuser.com) and the forums (http://forum.eeeuser.com). You can access each one at the top of EeeUser's main Web page by clicking their respective links.

Here is a quick look at what you'll find.

Wiki

A *wiki* is a Web site that allows users to collectively add and edit content. Wikipedia, the online encyclopedia, is the most well-known wiki (if you're wondering where the word *wiki* came from, it's based on *wiki wiki*, which is Hawaiian for *rapidly, rapidly*).

The EeeUser Wiki (as shown in Figure 10-6) is the go-to place for Eee PC information and how-to instruction. The large and comprehensive compilation of content has been assembled by experienced Eee PC users, eager to share their knowledge. Wikis are living, growing entities, and new information is always being added (and older information tweaked and refined).

There are two basic ways to navigate the wiki:

✔ **Table of contents:** At the right of the page is a Table of Contents organized by category (including Basics, Networking, and Installing Operating Systems). Click a category to view information associated with it.

✔ **Search:** At the top of the page is a text box next to a Search button. Type in something you're looking for and click Search. A list of wiki entries that match your search criteria is displayed. Click one that looks like it fits the bill.

Figure 10-6:
The Eee User.com Wiki.

If you are a new Eee PC owner, or even an experienced one, I highly recommend you spend some time reading the Wiki's Basics and Common Problems sections.

Forums

The wiki is a great source of encyclopedic knowledge, but if you're looking for more interactive, real-time help, the place to visit is the Eee PC forums (shown in Figure 10-7).

Over 35 forums are devoted to various aspects of the Eee PC. There are forums for different models, different operating systems, hardware hacking, accessories, and even foreign language forums for non-English speakers (Italiano is quite active).

Click a forum to view a list of posted subjects (posts are displayed chronologically, with the most recent appearing first) and then click a post title to read the complete thread (usually a question and subsequent replies).

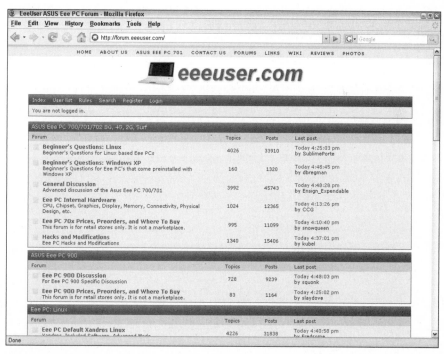

Figure 10-7:
Eee
User.com
forums.

Some of the forums receive a large amount of daily traffic, and it would take days or weeks to read through all the old posts. If you're looking for specific information, instead of scrolling through months of older posts, use the Search command at the top of the page. You can enter specific text associated with a question and get a list of posts that contain that text. For example if you wanted to know about connecting your iPod to your new Eee PC, you could do a search for *iPod*.

You don't need an account to browse through and search the forums (lurking is encouraged), but if you want to post a question or a reply, you need to sign up for a free account. This is a painless process that you can start by clicking Register at the top of the page.

Before you post a question, read the wiki and search the forums to see if someone else has already asked the same question and had it answered. This is simple common courtesy. Although the forum members are friendly, if you post a question without doing your homework first, don't be surprised if you get a few grumpy, scolding replies.

In addition to the ASUS and EeeUser.com Web sites, a number of blogs are devoted to the Eee PC that provide news and general information on using the mini-laptop. I share links to my favorite Eee PC blogs in Chapter 23.

Chapter 11

Eee PC and Windows XP

. . . .

. . . .

*W*hen the Eee PC was originally introduced, it was only available with the Linux operating system. Sure you could always install a copy of Windows over Linux, but that was a bit time-consuming and involved a number of steps. As the mini-laptop increased in popularity, ASUS decided to begin offering models that came installed with Microsoft Windows XP right out of the box.

In this chapter, I tell you all about Windows XP and the Eee PC — that has a nice ring, doesn't it? I start off by listing advantages of both Windows and Linux — just in case you're trying to make up your mind which type of Eee PC to buy. I then describe what programs you find preinstalled on a Windows Eee PC. And I finish up explaining how to replace Linux with a copy of Windows on your mini-laptop — including how to slim down the operating system to save space and get better performance.

Windows versus Linux

On a number of Eee PC models, you have a choice between preinstalled Linux or Microsoft Windows XP operating systems — keep in mind it's also possible to load Windows XP on just about any Eee PC, as I discuss later in the chapter. If you're thinking about getting an ASUS mini-laptop, you need to decide which operating system is best for you.

I'm not going to advocate for one system or the other (there are already enough flame wars on the Internet about this very subject). Like most things, each operating system has its pros and cons. To give you some perspective, here are a few key advantages of each.

Windows advantages

✔ More familiar user interface

✔ More programs available (including specialized applications)

✔ Commercial applications tend to have a more polished user interface

✔ Better hardware compatibility (especially with printers and scanners)

Linux advantages

✔ Free, resulting in a lower price compared to Windows Eee PC — some Linux mini-laptops may have more drive capacity than their same-priced Windows cousins.

✔ Many free, open-source programs (with similar functionality to popular Windows applications).

✔ More secure (fewer viruses, worms, and Trojans).

✔ Better performance on computers with slower processors and less memory.

Which to choose?

Because Windows is so widely used and known, much of this book is focused on Eee PCs running Linux — most people already know a fair amount about Windows. Skimming through the chapters should give you a pretty good idea of what using a Linux Eee PC is all about. You can then compare and contrast with your own Windows experience to decide which operating system is best for you.

If you're still having trouble making up your mind, here are a few suggestions to steer you in the right direction.

Pick Windows if you . . .

✔ Have experience with Windows and don't want to learn the nuances of a different operating system's user interface. (Be aware that the KDE Linux interface isn't really that difficult to use.)

✔ Plan on using Windows programs that aren't available for Linux

✔ Have hardware (printer, scanner, and so on) that isn't compatible with Linux.

Linux, Xandros, KDE, and Windows

On most Eee PC models, you have a choice between Linux and Microsoft Windows operating systems. Here's a little more information about your operating system options.

There are a number of Linux distributions — *distros* if you want to sound clued in. You may have heard or Ubuntu, Fedora (formerly RedHat), PCLinuxOS, or Slackware; to name a few. A company, organization or group of people creates a distribution based on a version of a common Linux kernel. It includes various packages and software. The distribution is packaged up and then released on CD-ROM, DVD, or for download. (Head over to www.linux.org to learn more about all the different distributions.)

ASUS uses a Linux distribution called Xandros, optimizing and customizing it for the Eee PC. Xandros (www.xandros.com) is based on a core distro named Debian. It uses a modified version of KDE (www.kde.org) as its graphical user interface. Linux, which is based on UNIX, started out as a command-line operating system. In an effort to modernize Linux with a desktop, windows, and menus, two graphical user interface projects were started: KDE and Gnome (www.gnome.org). Both generally work the same, but have a slightly different look-and-feel and associated programs. KDE is Windows-like; Gnome is more Mac-like. A Linux distribution typically uses either KDE or Gnome as its user interface.

For Windows models, Windows XP is used — it doesn't make sense to use Vista on the mini-laptop because the latest version of Windows requires a lot of system resources. Microsoft was planning on officially stopping distribution of XP at the end of June, 2008, but because of the growing mini-laptop market, it elected to continue making it available to manufacturers of small PCs.

If you decide a Windows Eee PC is for you, I highly recommend visiting the Windows XP section of the EeeUser.com forums located at http://forum.eeeuser.com/viewforum.php?id=13. There you find lots of information and tips for getting the most out of your Windows mini-laptop.

Pick Linux if you . . .

✔ Don't have much computer experience and want a simple-to-use computer to perform basic tasks (e-mail, Web browsing, and word processing).

✔ Like the idea of free, open-source software.

✔ Are technically inclined — you don't need to be a techie to use a Linux Eee PC, but being a little more technical just makes it easier to do advanced procedures at times.

If you buy a Linux Eee PC and have an old copy of a Windows XP installation disc lying around, it's fairly easy to replace Linux with Windows — and then restore Linux later if need be. Conversely, if you purchase a Windows Eee PC, you can replace the operating system with Linux — and reinstall Windows down the road.

Preinstalled Windows XP

If you purchase an Eee PC that has Microsoft Windows XP preinstalled, ASUS has added a few features in addition to the programs, accessories, and utilities that normally come with the operating system.

Be sure to check out Chapter 14, where I describe a number of free Windows programs you can download that are well-suited for the Eee PC.

Here is a brief summary of the preinstalled programs you find when you start your Windows XP Eee PC:

- **Acrobat Reader** — The ubiquitous utility for viewing PDF files.

- **ASUS Update** — A program for updating the Eee PC's BIOS.

  If you update the BIOS, be sure to have a fully charged battery and the mini-laptop plugged into an electrical outlet. If you lose power midway through a BIOS upgrade (or something goes wrong), there's a good chance you can turn your mini-laptop into a paperweight. I recommend updating the BIOS if you are experiencing a problem that only a newer version of the BIOS will fix, or if there is a significant new feature in a later BIOS release that you really need. Other than those two occasions, I say if it ain't broke, don't fix it.

- **Eee PC Tray** — This utility is accessed in the Windows system tray. With it you can change screen resolution, change the resolution of an external monitor or media projector, and enable/disable the WiFi card, Web cam, and Bluetooth (on models with the wireless service built in).

- **Ethernet Utility** — This program is for configuring the Ethernet network card.

- **Instant Key** *(on some models)* — A utility for configuring two Instant Keys (above the function keys) to run user-defined programs. By default these two keys launch Super Hybrid Engine and Skype.

- **InterVideo DVD XPack** *(on some models)* — A simple media and DVD player.

- **Microsoft Works** — This is a basic business suite of programs (word processor, spreadsheet, database, and calendar). The programs are fairly underpowered and I'd recommend uninstalling Works to save drive space and replacing it with OpenOffice (www.openoffice.org) — if your mini-laptop also came with Star Suite, use it instead. You can find out more about Microsoft Works at www.microsoft.com/PRODUCTS/works/default.mspx.

- ✔ **OS Cleaner** *(on some models)* — A utility that deletes the contents of various system directories to save drive space.

- ✔ **Outlook Express** *(on some models)* — A reduced-feature version of Microsoft's Outlook e-mail client. (I recommend using Thunderbird for your e-mail program at www.mozilla.com/en-US/thunderbird/.)

- ✔ **Skype** — The popular instant messaging and video conferencing program. If you don't have a Skye account, register for a free one before using (www.skype.com).

- ✔ **Star Suite** *(on some models)* — Star Suite is a commercial version of OpenOffice from Sun Microsystems — check out Chapter 5 for more on OpenOffice, which runs on both Linux and Windows. To learn all about Star Suite, visit www.sun.com/software/staroffice/index.jsp.

- ✔ **Super Hybrid Engine** *(on some models)* — A program that changes the clock speed of the processor in order to increase battery life. Super Performance mode runs at the highest processor speed. The other settings lower the clock speed, resulting in longer battery life.

- ✔ **U1 Utility** *(on some models)* — An application for configuring a USB Skype phone sold by ASUS.

- ✔ **YoStore** *(on some models)* — An online data storage service. If your Eee PC comes with this feature, activate it with a code found in your user manual. After you register, a virtual disk drive icon is created in the My Computer directory. You can use the virtual drive to transfer files between your mini-laptop and an Internet-hosted server.

Consult your user manual and online help for more information on all these programs and how to use them.

The Windows support DVD

In addition to preinstalled programs, your Windows XP comes with a support DVD. The DVD contains an image of the operating system, in case you need to restore it — I tell you how to reinstall Windows in Chapter 18. The disc also has copies of various programs, drivers, and utilities. The drivers, which are preinstalled on your Eee PC, are essential for hardware components such as the monitor, touchpad, Web cam, and network cards to work under Windows.

You need an external USB DVD drive to use the disc — I discuss selecting a drive in Chapter 15. Normally, the setup program automatically runs when you insert the support disc in the drive. If it doesn't, in Windows Explorer, look for a file named AsSetup.exe and double-click it. This runs the setup program. Select which drivers, utilities, or programs you'd like to install. I discuss using the AsSetup program in the section "Installing Windows on a Linux Eee PC."

Installing Windows on a Linux Eee PC

If you have a Windows XP Home installation CD-ROM from a computer you're no longer using, you can install the Microsoft operating system on a Linux Eee PC (as shown in Figure 11-1).

You need an installation disc with the Windows setup program. Some PCs come with CD-ROMs that contain a drive image of the operating system. If you need to reinstall Windows, the image is written to your hard drive instead of using the Microsoft installation program. You can't use a manufacturer-provided CD that contains a drive image to install Windows on your Eee PC.

Installing Windows is fairly easy, although it is a little time-consuming. If, after you install the operating system, you don't like it and decide you want Linux back, just use the recovery disc that came with your mini-laptop. I tell you how to do this in Chapter 18.

Hardware and software requirements

Before you change operating systems, gather up everything you need. Here is a list of the required components for installing Windows XP on your mini-laptop.

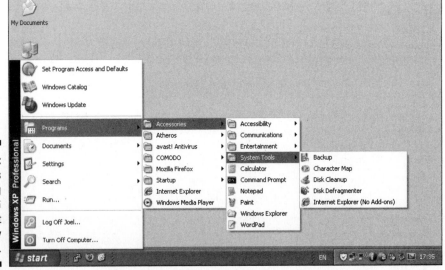

Figure 11-1:
Windows
XP running
on a 4G
Eee PC that
originally
ran Linux.

Eee PC

The first item on the list is a no-brainer. You can install Windows on any model of Eee PC; however, there are a few important things to note.

Even though the Eee PC 2G and 4G models use a 900 MHz Intel Celeron processor, they are not running at full speed — the chip speed is reduced to 571 and 630 MHz respectively; to limit power consumption. The Eee PC 900, which uses the same Celeron processor, runs at the full 900 MHz — you can optionally lower the processor speed in a BIOS setting to increase battery life.

After installing Windows XP on a 4G, I've found its performance isn't quite as snappy as when running the default Xandros Linux. In my opinion, the faster processor of the Eee PC 900 (and later models that use an Atom processor) makes these mini-laptops a better candidate for installing Windows.

It's possible to boost the processor speed of a 2G or 4G up to 900 MHz using a Windows program called eeectl (www.cpp.in/dev/eeectl/) — this is known as *overclocking*. This makes your Eee PC a little faster at the expense of shorter battery life and a higher amount of heat generated.

If you have a 2G or 4G, one of your biggest limitations is the small amount of drive storage space — especially on a 2G. With a little work, you can reduce the size of Windows XP to around 400 to 550MB (a normal installation is in the 800MB to 1GB range). I discuss slimming down Windows in an upcoming section.

DVD/CD Drive

Although it's possible to install a copy of Windows from an SD card or USB thumb drive, it's much easier to use an external CD or DVD drive, with a Windows installation CD — I discuss selecting DVD drives in Chapter 15.

If you don't have an external drive and would rather not purchase one, check this Web page for the lowdown on adding Windows XP installation files to an SD card: http://wiki.eeeuser.com/howto:installxp.

Windows XP

You need a copy of a Windows XP Home or Professional installation CD. This has to be an installation disc that includes at least the Service Pack 2 updates — the earlier version of XP won't support connecting an external USB DVD drive to the Eee PC.

A full Windows install takes up a lot of precious drive space. An alternative is to create a customized version of the installation CD with fewer features and files. See the "Shrinking Windows with nLite" sidebar for more information.

Eee PC Support DVD

You also need the support DVD that came with your Eee PC — it contains the Windows drivers and utilities for built-in Eee PC hardware. Alternatively, you can download the drivers and utilities from the ASUS support Web site (`http://support.asus.com/download`) and then install them.

Installing Windows XP

After you've got everything together, it's time to play operating system switcheroo. Here are the steps involved:

1. **Make sure you've backed up any files you want to keep.**

   Your drive is reformatted during the installation process.

2. **Connect an external CD or DVD drive to the Eee PC and insert the Windows installation disc.**

3. **Turn on your Eee PC.**

4. **Press Esc when the Eee PC startup screen appears.**

   This displays the boot device selection window.

5. **Select the USB external drive and press Enter.**

   The CD boots and the Windows setup program runs. Follow the on-screen instructions. Be patient, it takes awhile for all the files to load.

6. **Delete partitions and format the drive as NTFS.**

   By default, Linux Eee PCs can have up to four drive partitions. You must manually delete each partition — follow the on-screen directions. After you delete all the partitions, format the drive as NTFS. Setup begins by copying files from the installation CD to the internal drive.

 Some Eee PC models that use Solid State Drive (SSD) technology come with two drives. If an Eee PC is advertised as having 20GB of storage, it actually may have 4GB on one SSD and 16GB on a second drive. The operating system, whether Windows or Linux, resides on the smaller, faster drive. As SSD prices fall, I expect ASUS to start using single drives.

That's pretty much it for installation. Follow the directions and prompts and you should have a successful install. Upon completion, the setup program reboots the Eee PC, and Windows runs from the internal drive.

You're not quite done yet, however. You must still install a few drivers and utility programs, which is what I talk about next.

Installing Eee PC drivers

After you've installed Windows XP, you must install the Eee PC drivers and configuration utilities so the operating system can properly work with the mini-laptop hardware — including the Web cam, networking cards, and touchpad. These files are on the support DVD (or CD-ROM) that came with your Eee PC.

If you don't have the disc or an external drive, you can download the files on another PC from `http://support.asus.com/download` — copy them to a USB thumb drive and then install on your mini-laptop. The support site contains the latest versions of the drivers and utilities.

Insert the support disc into an external USB drive connected to your Eee PC. The ASUS Setup program should automatically run. If it doesn't, use Windows Explorer to locate AsSetup.exe (look in the Bin folder) and run the program.

ASUS Setup, as shown in Figure 11-2, has a tabbed interface. Click a tab to display options. You are primarily interested in the Drivers and Utilities tabs.

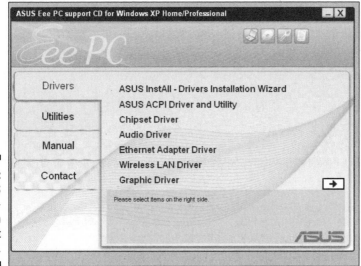

Figure 11-2: The ASUS Setup program on the support disc.

(Figure shows the ASUS Eee PC support CD for Windows XP Home/Professional window with tabs: Drivers, Utilities, Manual, Contact. Under Drivers: ASUS InstAll - Drivers Installation Wizard, ASUS ACPI Driver and Utility, Chipset Driver, Audio Driver, Ethernet Adapter Driver, Wireless LAN Driver, Graphic Driver. "Please select items on the right side.")

You have two choices for installing files from the support disc:

✔ **Install drivers and utilities individually** — Click a single driver or utility to install it.

✔ **Use ASUS InstAll Wizard** — This is a program for installing several files at once — see Figure 11-3. One version is for drivers and one for utilities. Click the wizard to start it, and then check which files you want to install. The wizard shows file version numbers and lists files that have already been installed.

Some drivers and utilities require the Eee PC to be rebooted after installation.

After you have installed the drivers and configuration utilities, your Windows Eee PC should be ready to use.

Figure 11-3:
The ASUS
InstAll
Wizard lets
you install
multiple files
at once.

Driver	Status	Available Version	Installed Version	Reboot
☐ ASUS ACPI Driver and Utility	Updated	1.0.0.0	1.0.0.0	No
☑ Chipset Driver	Not installed	8.3.0.1013	None	Yes
☐ Audio Driver	Updated	5.10.0.5477	5.10.0.5574	Yes
☐ Ethernet Adapter Driver	Updated	2.5.7.7	2.5.7.12	No
☐ Wireless LAN Driver	Updated	5.3.0.45	5.3.0.56	No
☐ Graphic Driver	Updated	6.14.10.4704	6.14.10.4764	No
☑ TouchPad Driver	Not installed	10.0.12.0	None	Yes

Please select the items you wish to install, and click GO to start the installation.

[Go] [Cancel]

Optimizing Windows XP for the Eee PC

With limited drive space and not the speediest processor in the world, some Eee PC models need all the help they can get when running Windows XP. Whether you're using a mini-laptop that came preinstalled with XP or you decided to install your own copy of Windows (I recommend using nLite — see the associated sidebar), you can use a variety of methods to free up drive space and increase performance.

Shrinking Windows with nLite

nLite (www.nliteos.com) is a slick utility for creating your own customized installation of Windows XP. You start with a Windows installation CD, run the nLite program, and then select what features and services you want to include. This is ideal for reducing the size of XP to shoehorn onto a limited capacity Eee PC drive. When you're finished, nLite creates a bootable installation CD that works just like the original version from Microsoft.

When using nLite, it's easy to get carried away when specifying programs and services not to include on the installation CD. If you eliminate certain things, Windows isn't going to work right (if at all) after you install it on your Eee PC. If that happens, go back to the drawing board and create a new installation CD — this time try not to remove critical components.

To help you figure out what should stay and what should go, here's a link to detailed steps (including screenshots) on using nLite to create a slimmed down version of Windows XP for the Eee PC: www.i64x.com/eeexp.php.

Some proven options to consider are

- ✔ **Disabling the pagefile (or setting it to a smaller size)**
- ✔ **Disabling hibernation**
- ✔ **Removing unneeded Windows programs and services**
- ✔ **Turning on File Compression**
- ✔ **Turning off System Restore**
- ✔ **Turning off indexing**
- ✔ **Turning off animated user interface elements**

For more information about these options (including how-to instructions) refer to: http://wiki.eeeuser.com/optimizingwinxp.

One of my favorite Web sites for information on tweaking Windows XP to improve its performance is appropriately called http://tweakxp.com. If you run Windows XP on any computer, not just the Eee PC, I highly recommend spending some time at this site.

Part III
Adding Software to the Eee PC

The 5th Wave   By Rich Tennant

AFTER INSTALLING LINUX, NED AND LORETTA SELECT THE COMPUTER'S BACKGROUND

"Oh – I like this background much better than the basement."

In this part . . .

*L*inux versions of the Eee PC come preinstalled with just about all the software you need for everyday office-type work and for accessing the Internet (whether it's e-mail, Web sites, instant messages, or Skype). But many more free, open-source Linux programs are available that you might be interested in. I begin this part by discussing the ins and outs of adding software to a Linux Eee PC (it's a little less straightforward than using Windows). I then describe some popular, open-source software you may want to consider installing.

For Eee PC Windows XP users, I devote a chapter to what I consider are the best free software titles for XP; covering Internet, productivity, entertainment, and security applications.

Chapter 12

Installing Linux Software

· ·

In This Chapter

▶ Fundamentals of Linux software installation

▶ Using the Add/Remove Software utility

▶ Installing programs with Synaptic Package Manager

▶ Command-line installation with Advanced Packaging Tool (APT)

· ·

So, you decided to go for a Linux Eee PC. Congratulations! You made a great choice. However if you're just getting started, and don't have much Linux experience, installing software on a Linux PC can seem a little intimidating compared to doing it on a Windows PC. With Linux you deal with things called packages and repositories, decide whether to use something known as pinning, and then choose from several installation utilities to do the actual downloading and installing.

That all sounds complicated, but in this chapter, I take the mystery and confusion out of installing programs on your Linux Eee PC. I explain fundamental installation concepts and give you the pros and cons of using various installation tools; including the default Add/Remove Software program, Synaptic Package Manager, and APT.

By the end of the chapter, you'll have it all figured out and will be able to confidently install, upgrade, and remove Linux programs from your Eee PC.

Let's get started with the basics.

Basic Installation Concepts

Before I tell you how to install Linux software on your Eee PC, I want to familiarize you with some basic concepts. Linux approaches installation differently than does Windows, and it's important to understand some of the differences. Here are a few key terms and concepts:

- **Package** — A package is software (and support files) compressed in a single file, using a specific file format. Think of it as a ZIP file with detailed installation instructions included. You download a package for a particular Linux program (or library) that you want to install. Different versions of Linux use different package formats. Eee PC packages have a .deb (for Debian) file extension. There are other package types, such as .rpm (Redhat Package Manager), but you can't use them with the Eee PC.

- **Package manager** — This is a program that installs, upgrades, configures, and removes packages. I describe three package managers you can use to manage software on your Eee PC in the next sections.

- **Repository** — An Internet server that contains a collection of packages. Packages can be downloaded with a package manager or manually transferred from a Web site or FTP server. I show you how to access repositories containing Eee PC–compatible software later in the chapter.

- **Pinning** — Because various repositories may have different versions of the same package, *pinning* prioritizes which repositories to use when downloading. Pinning protects you from accidentally downloading and installing packages that might make your system unstable. I explain how to *pin* repositories coming up.

With these concepts in mind, let's now discuss the different options you have for installing and managing software.

Eee PC eccentricities

When it comes to installing new Linux software or upgrading existing programs on your Eee PC, be aware of a few of its eccentricities. Don't worry about these peculiarities; just recognize them for what they're worth.

- **Limited drive space** — Because most Eee PC models have considerably less drive capacity than a traditional laptop, storage space is at a premium. Be aware of available space to ensure you don't fill the drive up with too many newly installed packages. If you run out of space, a package manager will tell you. But it's better to be aware ahead of time.

- **UnionFS** — Because of UnionFS (which I fully describe in Chapter 18), you cannot

remove programs and operating system components that are preinstalled on Linux Eee PCs. The operating system and default programs are stored on a read-only drive partition; which allows F9 system recoveries. This means if you update a preinstalled program to a new version, you end up with two copies — both the old version of the program (on the read-only partition) and the new version (on the user partition). This restricts available drive space even further. (It's possible to remove UnionFS, but this is an advanced move, and you'll lose the capability to use F9.)

- **Xandros** — The Eee PC uses a variation of Xandros Linux. Xandros doesn't update packages as often as other Linux distributions, so newer versions of some programs may not be available in the Xandros and Eee PC repositories. (If you don't like this, you can always install a different version of Linux or even Windows.)

✔ **Add/Remove Software** — This is the default Linux Eee PC program for installing software — it's located in the Settings tab. Some users have reported the utility can cause system problems. I provide more details in the "Installing and Uninstalling with Add/Remove Software" section in this chapter.

When it's time to install software, I like to think of the Eee PC as a favorite, semi-eccentric uncle. It's got a few quirks, but overall it's still friendly and fun to be around.

Installing and Uninstalling with Add/Remove Software

The Add/Remove Software utility in the desktop Settings tab is the ASUS default method of installing and uninstalling Eee PC Linux software. It's a very simplified, easy-to-use package manager designed to fit well with the Easy Mode user interface. To use the program, make sure you have an Internet connection and then follow these steps:

1. **In the desktop Settings tab, click Add/Remove Software.**

   A dialog box is displayed as the Eee PC checks for software updates — the program compares what is installed on your mini-laptop to what is available in the official ASUS repository. This can take awhile, depending on the server load.

2. **Click a tab (as shown in Figure 12-1) to display updated software associated with that tab.**

   Packages that are available for download and installation are organized by tab. The name of a program, its version number, and a brief description is shown.

Don't expect to see every Linux program on the planet — far from it actually. Add/Remove Software only displays a very small collection of supported programs that reside in ASUS repositories. Use Synaptic Package Manager or APT if you want to install other programs that aren't listed.

Just because Add/Remove Software says a package is available for download doesn't mean you should automatically install it. If you don't know what it is or don't have a use for it, resist the temptation. The same is true for upgraded versions of programs, system files, and the BIOS.

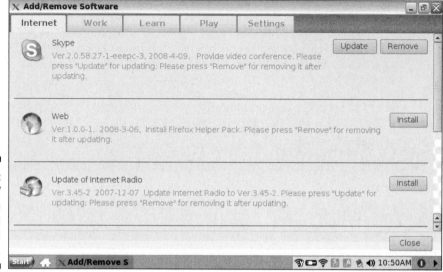

Figure 12-1:
Add/
Remove
Software
tabs and
programs.

Use a command button to carry out an installation action. Command buttons are displayed to the right of each package icon. The following buttons are available:

✔ **Open** — If multiple packages are present, click the Open button to display them. You can then use the other buttons listed next for installing.

✔ **Install** — Downloads and installs a package.

✔ **Update** — Updates a previously installed package.

✔ **Remove** — Removes a previously installed package.

The Remove button only uninstalls and deletes packages you have personally installed. You cannot use it to remove preinstalled programs — if, for example, you're trying to free up space. Default Linux Eee PC programs are kept on a read-only partition. New programs and updates are saved to a user partition, which is read-write.

Available command buttons depend on the package's status. For example, if a new package is listed that hasn't been installed yet, the Remove button is not shown.

Despite its simple-to-use appearance, the Add/Remove Software utility has caused grief for some Eee PC users — I've personally been burned a time or two by the program myself. Here's what you need to know about it.

If you visit the EeeUser.com forums, you find a number of posts from users who have run into problems using Add/Remove Software. Program icons disappear, programs don't work correctly, and some users have been forced to use F9 to restore their computer to factory settings. (On the other hand, other users report successfully using Add/Remove Software with no troubles.)

Because of these currently mixed reviews (with no causes identified or fixes suggested), I recommend that if you plan to install or update software on your Eee PC, you use Synaptic Package Manager or APT instead of Add/Remove Software. (Or, don't worry about updating as I discuss in the "Update nation" sidebar.)

If you do decide to use the Add/Remove Software program and your Eee PC doesn't work properly afterwards, here are your options to get things back to normal:

- ✔ Try restoring lost program icons with the methods I describe in Chapter 21.

- ✔ Perform an F9 system recovery, which I discuss in Chapter 18. If that doesn't work, you can reinstall the operating system — which I also detail in the same chapter. Just remember, all your files will be deleted with F9 and DVD recovery methods, so be sure to back them up first.

Update nation

The Internet has fueled a psychosis I like to call update-itis. On most PCs, at least a couple of times a week, a dialog box appears that proclaims, "New version available. Update now?" (or something like that). Maybe it's an operating system security patch or perhaps a new feature update for a program. If you have a Net connection and you're not seeing these dialog boxes, it's probably because at some point you elected to automatically install updates, so you aren't constantly bothered by the annoying messages.

Most people's reaction is, "They're telling me I should update, so there must be a good reason for it." Or, "If I don't update, the hackers will get in."

Call me a Luddite, but I think the "newer must be better" attitude is out of control. Most software updates contain "nice-to-have" versus "need-to-have" features. And the bulk of security patches are fixes for theoretical versus realistic threats. (I'm convinced the keys to effective computer security are simple common sense about where you visit and what you download, a good firewall, and decent anti-virus software. It's as simple as that.)

How does this apply to the Eee PC? I say if your mini-laptop is running and working fine, don't feel compelled to update it (especially with Add/Remove Software). Out of the box, I view the Eee PC as a computing appliance. And how often do you update your TV, cell phone, or blender? If it's not broken, don't fix it.

Installing with Synaptic Package Manager

Synaptic Package Manager, or Synaptic for short (see Figure 12-2), is a user-friendly, graphical user interface for the command-line Advanced Packaging Tool (APT), which I discuss in the next section.

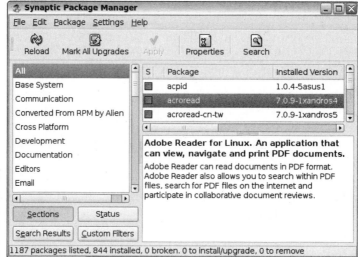

Figure 12-2:
Synaptic
Package
Manager.

Synaptic displays available packages (based on selected repositories), shows which packages your Eee PC has installed, and can automatically download and install programs for you. It's considerably more advanced and powerful than the Add/Remove Software utility and doesn't seem to cause the random system problems that some users encounter when installing new software and upgrades.

For lots more on using Synaptic, because I don't have the space in this chapter to fully cover all its features, check out this how-to: `https://help.ubuntu.com/community/SynapticHowto`.

The Easy Mode desktop doesn't have an icon for Synaptic Package Manager, so you start a console session to run it. Here's how:

1. **Press Ctrl+Alt+T.**

2. **Enter** sudo synaptic.

3. **Use Synaptic to install and remove software.**

When Synaptic is loaded, a window like the one shown in Figure 12-2 is displayed. The primary elements of the window are:

✔ **Sections:** The Sections list allows you to filter which packages are displayed, by type — in Figure 12-2, All, Base System, Communication, and so on are sections. By default, All is selected; which shows all packages. Select a Section type for the packages you are interested in seeing. For example if you select the Editors section, only text editor packages are shown.

Click the Status button below the Sections list to display all packages currently installed, uninstalled, or those that can be upgraded. Click the Sections button to return to the Sections list.

✔ **Packages:** To the right of the Sections list is a list of packages corresponding to the currently selected Section — in Figure 12-2, acpid, acroread, and so on are packages. If a package has a filled box to the left of its name, it has been installed. Unfilled boxes indicate a package hasn't been installed. All the packages shown in the Add/Remove Software program are available, plus more. (If you know the name of a program or package, you can search for it to see if it's available in a repository.)

✔ **Description:** When you select a package, a description is shown in the text box below the list of packages. In Figure 12-2, the description for the Adobe Reader (acroread) package is displayed.

Right-click a package and select Properties to get more detailed information about a package, including its size, version, and file dependencies.

Installing and removing packages

The first thing you should always do when running Synaptic is click the Reload button in the toolbar. This downloads the latest repository information, which is important to keep up-to-date.

If you see a program that you'd like to download in the Packages list, here is how to install it on your Eee PC:

1. **Select the package you want to install.**

2. **Right-click and choose Mark for Installation.**

3. **Click the Apply button in the Synaptic toolbar.**

   A dialog box appears with information about the package.

4. **Click Apply in the dialog box.**

   You may need to hold down the Alt key and drag the cursor because the Apply button may appear at the bottom, off the screen.

Status information is shown as the package downloads, and the program is installed. When installation is successfully completed, you can run the new (or upgraded) program.

In case you're thinking of installing a program on an SD card to save drive space, hold on a minute. If you are using Synaptic or APT, Eee PCs running the default version of Xandros Linux cannot install programs to an SD card or other external device. It's possible to mount an SD card as the user partition, which would allow you to install programs to the card, but this is a fairly involved process. If you're up for the challenge, read this comprehensive message thread in the EeeUser.com forums: `http://forum.eeeuser.com/viewtopic.php?id=7694`.

If you've downloaded an Eee PC–compatible package (with a `.deb` extension) from a Web site or FTP server, you can install the program with File Manager. Select the `.deb` file, right-click, and choose Install DEB File from the pop-up menu. Just be forewarned that if there are dependent files and libraries not included inside the package, they won't be installed — if you used a package manager they would be. If dependent files aren't installed, the program won't run correctly.

Uninstalling a program with Synaptic follows the same procedure as installing:

1. **Select the package you want to uninstall.**
2. **Right-click and choose Mark for Removal.**
3. **Click the Apply button in the Synaptic toolbar.**
4. **Click Apply in the dialog box.**

If you don't exactly know what a package is and does, don't remove it. You can potentially make your system unstable if you remove something you shouldn't. If that happens, it's probably time to perform an F9 or DVD restore.

Creating desktop shortcuts

After a package has been installed, create a desktop icon so you can run the program (the alternative is to use the console and type the program's name each time you run it).

Unfortunately, Synaptic doesn't create these icons for you (or add them to one of the desktop tabs). Instead you can use SimpleUI Editor or one of the other tools I describe in Chapter 21. This is usually a straightforward process.

Because package names aren't always the same as program names, at times finding where a program was installed can be a little challenging — if you don't know the program path, you can't create a desktop icon for it. Use File Manager for your search. Programs are typically installed in the /usr directory, often in the /bin subdirectory.

Adding a repository

By default, Synaptic only uses official ASUS repositories — which include only a small number of ASUS-supported programs. If a program you'd like to install isn't shown in the list of available packages, get it from another Eee PC–compatible repository.

To manually add a single repository to Synaptic, make sure you have an Internet connection and then do the following:

1. In Synaptic's Settings menu, select Repositories.

The Repositories window is displayed showing a list of currently referenced repositories.

2. Click the New button.

Text boxes for filling in information about the repository you want to add are displayed (as shown in Figure 12-3).

Figure 12-3:
Synaptic's
Repositories
window —
adding
a new
repository.

Repositories
Enabled	Type	URI	Distribution	Se
☑	deb	http://update.eeepc.asus.com/p701/	p701	m
☑	deb	http://update.eeepc.asus.com/p701/en/	p701	m
☑				

⬆ Up
⬇ Down

Binary (deb) ▾

URI: http://download.tuxfamily.org/eeepcrepos/

Distribution: p701

Section(s): |

New   Delete   ✗ Cancel   ✔ OK

3. **Enter a URL for the new repository.**

   For example, **http://download.tuxfamily.org/eeepcrepos/**.

4. **Enter the Distribution.**

   Such as **p701**.

5. **Enter the Section.**

   In most cases, this will be **main**.

6. **Click OK.**

   The new repository is added to the list.

Click the Reload button in the Synaptic toolbar to update the list of available packages.

When the Repositories window is displayed, repositories that have a check box are enabled. Check and uncheck repositories to choose which ones you want to access.

 I show you how to edit several configuration files to add repositories as well as *pin* them (prioritize for downloading) in the section, "Adding More Repositories" at the end of the chapter. There I provide instructions for including several repositories at once as well as the important instructions for *pinning*.

All about APT

APT stands for Advanced Packaging Tool. This command-line installation utility is found in many Linux distributions — including the Eee PC.

APT isn't a standalone program, but a collection of function libraries for managing packages. If you're comfortable using the console, which I describe in Chapter 20, APT is a fast and efficient way to install, remove, and update Eee PC software.

When you run an APT command, status messages appear in the console. During the install process, APT may also ask you to confirm some operations.

 Synaptic Package Manager is a graphical user interface for APT — it uses APT settings files and transparently passes commands to the function library. Synaptic is much easier to use because of its point-and-click nature. APT is faster.

Here is a list of some commonly used APT commands that you enter in the console:

- ✔ `apt-cache search packagename` — Searches repositories for a named package. Package names and their descriptions are examined for a match (searches are not case-sensitive).

  If you search for a common term, such as *xandros*, you need to pipe to the Less command to see all the results — if none of that made sense, check out Chapter 20.

- ✔ `apt-get clean` — Cleans up the package cache. Do this every so often to save disk space.

  Because `apt-get` commands require administrative privileges, precede them with the word *sudo*. For example, `sudo apt-get clean`.

- ✔ `apt-get install` *packagename* — Installs the named package. If other packages are required for the program to run correctly, APT automatically downloads and installs them.

- ✔ `apt-get remove` *packagename* — Uninstalls a package.

- ✔ `apt-get update` — Updates repository information. Always run this command before you install a package.

There's much more to APT, and the best way to come up to speed is to visit the official how-to site at `www.debian.org/doc/manuals/apt-howto/`.

Adding More Repositories

The ASUS repositories used by Synaptic Package Manager and APT contain Eee PC system and program updates and new, officially supported programs for the mini-laptop. In keeping with the theme of the Eee PC as a computing appliance, these repositories are fairly small — which makes the mini-laptop easy to use and support.

However, as you already may know, a large amount of free, open-source Linux software is available on the Internet. To download and install these programs, you should make additional repositories available to the package managers.

Previously in this chapter, I told you how to add a single repository to Synaptic. I now want to show you can access the most popular, current Eee PC–compatible repositories and ensure that you get the most optimal package versions by using *pinning*.

Adding multiple repositories

Here's how to add all the current Eee PC–compatible repositories at once. After you do this, you can to download many more Eee PC programs with Synaptic or APT.

1. **Start a console session by pressing Ctrl+Alt+T.**

2. **Enter** `sudo kwrite /etc/apt/sources.list.`

   This opens a configuration file used by both Synaptic and APT with the KWrite word processor. The ASUS repositories are listed at the beginning.

3. **Add the following four lines to the file:**

   ```
   deb http://xnv4.xandros.com/xs2.0/upkg-srv2 etch main contrib non-free
   deb http://dccamirror.xandros.com/dccri/ dccri-3.0 main
   deb http://www.geekconnection.org/ xandros4 main
   deb http://download.tuxfamily.org/eeepcrepos/ p701 main etch
   ```

   These are Web site references and description information for each of the repositories. All the repositories contain Eee PC–compatible software. Be sure not to accidentally remove the reference to the ASUS repository.

   If you don't feel like risking a typo, go to this link and copy and paste the four lines: `http://wiki.eeeuser.com/addingxandrosrepos.`

4. **Save the file and quit KWrite.**

The four additional repositories are now available to Synaptic and APT.

To view all the available packages, click the Reload button in Synaptic or the Apt-Get Update command to refresh the repository list. If you get a warning message about an invalid public key, just ignore it.

As you hear about new Eee PC–compatible repositories, just add a new entry to the sources.list file with a text editor. You can also use Synaptic to add a repository as I described earlier, because it uses `sources.list.`

Pinning repositories

Before you start downloading packages, I highly recommend that you *pin* the repositories — and no, I'm not talking about using your ATM personal identification number. *Pinning* forces the package manager to select specific package versions that may be available in different versions on multiple repositories. This ensures that packages are not upgraded to versions which may conflict with other packages or the system.

If you're just using the default ASUS repositories, you don't need to worry about pinning.

If repositories aren't pinned and copies of the same-named package exist on several repositories (but with different versions), the package manager always chooses the package with the highest version number. This can cause problems if a newer package hasn't been fully tested or perhaps is not compatible with the system.

Pinning involves assigning a number to a repository that sets its priority when a package is downloaded. A package from a repository with the highest number always takes greater download precedence over other repositories that have the same package. For example, the primary ASUS repository should always get the highest pin-priority number.

Here's how to pin the repositories you just added:

1. **Start a console session by pressing Ctrl+Alt+T.**

2. **Enter** `sudo kwrite /etc/apt/preferences`.

   Pinned repositories are set in the file. This command opens the file (or creates it if it doesn't exist).

3. **Add the pin information.**

   You must enter quite a bit of text in the file, so instead of listing it here and asking you to type it, go to: `http://wiki.eeeuser.com/adding xandrosrepos` and copy the pin information to paste into the preferences file.

4. **Save the file and exit KWrite.**

That's it. Now when you use Synaptic or APT, you can be assured you always get the right package from the right repository.

For lots more information on repositories and the Eee PC, spend some time reading this excellent how-to at the EeeUser.com Wiki: `http://wiki.eeeuser.com/addingxandrosrepos`.

Automating the process

Now that you know how to manually add repositories and pin them, I have to tell you that the Tweakeee and Pimpmyeee.sh utilities, which I describe in Chapter 21, both have options that add Eee PC–compatible repositories to the `sources.list` file and then pin them.

Why didn't I tell you earlier, and save you all of that work (and reading)? I'm not being mean (really). I just think it's important to understand how things work before you break out the black box tools and put them to work.

Eee Download Web site

As I put the finishing touches on this chapter, a new Web site from ASUS has appeared. Dubbed *Eee Download* (`http://eee download.asus.com`), the Web site offers yet another alternative for installing programs on Linux Eee PCs.

The official ASUS site claims to have over 3,000 programs that can be installed with just a few mouse clicks. A large number of productivity applications, games, and utilities are listed and described. You need a copy of Eee PC Linux version 1.6 or later to use the site, but there's presently little to no information on how to upgrade to this release or use the download site.

My guess is Eee Download is currently a work in progress, and at this point, it isn't ready for prime time. However I encourage you to pay a visit to the site when you read this, to see if it's live and has information on how to use it. From initial appearances, Eee Download just might provide the easiest and fastest way to download and install programs on your Linux Eee PC.

Chapter 13

Popular Linux Programs

· ·

In This Chapter

▶ Editing graphics with GIMP

▶ Cataloging digital photos with Picasa

▶ Traveling the world with Google Earth

▶ Editing sound files with Audacity

▶ Playing media with VLC

▶ BitTorrenting with FrostWire

▶ Stargazing with Stellarium

▶ Balancing your checkbook with GnuCash

▶ Word processing with AbiWord

▶ Running Windows programs with Wine

· ·

*I*n Chapter 12, I tell you how to install Linux programs with Synaptic Package Manager and APT. But what's the use of knowing how to install programs if you don't know which cool Linux programs to run on your Eee PC?

That's what this chapter is about. I tell you about a variety of cool programs for your Linux Eee PC. In addition to briefly describing the programs, I also tell you how to download and install (and uninstall) them. To be successful at this, I make a few assumptions:

✔ You're connected to the Internet.

✔ You've added the repositories I mention in Chapter 12 (and pinned them). It wouldn't hurt to have skimmed through that chapter so you have an idea of how Linux software installation works.

✔ You know how to start a console session — just press Ctrl+Alt+T. I show you some simple APT commands for installing the programs. Although you can certainly use Synaptic, apt-get is faster (and easier to use because you don't have to mess with a bunch of menu items, buttons, and lists). To come up to speed on command-line Linux, visit Chapter 20.

✔ You understand these programs aren't supported by ASUS. You should go to Web sites and community forums if you have questions.

After you install a program, you want to create a desktop icon for it. I explain how to create program icons in Chapter 21. Or you can always run the program by entering its name at the console — I show you the command you type to run the program.

Many Linux programs weren't designed for the tiny 7-inch Eee PC screen. If a dialog box appears off the bottom of the screen, hold down the Alt key and use the cursor to drag the window up so you can see the rest of the dialog box.

Editing Graphics with GIMP

If you need a little more oomph than the preinstalled paint programs on your Linux Eee PC can provide, consider the GIMP. GIMP stands for the Gnu Image Manipulation Program (as shown in Figure 13-1). It's a powerful, raster graphics image editor — think of it as a free, open-source alternative to Adobe Photoshop.

If you're a photographer, be sure to read this how-to for using GIMP with the Eee PC to edit RAW format images: http://wiki.eeeuser.com/howto:addrawphotoediting.

To find out more about GIMP and how to use it, visit: www.gimp.org.

Figure 13-1:
The GIMP graphics editor.

In the Gnus

When you start using Linux, you see a lot of references to Gnu. Gnu-this, Gnu-that. Here's the news on all of those Gnus.

GNU (for GNU's Not Unix) is a UNIX-compatible operating system composed of entirely free software that dates back to the mid-1980s. It was fathered by Richard Stallman, a programmer and founder of the Free Software Foundation (www.fsf.org). In addition to the operating system, the GNU Project also created a compiler and other utilities. In 1991, Linus Torvalds used GNU development tools to create the Linux kernel.

GNU is as much a philosophy as it is an expression of technology, and over the years a number of programs have adopted the GNU moniker in their names to support and promote the notion of free software.

For more on GNU, visit: www.gnu.org.

Here's what you need to type at the command line:

To install GIMP: sudo apt-get install gimp.

The GIMP relies on a number of different libraries and support files, so be patient as it downloads.

To run GIMP: gimp

To uninstall GIMP: sudo apt-get remove gimp

Cataloging Digital Photos with Picasa

Picasa is a popular program for organizing and editing digital photos and graphic images (you can see a sample screen in Figure 13-2). The name is a play on the name of the artist Pablo Picasso as well as combining *pic* (pictures) and *casa* (Spanish for house). You can catalog, view, and sort images by different criteria and perform basic edit functions (red-eye removal, color correction, special effects).

A similar Linux program called Gwenview is already installed on your Eee PC — I tell you all about it in Chapter 8.

Don't scan the entire drive when Picasa first starts up. If you do, be prepared for a lengthy wait. You'll be amazed at all the small graphics files (icons, buttons, window ornaments, and so on) that are tucked away inside various Eee PC directories.

To learn more about Picasa features and how to use the program, visit: http://picasa.google.com/.

Here's what you need to type at the command line:

To install Picasa: sudo apt-get install picasa

To run Picasa: picasa

To uninstall Picasa: sudo apt-get remove picasa

Some Eee PC models might have Picasa pre-installed. If it's already on your mini-laptop, there's no need to install it again.

Traveling the World with Google Earth

Google Earth (as shown in Figure 13-3) is a free program that displays satellite imagery of the entire planet. You can zoom in on a location and get a detailed bird's-eye view of a place — resolution varies, depending on available satellite data. It's an amazing program, kind of like having your own personal spy satellite, and it is indispensable if you travel with your mini-laptop.

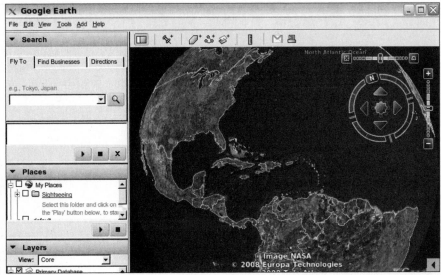

Figure 13-3:
Viewing
satellite
images
with Google
Earth.

Google Earth is designed to run on at least a 1024-x-768 screen, but still works on the Eee PC — performance can be a bit pokey though, considering the Eee PC's relatively under-powered processor.

If, after you install Google Earth, it's running as slow as molasses, here's what to do:

- ✔ If you have a pre-4.3 version of the program, apply some speed patches that are documented at `http://wiki.eeeuser.com/howto:fixgoogleearthspeed`.

- ✔ If you have version 4.3 or later, try unchecking Atmosphere in the View menu. (The speed patches for older versions don't noticeably improve performance.)

To find out more about Google Earth, go to `http://earth.google.com`.

Here's what you need to type at the command line:

To install Google Earth: sudo apt-get install googleearth

To run Google Earth: googleearth

To uninstall Google Earth: sudo apt-get remove googleearth

Editing Sound Files with Audacity

Audacity (as shown in Figure 13-4) is a powerful, digital sound editor. It's a souped-up version of the Sound Recorder found in the Play tab that can record sounds and edit the generated WAV file. The program can also save WAV files in compressed MP3 format — a space-saving must if you're using your Eee PC to take and save lecture notes.

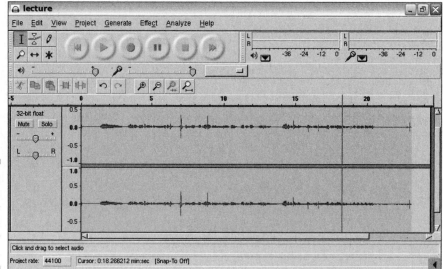

Figure 13-4: The Audacity sound recorder and editor.

For more about Audacity, including how to use the program, visit http://audacity.sourceforge.net/.

Here's what you need to type at the command line:

To install Audacity: sudo apt-get install audacity

To run Audacity: audacity

To uninstall Audacity: sudo apt-get remove audacity

Playing Media with VLC

VLC is a popular, free media player developed by the VideoLAN Project (a program screen is shown in Figure 13-5). Available for a number of different computer platforms, the program can play audio and video files and encode and stream media. It comes with a large number of audio and video codecs, which means it supports playback for many types of media formats.

Figure 13-5:
The VLC
media
player.

To find out more about VLC features and how to use the program, visit `www.videolan.org/vlc/`.

Here's what you need to type at the command line:

To install VLC: sudo apt-get install vlc

To run VLC: vlc

To uninstall VLC: sudo apt-get remove vlc

BitTorrenting with FrostWire

FrostWire is a peer-to-peer (Gnutella and BitTorrent) file-sharing program. The open-source application, shown in Figure 13-6, is written in Java and is a variation of LimeWire; a popular Gnutella client. In addition to many advanced P2P features, it also includes a built-in media player.

In the Tools menu, select Options. Here you can specify whether to save downloaded files to an SD card or to a USB thumb drive. If you do a lot of BitTorrenting, the Eee PC's small internal drive can fill up pretty fast.

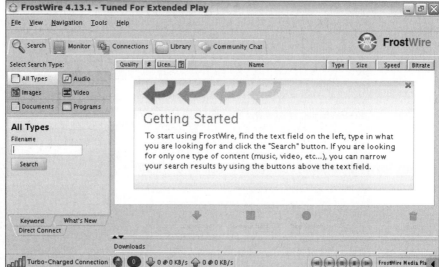

Figure 13-6:
The
FrostWire
BitTorrent
client.

To find out more about FrostWire (including getting support from a large user community), visit: www.frostwire.com.

Here's what you need to type at the command line:

To install FrostWire: sudo apt-get install frostwire

To run FrostWire: frostwire

To uninstall FrostWire: sudo apt-get remove frostwire

Stargazing with Stellarium

I'm kind of a sucker for astronomy programs. Although Planetarium/KStars in the Learn tab is pretty cool (I tell you all about it in Chapter 7), an even better sky-watching tool is called Stellarium, shown in Figure 13-7.

Stellarium is an open-source planetarium program that gives you a photo-realistic view of the night sky. It's just like looking at the stars (and planets) with binoculars or a telescope. Set coordinates for any place on earth, and see what the sky looks like at a certain date and time.

Figure 13-7:
Look to the
skies with
Stellarium.

Initially, Stellarium won't run on an Eee PC and displays an error message about an incorrect screen size. To use the program, you need to make a few changes to a configuration file. Here's how:

1. **Using File Manager (in the desktop Work tab), go to your Home directory.**

   In the View menu, make sure Show Hidden Files is checked.

2. **Open the .stellarium directory.**

3. **Double-click config.ini.**

4. **Change settings to the following:**

   ```
   [video]
   fullscreen = true
   screen_w = 800
   screen_h = 480
   bbp_mode  = 16
   ```

5. **Save the file and run Stellarium again.**

You should now see stars.

To find out more about Stellarium features and how to use the program, point your browser to www.stellarium.org.

Here's what you need to type at the command line:

To install Stellarium: sudo apt-get install stellarium

To run Stellarium: stellarium

To uninstall Stellarium: sudo apt-get remove stellarium

Some Eee PC models might have Stellarium pre-installed. If it's already on your mini-laptop, there's no need to install it again.

Balancing Your Checkbook with GnuCash

If you want to track finances on your Eee PC, check out an open-source program called GnuCash — think of it as a free alternative to Quicken or QuickBooks. GnuCash (a sample screen is shown in Figure 13-8) allows you to track bank accounts, stocks, income, and expenses. You can use it for personal or business finances.

To find out more about GnuCash, visit www.gnucash.org.

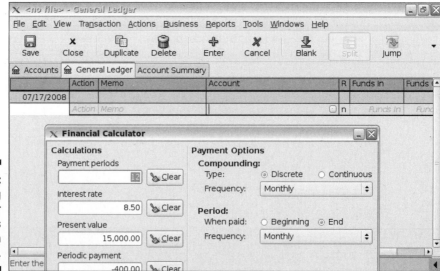

Figure 13-8: Tracking your finances with GnuCash.

Here's what you need to type at the command line:

To install GnuCash: sudo apt-get install gnucash

To run GnuCash: gnucash

To uninstall GnuCash: sudo apt-get remove gnucash

Word Processing with AbiWord

If you don't like the OpenOffice word processor, try a popular free alternative called AbiWord (shown in Figure 13-9). AbiWord is a fast and easy-to-use word processor with all the features you need to write papers and reports.

If you want to exchange documents with Microsoft Word, your best bet is to use Rich Text Format (RTF). Keep in mind that OpenOffice supports many more import file formats than AbiWord.

After installation, the only configuration you may need to perform to get AbiWord working with your Eee PC involves the spell checker.

If *Check spelling as you type* is enabled in the Preferences dialog box (in the Edit menu, select Preferences), the Check Spelling item in the Tools menu is dimmed. Turn off automatic checking and try spell checking the document.

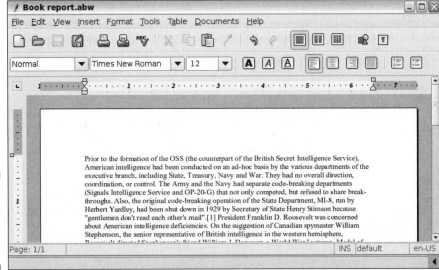

Figure 13-9:
The AbiWord word processor.

If spell checking still isn't working, download a spell checker package and create a link to it. This is a simple task. Quit AbiWord, and in the console, enter these commands:

```
sudo apt-get install ispell
sudo ln -s /usr/lib/ispell /usr/share/enchant/ispell
```

The next time you run AbiWord, spell checking should work.

To learn more about AbiWord, go to www.abisource.com/.

Here's what you need to type at the command line:

To install AbiWord: sudo apt-get install abiword

To run AbiWord: abiword

To uninstall AbiWord: sudo apt-get remove abiword

Running Windows Programs with Wine

Wine is a program that enables you to run Windows programs inside of Linux — Wine stands for Wine Is Not an Emulator, in case you're curious. Wine started development back in 1993, and the 1.0 version was finally released in the summer of 2008. Its goal is to allow many different types of Windows programs to function under Linux — for example, a Windows utility running on a Linux Eee PC is shown in Figure 13-10.

Figure 13-10: Wine running a Windows utility on a Linux Eee PC.

Keep in mind that not all Windows programs work with Wine, and there are some limitations in using it. I recommend that, if you regularly run Windows applications, you're probably better off getting a Windows XP Eee PC — despite what Linux fanboys say.

To learn more about Wine, visit the official project site at `www.winehq.org`. There's also an extensive tutorial on installing and running Wine on the Eee PC at `http://wiki.eeeuser.com/howto:wine`.

To install Wine, type this at the command line: sudo apt-get install wine.

If you want to use Synaptic to install Wine on your Eee PC, check out Laptop Magazine's easy-to-follow how-to at `www.laptopmag.com/advice/how-to/eee-pc-wine.aspx`.

To run a Windows program after you've installed Wine, follow these steps:

1. **In File Manager, choose the Windows program.**

2. **Right-click and select Open With.**

3. **In the /usr/bin directory, choose Wine**

   If the program is compatible with Wine and the emulator is configured correctly, the program opens up in a window and runs just like a Linux application.

To uninstall Wine, type this at the command line: sudo apt-get remove wine.

Got game?

I couldn't end this chapter without mentioning games. Although Linux Eee PCs come with a few fun games, if you're a serious gamer, you might find them, well, rather lame. Granted, the small screen and limited processor and graphics card don't make the Eee PC the most killer game machine, but you can play a surprising number of "real" games on the mini-laptop. Here are a few resources to consult to get game:

✔ **Linux Gaming forum** — The EeeUser. com forums host a forum devoted to Linux games: `http://forum.eeeuser. com/viewforum.php?id=29`.

✔ **List of Eee PC compatible games** — `http://wiki.eeeuser.com/ list:games`.

✔ **Eee PC Crysis and Quake 4** — A little hard to believe you say? Here's a YouTube video with proof (`www.youtube.com/ watch?v=Y4cU19WFv7g`). This magic is made possible by streaming the game from a Windows PC to the Eee PC. Check out StreamMyGame (`www.streammyg-ame.com`) for details.

Chapter 14

Popular Free Windows Programs

. . . .

. . . .

*L*et's face it. Linux Eee PCs come with a lot more preinstalled software than their Windows cousins. That's a benefit of open-source software; ASUS can load Linux mini-laptops up with all sorts of free and useful programs.

If you're running Windows XP, don't feel slighted. You still have several options for loading up your Eee PC with more software. You can do the following:

✔ Buy commercial software (however, hold off for a minute and read this chapter before you do that).

✔ Install commercial software you already own (following the licensing agreements of course).

✔ Download some great free programs.

That last option is what this chapter is all about. I list and describe what I feel are the best free Windows programs in a variety of categories. Many of these programs are especially well-suited to the Eee PC because they are fairly *lightweight* — that means they don't consume a lot of system resources like memory, CPU cycles, and drive space; all of which are at a premium in the mini-laptop.

In addition to the top 20 or so applications, I also point you to a number of Web sites that contain even more free Windows software. By the end of this chapter, you'll investigate some new and useful programs for your Eee PC — and your other Windows desktops or laptops for that matter. So read on.

Some software installs a program only to a hard (or solid state) drive. If you want to install a program to an SD card to save drive space, an installation program may prevent you from browsing to and choosing the card as the destination. To get around this, determine the card reader's drive letter (for example, D:), and then type in the path where you want the program installed — such as, D:/CoolProgram.

Essential Internet Programs

The Eee PC shines as a highly portable and easy-to-use appliance for accessing the Internet. You want to have the mini-laptop loaded with everything you need to browse, e-mail, download, and chat. Although Windows XP models do come bundled with several Net programs, I recommend a few alternatives that work quite well on the Eee PC.

Firefox (browser)

Yes, I know. Windows XP already comes with the Internet Explorer Web browser. So why should you take up precious drive space installing another browser? I have three words for you, "Speed, security, and features." The Firefox browser is faster (and consumes less system memory), is more secure, and has a whole lot of innovative features that makes browsing easier.

You owe it to yourself to give Firefox a spin — especially the 3.0 and later versions. Try it, you'll like it. And if you don't, it's easy to uninstall. For more information and to download the browser, go to www.mozilla.com/firefox/.

I briefly discuss Firefox running under Linux in Chapter 4, so if you've never used the browser, you might want to give the section a quick read. The Linux version has the same basic features and interface as the Windows release. I also discuss some add-on programs that make it easier to use Firefox on the Eee PC's small screen; regardless of whether you're running Linux or Windows.

Opera (browser)

Another free Internet Explorer alternative to consider is the Opera browser. Actually Opera is more than a browser because it can send and receive e-mail, manage RSS and newsfeeds, download files with BitTorrent, and a whole lot more. Opera is fast, and its screen configuration and keyboard commands lend themselves quite well to the Eee PC.

Check this multiplatform browser out at www.opera.com.

Thunderbird (e-mail)

For your e-mail needs, instead of Windows Mail or Outlook, consider Thunderbird; a popular open-source e-mail client. To learn more about Thunderbird, refer to Chapter 4 where I cover the Linux version of the e-mail program — which has the same basic features and interface as the one for Windows. Or, visit the project Web site at www.mozilla.com/thunderbird.

μTorrent (BitTorrent)

If you use BitTorrent, you may already have a favorite Windows client. Just be aware, however, some BitTorrent clients use a lot of system resources (Azureus and BitComet both come to mind) and really aren't well-designed for use on small-screen laptops.

For torrenting on a Windows Eee PC, I recommend using μTorrent, which is both small and stingy with system resources.

μTorrent is also known as *Micro Torrent* (the little squiggly character at the front is the Greek letter *Mu*, which is used in science to represent *micro*; one-millionth) or *You Torrent* (μ looks like *you*, and because μ is hard to find on the keyboard, many people use the letter *u* as in uTorrent).

To learn more about μTorrent and download the program, visit www.utorrent.com.

Your Eee PC doesn't have hundreds of gigabytes of free drive space available like your primary PC. So remember to go easy with the torrent downloading.

Pidgin (instant messaging)

For instant messaging (IM), Windows comes with Live Messenger (formerly called MSN Messenger). If you use MSN for your chatting, this IM client is sufficient (although I personally like an open-source program called aMSN, which has more features — download it from www.amsn-project.net). If you're wondering what aMSN stands for, it's Alvaro's Messenger (MSN) — the name of original developer Alvaro Iradier.

If you're using AIM, Yahoo, or another IM network, you can obviously use the network's proprietary software, or better yet, give a multinetwork IM client called Pidgin a try (www.pidgin.im). I describe the Linux release of Pidgin in Chapter 4 — it has the same basic features and interface as the Windows version.

Portable apps

Back in the old days of personal computing, most programs were truly standalone. You could copy a program on to a floppy disk, insert it in any compatible PC, and then run the program. In those long ago days, programs had to be small and efficient because memory and drive space was limited. Then came lots of memory, big hard drives, and complex operating systems which led to bigger programs and more complicated installations (because of support libraries and registries). Just like the floppy disk, the days of simply being able to move a program from one computer to another went by the wayside.

But lately, thanks to cheap USB thumb drives, portable applications are making a comeback. The general idea is to put a Windows program on a thumb drive, plug the drive into any PC, and then run the program without worrying about registry entries, support files, and other issues that typically keep a program chained to the C: drive.

In order to do this, an application needs to be rewritten or be initially developed with portability in mind. The good news is that many free and open-source Windows programs are jumping on the portability bandwagon, including a fair number of the ones I mention in this chapter (such as Firefox, Thunderbird, Pidgin, and OpenOffice).

This is a pretty slick solution for a space-constrained Windows Eee PC because you can install your favorite programs on a USB thumb drive or SD card, thus freeing up internal drive space. You can then move the drive or card between computers and always have your favorite programs handy.

For free Windows portable apps, check out http://portableapps.com, www.pendriveapps.com, and www.portablefreeware.com. Here you find complete collections of take-anywhere, essential programs.

For Internet phone calls, Skype comes bundled with Windows XP Eee PCs. If you installed Windows on a Linux mini-laptop and need Skype, you can download it at www.skype.com.

Work and Entertainment Applications

If you purchased an Eee PC with Windows, you'll find it has Microsoft Works (a very basic office suite that's not fully compatible with Microsoft Office), StarSuite (a proprietary office product that shares OpenOffice programs), and Adobe Reader. That's it for the work-related programs. For entertainment, you've got the old, standard-issue Windows games and accessories and Windows Media Player.

Now just because these programs are preinstalled, that doesn't necessarily mean you have to use them — especially when there are alternatives available, such as those I discuss in the following sections.

OpenOffice (office suite)

My first piece of advice is, unless you have very limited and simple computing needs, forget about Microsoft Works. It's not a serious office suite.

That leaves you with the preinstalled StarSuite, which is based on OpenOffice (I tell you all about that open-source project in Chapter 5). I'd get rid of that program, too, and opt for the latest release of OpenOffice. Although StarSuite and OpenOffice share the same programs, support is better with OpenOffice, thanks to an extensive user community. You also get more frequent updates. You can download OpenOffice and get more information at `www.open office.org`.

As you may have guessed, I'm a big fan of open-source software. However, I still give a slight node to older versions of Microsoft Office over OpenOffice for speed and usability on an Eee PC. OpenOffice is a great free alternative to Microsoft Office, but if you have an older version of Office lying around (specifically the 1997, 2000, or the XP version — later releases are kind of resource hogs, to put it bluntly), you'll probably prefer it over OpenOffice.

FoxIt (PDF reader)

How do I put this politely? Adobe Reader has gotten, er, rather bloated in its old age. It consumes a lot of system resources and has a number of features the average user never touches. So for reading PDF files, I recommend FoxIt, a free, slick little PDF reader that's less filling and tastes great. You can download it at `www.foxitsoftware.com`.

Paint.Net (graphics)

Although the Paint accessory that comes with Windows XP is perfectly fine for doing basic graphics work, if you want a program that's a little more Photoshop-like in terms of features, check out Paint.net (`www.getpaint.net`). Paint.net is free, and (for all its whistles, bells, and tools) it runs pretty well on an Eee PC.

AsTray Plus

AsTray Plus is a free Windows utility that increases an Eee PC's screen resolution. Although it's impossible for any software package to add more pixels to a display monitor, it is possible for a clever programmer to do some tricks with fonts, color depth, and other settings to make it appear that you've got a larger screen (although if you set the resolution to 1024 x 768, I challenge you to make out any text that appears on a 7-inch screen).

For more on installing AsTray Plus, visit the EeeUser.com Wiki article at `http://wiki.eeeuser.com/astrayplus`.

There's also a forum thread devoted to discussing the program, including the latest on new releases, at `http://forum.eeeuser.com/viewtopic.php?id=18260&p=1`.

VLC (video player)

Instead of using the default Windows Media Player, give VLC a try. VLC is a popular, free, cross-platform media player that supports all the common video formats, streaming video and playing DVD movies (plus, it's not as resource intensive as Windows Media Player). You can download VLC and learn more about it at `www.videolan.org/vlc`.

Another alternative media player that's not as widely known, but still is well suited to the Eee PC because of its low resource usage, is the GOM Media Player. Check it out at `www.gomlab.com/eng/`.

Freeware XP games

Linux Eee PCs come with a pretty decent collection of games. The games that are bundled with Windows XP, are, well, just a little bit stale. Even Solitaire and Mine Sweeper get old after awhile. Although you can plunk down some hard-earned cash for commercial game software, before you do, just be aware there are thousands of free Windows games out there.

One of the best places to find Windows games is Andrew K's XP Games Web page at `http://home.comcast.net/~SupportCD/`

`XPGames.html`. This is a comprehensive list of many of the better freeware Windows games — conveniently organized by type, with a brief description and download link.

Another place to check out is Gameeer (`www.bourdeaux.net/eeepc/`), a Web page that focuses on playing Windows games exclusively on the Eee PC.

If you want to get your game on, both of these sites are well worth the visit.

foobar2000 (music player)

Although Windows Media Player can play MP3 and other audio files, for the Eee PC, I prefer a free audio player called foobar2000 (*foobar* is an inside joke among programmers because *foo* and *foobar* are often used as temporary variable names in programs). Foobar2000 has all the options you'd expect to find in an audio player, plus it is resource frugal, has a great user interface, and an extensive feature set. To find out more, head to http:// foobar2000.org.

Safety and Security Utilities

One of the advantages to running Linux is that you don't worry about the large amount of malicious software that continuously plagues Windows users. If you run Windows and use the Internet (or come in contact with files from other people), it's essential that you have a collection of good security programs to keep you and your computer safe.

Although you can go the standard security suite route with Norton or MacAfee, keep in mind these commercial products often consume a tremendous amount of system resources (which are at a premium on the Eee PC). They also tie you to yearly subscription fees.

Instead I suggest using a combination of lightweight, free security programs that have a proven track record. In this section, I give you my picks for Eee-PC–suitable anti-virus, firewall, and spyware software.

Many security software companies offer both free and commercial versions of their products. The commercial software tends to have more features, but for the average user, the basic features in a free version usually provide an adequate level of protection.

Virus defenders

Because Windows XP doesn't come preinstalled with software to protect you from viruses, one of the first things I'd suggest doing after you get your Eee PC is to install some anti-virus software. Two free Windows programs fit the bill, providing you with real-time virus protection (the software runs in the background and is always on the lookout for viruses).

Avast!

Avast! is a very popular anti-virus program that hails from the Czech Republic. It was first made available in 1988 and, as of the spring of 2008, it has over 50 million registered users worldwide. The software has a number of different features that protect you from all sorts of malicious threats. Download the free version and get more information at www.avast.com.

AVG

AVG is another widely used anti-virus application from the former Czechoslovakia (do the Czechs know viruses or what?). Avast! has a few more features and a cleaner interface in my opinion, but I always recommend downloading and evaluating both these programs to see which works best for you. AVG's Web site is http://free.grisoft.com/.

Your Eee PC's start-up time increases when you use anti-virus software that provides real-time protection — more system resources are also used because the program is always running. An alternative is to use the open-source ClamAV utility (www.clamav.net). ClamAV only searches for viruses and Trojans when you run the program (that means no real-time protection). If you have a low risk of picking up a virus, use this program to scan your drive every week or so to check for infections.

Firewall shields

When you're computing at home, I highly recommend you have a router or a switch between your computer and the broadband connection. Routers and switches provide a hardware firewall that keeps the bad guys out and makes your PCs fairly invisible to the rest of the world.

In addition you should also be running some type of software firewall. If your computer becomes infected and covertly tries to send data to someone, the firewall lets you know and blocks any outgoing traffic. A software firewall is also essential if you're on the road, accessing the Internet through a wired or wireless connection.

Although you can use Microsoft's firewall that comes with Windows XP, it doesn't support blocking outbound connections. Because of this, I recommend two free firewalls (both of which have received high marks in independent evaluations).

Comodo

Comodo's free personal firewall has scored number one in several tests designed to measure firewall effectiveness (beating out a number of commercial products I might add). Strong security, relative ease of use, and frequent updates make this Windows firewall my personal pick. For more information, go to www.personalfirewall.comodo.com.

Online Armor

This is another highly regarded firewall with a simpler user interface than Comodo. To read about its features or download it, visit `www.tallemu.com`.

Spyware protectors

Spyware is a broad term that relates to any ill-intentioned program or file that is installed on your PC without your knowing about it. Spyware is designed to take control or monitor your computer — without your permission.

Adware is often lumped together with *spyware* and refers to surreptitiously installed programs that display unwanted advertisements. Some people also consider cookies that are used for tracking Web site visits a form of spyware.

Spyware can be covertly installed on your computer when you run a program or visit a Web site. It is so pervasive these days (especially targeted at Windows PCs), a number of both free and commercial utilities are available for detecting and removing unwanted pests.

Ad-Aware Free

Ad-Aware Free started out as a utility for alerting you to advertising Web sites that were secretly tracking your visits. Since then, the program has evolved into a complete spyware detection and removal tool — it identifies dialers, Trojan horses, keyloggers, browser hijackers, and other privacy-violating malware. For more information and to download the program, visit `www.lavasoft.com`.

Spybot SD

Spybot SD (for Search and Destroy) is the granddaddy of spyware detection and removal programs. Although it's been around forever, it's still a valuable tool to have in your protection arsenal. You can learn about it at `www.safer-networking.org`.

CCleaner

CCleaner (the first C stands for Crap), really isn't a dedicated spyware detector, *per se*. Instead it cleans up temporary files, browser histories, cookies, and unused registry entries. Although spyware can hide data in some of these places, CCleaner is even more indispensable on a Windows Eee PC for getting rid of unneeded files that take up valuable drive space. To download the utility, go to `www.ccleaner.com`.

Call me paranoid, but I have all three of these programs installed on my Windows PCs. In the past there have been times when I've found one utility will detect and deal with something malicious that the others missed.

Encryption

The small form factor of the Eee PC makes it easy to carry around. It also makes it easy to lose or steal. If you store sensitive information on your mini-laptop, I highly recommend you use some type of encryption to secure the data. (Encryption software scrambles files, requiring a password to restore them.)

By far the best encryption application for keeping your files safe is called TrueCrypt. The program is an on-the-fly encryption utility — any files you copy, move, or write to a protected volume are automatically encrypted. TrueCrypt uses several strong encryption algorithms that even the NSA would have difficulty cracking.

To get the lowdown on the program (you don't need a top secret clearance), visit www.truecrypt.org.

More free Windows software

This chapter contains just a sampling of great, free Windows programs for your Eee PC. Many, many more free applications of all types are available.

Here is a list of additional Internet resources for downloading free Windows programs:

✔ **Open Source Windows** (www.open sourcewindows.org) — A list of the best open-source applications for Microsoft's operating system.

✔ **Mohawke's Best of the Best** (www. digitaldarknet.net/thelist/ index.php?page=windows) — An extensive list of Windows freeware (you can check out gratis-ware for other operating systems too).

✔ **WinFiles** (www.winfiles.com) — A large CNET site devoted to free Windows software.

✔ **Tiny Apps** (www.tinyapps.org) — Programs so small that if you sneeze they blow away.

✔ **Microsoft Power Toys for Windows XP** (www.microsoft.com/windowsxp/ downloads/powertoys/xppower toys.mspx) — A collection of nifty utilities straight from the Redmond homeland.

✔ **Windows Sysinternals** (http://tech net.microsoft.com/en-us/ sysinternals/default.aspx) — Essential system administration tools and security utilities.

Happy downloading!

Part IV
Hardware and Accessories for the Eee PC

The 5th Wave   By Rich Tennant

"He saw your Eee PC and wants to know if he can check his e-mail."

In this part . . .

The Eee PC contains a surprising number of features for such a small and affordable laptop. But you might want to consider a variety of accessories and hardware add-ons to enhance your Eee PC's functionality and usability. That's what this part of the book is about.

You learn about expanding storage and memory, how to connect all sorts of different peripherals (including monitors, keyboards, modems, Bluetooth, and more), and what you need to keep your mini-laptop powered up on the road (spare batteries, car chargers, and even solar power if you end up far off the beaten track). I also cover options for toting your Eee PC around town and include some tips on turning your mini-laptop into a fashion statement.

Chapter 15

Expanding Storage and Memory

· ·

· ·

*Y*ou have to make compromises when designing a small, light, and energy-efficient computer. One of those compromises in mini-laptops like the Eee PC is the amount of internal storage. Presently, you can't shoehorn a hard drive with the kind of gigabytes you find in a larger laptop into a small platform — the physical dimensions of the drive are too big, and they consume too much power. That will change in the future as technologies such as Solid State Drives offer more capacity at affordable prices, but in the meantime you have to make do with a limited amount of storage.

The good news is that, if the Eee PC's internal drive is just too miniscule for your needs, you have a number of ways to get around the gigabyte crunch. ASUS didn't compromise on including a number of ways to inexpensively expand storage.

That's what this chapter is about. In it, I explore SD cards, USB thumb drives, and other types of external USB drives you can use to save your files. The nice thing about all these storage options is they allow you to easily transfer data back and forth between your Eee PC and traditional desktop and laptop PCs.

In addition to telling you about ways to expand storage, I also cover expanding your Eee PC's internal memory with up to 2GB of RAM (that's a bunch of memory in such a small computer).

That's enough of an introduction; let's get the show on the road.

Secure Digital Card Tricks

Because of the small amount of drive space available on Eee PC models, many users find the mini-laptop's MMC/SD card reader essential for storing programs and data. At under $25 for a 4GB, with prices always seeming to be going down, SD cards (one is shown in Figure 15-1 later in this chapter) are a cheap way to expand storage. This section explains what you need to know about using them.

When you're done using a SD card, be sure to use the Safely Remove (Linux) or Safely Remove Hardware (Windows) taskbar commands before ejecting the card.

Supported cards

You can use several types of memory cards with your Eee PC. They include

- ✔ **SD** — Secure Digital. Flash memory cards that range from 8MB to 4GB.

- ✔ **SDHC** — Secure Digital High Capacity. This is an extension of the SD standard that debuted in 2006. It allows for memory cards with capacities higher than 4GB. The size and shape of SDHC cards are identical to those of SD cards; however older card readers can't read the new format. (High capacity cards are labeled SDHC, so you can tell the two cards apart.)

Based on the SDHC specification, these cards can theoretically have up to 2,048GB of storage. Wow! However, at present, card manufacturers have set a maximum limit of 32GB. Don't be surprised if that goes up in the future.

- ✔ **MMC** — SD and SDHC cards are derived from an older standard known as MultiMedia Cards. MMCs are slower and have less storage capacity. SD and SDHC cards have surpassed MMCs in popularity.

Check your Eee PC user manual for an official list of supported SD cards (by manufacturer and model) — just keep in mind this list isn't complete. These are only the cards ASUS had tested when the manual was written. The EeeUser.com Wiki also maintains a user-submitted list of SD cards that work with Eee PCs at http://wiki.eeeuser.com/hardware:eee_un_supported_devices.

If you can't save files to an SD card, check that the write protection tab hasn't been switched on accidentally. If you still can't write data, check out Chapter 22 where I present additional troubleshooting tips.

The heat is on?

If you're having problems with corrupted files on an SD card or one that refuses to format correctly, the cause may be heat. Some users on the EeeUser.com forums (http://forum.eeeuser.com) speculate that after the Eee PC has been running awhile, the card reader controller chip starts to overheat and cause troubles; especially when writing large files. Whereas various users have reported solving SD card problems by temporarily placing their Eee PC in a refrigerator or next to a fan or air conditioner, others have tried these cooling solutions and still had problems.

This seems to be an intermittent issue that doesn't affect all Eee PCs. If you're having SD card issues similar to the ones I just mentioned, before you put your Eee PC on ice, here are some things to try:

- Make sure the card isn't defective. It's not uncommon to get a bad SD card. Try using it on another computer. If it doesn't work on any computers, then you've got a bad card.

- Make sure the card reader on the Eee PC isn't defective. Again, try using the card with another PC. If it works on another computer, you've got a bad card reader.

- Reformat the card (see the section "Formatting SD cards" in this chapter).

- Placing an Eee PC on a soft surface can block the cooling vents, so keep it on a hard surface.

- For Windows Eee PCs, try running eeectl (www.cpp.in/dev/eeectl/) and setting CPU voltage to medium. The lower voltage decreases CPU temperature, which lowers the overall heat.

- If you need to transfer large files, do so before the mini-laptop starts to warm up.

Formatting SD cards

You might think with an SD card, you can easily move it from your Linux Eee PC, to your digital camera, to a Windows or Mac PC. After all, it fits in all three devices. Just keep in mind these two gotchas:

- **SDHC compatibility** — The Eee PC can read and write SDHC cards, but your camera or the card reader on your Windows PC may not.

- **Formatting** — MMC, SD, and SDHC cards can be formatted several different ways. Depending on how you format a card, it might not be readable by another device.

Eee PC file system formatting options include

- **Ext2** — A Linux file system (as in second extended file system)
- **Ext3** — An enhanced version of ext2

If you have a Linux computer and format a SC card as ext2 or ext3, Macs, Windows PCs or digital cameras are not able to read the card unless special drivers are installed.

> ✔ **FAT16** — FAT stands for File Allocation Table — in this case, 16-bit. This format goes dates back to the mid-1970s and is the primary file system for DOS and Windows. Maximum file size is 2GB.

> ✔ **FAT32** — An enhanced, 32-bit version of FAT that debuted in 1996 offering larger volume and maximum file sizes.

Most SD and SDHC cards come formatted as FAT16 or FAT32. You shouldn't need to format them before using.

If you need to reformat an SD card (if it somehow gets corrupted or is in a different format), here's how to do it with your Eee PC. First, insert the card and then follow these steps:

Formatting with Windows

To format an SD card with a Windows Eee PC

1. **Right-click the Start button and select Explore.**

2. **In Windows Explorer, select the drive letter associated with the card you want to format.**

3. **Right-click and select Format from the pop-up menu.**

4. **Select the format type and give the card a name.**

   One of the options is NTFS. For compatibility with the Eee PC and other devices, don't use this option. Stick with one of the versions of FAT instead.

5. **Click Start.**

If you want to use the SD Card Association's (the SD standards group) official formatting utility, you can download a Windows version at this site: www.sdcard.org/about/downloads/.

Formatting with Linux

On a Linux Eee PC, use the command line to format an SD card.

For example, the following console commands format an SD card as FAT32:

```
sudo -i
umount /dev/sdb1
mkdosfs -F 32 -n volume_name /dev/sdb1
```

Replace *volume_name* with whatever you want to call the card (up to 11 characters). If there's a space in the name, enclose it in quotes.

Here's a link to a tutorial for formatting a card to other formats: `http://wiki.eeeuser.com/howto:format_sd`.

TIP

If you need to format an SD or SDHC card, instead of using your Linux Eee PC, use a Windows PC or Mac. It's easier and as long as you format the card as FAT16 or FAT32, you can use it with Linux, Mac, and Windows PCs, digital cameras, and other electronic devices.

Disabling the Device Detection dialog box

Whenever you insert an SD card or USB device into the Linux Eee PC, a dialog box appears and politely asks you if you'd like to run a program to open files (such as music or videos) or use File Manager to view the contents of the device. This is nice and user-friendly, but can get a little annoying if you leave an SD card in the reader and the dialog box always shows up when you turn the mini-laptop on. If you have a 2G, 4G, or 8G Linux Eee PC, here's how to disable the feature:

1. **Start a command-line console session by pressing Ctrl+Alt+T.**

2. **At the command line, enter sudo chmod a-x /usr/bin/xandros_device_ detection_dialog.**

`chmod a-x` is a file permission command that changes a program (the Device Detection dialog box, in this case) setting so it is no longer executable. To restore the program, in the console, enter:

```
sudo chmod a+x /usr/bin/xandros_device_detection_dialog
```

This simple command disables the dialog box whenever a SD card or USB device is inserted. But if you just want to disable the dialog box when the Eee PC starts up (if there's an SD card already in place), it's a little more complicated. Here's how you do it:

1. **Start a command-line console session by pressing Ctrl+Alt+T.**

2. **Enter:** sudo mv /usr/bin/xandros_device_detection_dialog /usr/bin/ xandros_device_detection_dialog.bak

   This renames the file that contains the Device Detection dialog code.

3. **Enter** sudo kwrite /usr/bin/xandros_device_detection_dialog.

   Now create a new file, with the same name as the original.

4. **Add the following to the new file:**

```
#!/bin/sh
awk ë$1 < 40 { exit 1 }í /proc/uptime && xandros_device_
        detection_dialog.bak i$@î &.
```

You can also go to this link, where you can copy the preceding text and paste it directly into the new file: `http://wiki.eeeuser.com/howto:` `tempdisabledevicedetection`.

5. **Save the file.**

6. **At the console, enter the following:**

```
sudo chmod a+x /usr/bin/xandros_device_detection_dialog
```

This sets the permission so the new file is executable.

The modified code checks if the Eee PC has just started up when an SD card is present. If it has, it doesn't display the Device Detection dialog box. If the Eee PC has been running for awhile and a card is inserted, the Device Detection dialog box is displayed.

In a Flash: USB Thumb Drives

Back in the day, floppy disks were the technology of choice for saving files and moving data between computers. In 2000, IBM and Trek Technology introduced a slick alternative to the floppy disk that would change the course of personal computing. Dubbed the *thumb drive* the product was a flash memory card with a USB connector, enclosed in a small plastic case. Plugged into a PC's USB port, the drive offered a whopping 8MB of storage (around five times more than a 3.5-inch floppy disk).

The rest is history, and USB thumb drives (also known as flash drives, pen drives, jump drives, key drives, and UFDs — USB Flash Drives) have become a ubiquitous part of everyday computing (several drives are shown in Figure 15-1). Now small storage devices are available in sizes up to 32GB (it's difficult to find new drives under 1GB these days). Capacities seem to always be rising with prices falling. As I write this, if you shop around you can get a 4GB thumb drive for around $30.

The Eee PC has three USB 2.0 ports (which are compatible with older and slower 1.1 USB thumb drives, as well as the more modern, faster 2.0 drives). Just plug a thumb drive into either Linux or Windows versions of the mini-laptop and use File Manager or Windows Explorer respectively to access your files.

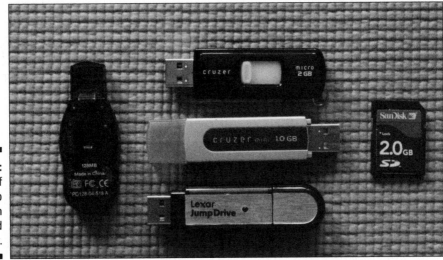

Figure 15-1:
A variety of
USB thumb
drives with
an SD card
on the right.

When you're done using a thumb drive, be sure to use the Safely Remove (Linux) or Safely Remove Hardware (Windows) taskbar commands before removing the drive.

Thumb drive life cycles

Nothing lasts forever, and that statement holds true for thumb drives. Several criteria determine the life span of a thumb drive.

The first is the type of flash memory used. The most common is called MLC (multilevel cell). There's also SLC (single-level cell), which is twice as fast (as well as twice as expensive). SLC also boasts a longer life cycle of 100,000 write/erase cycles compared to MLC's 10,000 write cycles. (Unfortunately, most manufacturers don't label their products, so you won't know if a more expensive thumb drive is using SLC or not.)

Right around the maximum number of write cycles, a thumb drive slowly starts to fail —

parts of its memory can no longer be used. Many thumb drives have a five-year warranty, and under normal use should last beyond that.

The other factor that limits a thumb drive's life is the USB connector. Manufacturers use a figure known as *mating durability* (I'm not kidding) to predict the maximum number of connections before failure. That number is about 1,500.

I wouldn't get too concerned about thumb drive cycles. I'm convinced the biggest risks for thumb drives to be cut down in the prime of their lives comes from the owner's losing the darn things or accidentally sending them through the wash.

I've yet to find a thumb drive that doesn't work with the Eee PC, but check your Eee PC user manual for the official list of supported USB drives (by manufacturer and model) — just keep in mind, the list is far from complete. The EeeUser.com Wiki also maintains a list of thumb drives users have had success with at `http://wiki.eeeuser.com/hardware:eee_un_supported_devices`.

If your MP3 player can serve as a USB mass storage device (often referred to as MSC or UMS), you can use it with your Eee PC to transfer and save files. Just connect the player to the mini-laptop with a USB cable, and the player's memory or drive appears as a volume in File Manager (Linux) or Windows Explorer (Windows XP).

If you're a Windows user who frequently defragments your hard drive to keep it running well, you may have thought about defragmenting your USB thumb drive. Don't bother. Defragmentation works by optimizing access to data on a drive with spinning platters and moving heads. Flash memory is random-access, and you don't get any performance gains with defragmenting. Additionally, because defragmentation moves data around for optimization, the write/erases decrease the flash memory's life (see the "Thumb drive life cycles" sidebar).

USB "Not That Hard" Drives

If an SD card or thumb drive doesn't meet your storage needs, a simple solution is to use a portable USB hard drive. These are traditional external hard drives, with smaller enclosures, designed to be easily moved around (an example is shown in Figure 15-2). Just plug a drive into your mini-laptop and, voilà, you've got hundreds of gigabytes at your disposal. Plus, the drive is easy to move between different computers.

USB hard drives come in a variety of sizes, but I like the small ones you can easily slip inside a pocket. These portable devices use small hard drives that limit the amount of available space (generally in the 120 to 320GB size range). If you don't plan on taking your hard drive on the road much, you can always opt for a physically larger drive with more storage space (just be aware that a larger drive may require two USB ports as I discuss in the "USB power considerations" sidebar).

When you're done using a USB hard drive, be sure to use the Safely Remove (Linux) or Safely Remove Hardware (Windows) taskbar commands before removing the drive.

Figure 15-2:
An EeePC
and a por-
table USB
hard drive.

USB power considerations

USB ports not only transfer data back and forth, but can also provide power to a connected device. (That's where an external drive is getting its juice from, unless it uses its own power supply.)

Ideally, you plug a USB hard drive or DVD into your Eee PC and everything works, with the files and folders all displayed in File Manager (Linux) or Windows Explorer. However, to function correctly, some drives need more power than a single USB port can provide.

This is addressed with a special USB Y-cable. You plug the two ends of the cable into two Eee PC USB ports and the single end into the hard drive. This supplies enough power to run the drive from the two ports.

Drives that require power from a single USB port are more energy efficient, which means longer battery life when you're not plugged into a wall socket. They also don't tie up a second USB port. If you have a choice, always go with a drive that only needs a single cable.

Swapping SSDs

Some Eee PCs (notably the 900 and later models) come with a socketed slot that makes it easy to replace the Solid State Drive (SSD). As this book goes to press, third-party SSDs are starting to appear that offer more storage and faster data read and write speeds than the default ASUS drives. Do-it-yourself installation is simple. You open the bottom of your Eee PC, unplug the old drive, and swap it with the new one. Prices depend on the type of flash memory (faster SLC memory is more expensive than slower MLC) and the amount of memory you want. Since the third-party SSD market is in its infancy, don't expect the cheap prices you'd pay for a conventional hard drive. A 16GB SLC drive currently runs around $200. Prices will fall as SSDs become more widely used, but for now, you are charged a premium price.

Prices for smaller portable drives range from around $100 to $200. Popular USB drive manufacturers include

- **Iomega** — www.iomega.com
- **Maxtor** — www.maxtor.com
- **Seagate** — www.seagate.com
- **SimpleTech** — www.simpletech.com
- **Western Digital** — www.westerndigital.com

If you have an IDE or SATA internal hard drive from an old PC lying around collecting dust, consider turning it into a cheap storage device for your Eee PC. Just pick up a USB IDE adaptor. Plug one end into the old hard drive (or an old internal CD or DVD drive for that matter), hook up the included power supply if needed, and then plug the USB connector into the Eee PC. The adaptors are reasonably priced at under $25 and are available from a number of online retailers. Do a Google search for *usb ide adaptor*.

Check your Eee PC user manual for an official list of supported USB hard drives (by manufacturer and model) — remember the list doesn't give you everything that works. Visit the EeeUser.com Wiki for a user-submitted record of compatible USB hard drives: http://wiki.eeeuser.com/hardware:eee_un_supported_devices.

DVD Drives for Dummies

Unlike traditional laptops, and Eee PC doesn't come with a built-in DVD drive — considering the size, there's no place to put it. Realistically, because of Eee PC's role as an ultra-portable laptop, you can easily get by without a DVD drive for it.

A couple of reasons might lead you to purchasing a DVD drive, however. For example, if you want to do any the following:

- ✔ **Watch movies on commercial DVDs.** If you want to watch rented or purchased movies on your Eee PC's DVD player, you must add some additional files to your Linux Eee PC. I tell you how in Chapter 8.

- ✔ **Restore your system from the recovery DVD that came with your computer.** With a Linux Eee PC you can create a recovery USB thumb drive on a Windows PC that has a DVD drive. However, if you have a Windows Eee PC and you want to restore your system, you need an external DVD drive connected to the mini-laptop to use the recovery DVD. (I discuss restoring your Eee PC in Chapter 18.)

- ✔ **Access files you have stored on DVDs.**

To use DVDs with your Eee PC, you need a portable, USB DVD drive such as the one shown in Figure 15-3. (This is an LG model GSA-E50N by the way, which is very popular with Eee PC users and works quite well with both Linux and Windows models.) Portable DVD drives are priced between $100 and $150 and are available online or from most large electronics retailers.

If you have an old internal DVD drive from a desktop PC or laptop, you may be able to connect it to your Eee PC with an IDE to USB converter. See the previous section on hard drives to find out more.

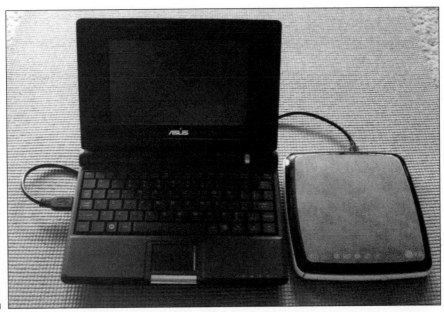

Figure 15-3:
An LG Slimline USB DVD drive and an Eee PC.

Check your Eee PC user manual for an official list of supported USB DVD drives (by manufacturer and model) — remember, just because a drive doesn't appear on the list doesn't mean it's not compatible. Check out the EeeUser.com Wiki for DVD drives users have had success with: `http://wiki.eeeuser.com/hardware:eee_un_supported_devices`.

More Memory

With most Eee PC models, you can expand the system memory up to 2GB — the 2G Surf is the exception because its 512K of memory is soldered into place. Here's everything you need to know about purchasing and installing memory.

Eee PCs use DDR2-667 SODIMM memory chips — DDR2 laptop memory that runs at a speed of 667 MHz (also known as PC2-5300). This memory is commonly used in many different laptops. Depending on the brand, where you purchase it, and how much memory you buy (1 or 2GB), expect to pay between $20 and $50. (Like the stock market, memory prices seem to always be going up or down.)

A number of different memory brands are available. Check out this active and ongoing forum thread for a discussion of what brands have worked well (and not so well) for Eee PC users: `http://forum.eeeuser.com/viewtopic.php?id=26317&p=1`.

Is more memory worth it?

Is boosting your Eee PC's memory really worth it? It depends on what model of mini-laptop you have and how you use it. For most people, the amount of memory that comes with their Eee PC is more than adequate for day-to-day use. But, if you're thinking about upgrading your memory, here are my recommendations.

If you're running Linux on an Eee PC with 512K of RAM, you may see a small performance increase if you upgrade RAM (especially if you frequently run multiple programs at the same time). For what it's worth, I've been perfectly happy with the performance of a 512K Linux 4G.

If you're running Windows XP on an Eee PC with 512K of RAM, you get an increase in performance with more memory (not a difference of day-and-night, but one that is noticeable). I'd lean toward upgrading if you're comfortable installing the memory yourself.

If your Eee PC comes with a gigabyte of memory, 2GB gives you a bit more performance (but not much). Unless you have a real need for another gigabyte (or must always have the most available memory), I'd pass on upgrading.

Memory does help, but remember you still have a relatively underpowered processor that's holding you back from having a machine as fast as your primary desktop PC or laptop.

Beating the 1GB limit

On 2G, 4G, and 8G Eee PCs running Linux, the Xandros system can only access up to 1GB of RAM (900 and later models don't have this issue). That means if you buy 2GB of RAM, your Eee PC will only use half of it. (This doesn't apply to these mini-laptops if they're running Windows or other versions of Linux.)

To get around this barrier, recompile the Linux kernel. This is a pretty advanced move (even for the average techie), requiring you to make a few changes in the operating system source code, use a compiler to create new binary code, and then install the new kernel on your Eee PC. Definitely not for the faint of heart!

If you're a little technically inclined though and want to max out your RAM, you can download and install a precompiled version of the kernel with the necessary changes and use instructions from this how-to: `http://wiki.eeeuser.com/howto:install2gigkernel`.

If this whole process looks intimidating, don't sweat it. Be happy with 1GB of RAM. The extra GB doesn't make that much of a difference.

The Eee PC doesn't have empty slots to add more memory. To expand your RAM, replace the existing memory with a larger amount — which means a 1GB or 2GB module. If you have a 512K Linux model, you can currently only expand to 1GB of memory (I describe a way around this in the "Beating the 1GB limit" sidebar). Also, don't bother spending the extra money to get RAM faster than 667 MHz, as the performance gains don't justify the additional cost.

After you've purchased memory, installation is a quick (couple of minutes) and easy process that consists of these steps:

1. **Turn off the Eee PC.**

2. **Open the panel on the bottom of the Eee PC (held in place with several screws).**

3. **Remove the old memory.**

4. **Put the new memory into the empty slot.**

5. **Reattach the panel.**

6. **Turn the Eee PC on and check that it works.**

If you want to see what upgrading memory on an Eee PC is all about, check out this great Web tutorial with detailed instructions (including photos and a video) at: `www.wikihow.com/Upgrade-Memory-in-an-Asus-Eee-PC`.

Chapter 16

Essential Eee PC Accessories

. . . .

. . . .

The Eee PC is ready to use out of the box. But if you're like most people, you probably want to pick up some accessories to go with your mini-laptop. Some popular accessories include carrying cases, wireless mice, Bluetooth gadgets, and GPS receivers.

In this chapter, I give you the lowdown on these Eee PC accessories and more — including keyboards, dial-up modems, external monitors, and presentation projectors. I even tell you how to personalize the outside of your Eee PC and turn it into the ultimate fashion accessory.

The most widely used type of Eee PC accessory is some form of external storage device — such as an SD card, USB thumb drive, or DVD drive. I devote Chapter 15 to discussing these and other storage-related accessories.

Getting Carried Away

Although the Eee PC is small and light enough to carry around in your hand, I recommend using some type of a case when it's time to leave the house or office. A carrying case offers added protection from bumps and drops, isn't as likely to slip out of your hands, and can provide much-needed room for your wall charger, spare battery, and other accessories.

Because of the Eee PC's diminutive size, you have many options available when selecting a suitable carrying case — especially compared to larger laptops. Sure you can always buy a laptop case fitted for the Eee PC (as mini-laptops become more popular, expect lots of options), but don't discount more frugal alternatives. Some of the creative ways Eee PC users are toting around their mini-laptops include

- **DVD player cases**
- **Hardware store tool bags**
- **Padded lunch sacks**
- **Camera bags**
- **Bible cases** (from Christian bookstores)
- **Shoulder travel bags and purses**
- **Mailing envelopes** (with bubblewrap padding)

My favorite way to protect and carry an Eee PC is with a case designed for a portable DVD player. The smaller model Eee PCs match the general dimensions of many travel DVD players, and there are a lot of nice, padded cases on the market — I personally like the Case Logic brand. These products don't cost an arm and a leg; they can be had for under $20 — an example is shown in Figure 16-1.

Figure 16-1:
A Case Logic DVD case that fits an Eee PC.

If you have a sewing machine in the house, and someone who knows how to use it, here's a great illustrated tutorial for making your own Eee PC carrying case out of fabric: `http://forum.eeeuser.com/viewtopic.php?id =13300`.

If whatever you carry your Eee PC in isn't padded, use a protective sleeve — priced around $10 or less. I like neoprene sleeves (the same material used in wetsuits) the best because of the extra padding and water-shedding qualities. Custom-fit sleeves for the Eee PC are available from many online retailers who stock accessories for the mini-laptop.

Mice and Keyboards

If the Eee PC's touchpad or keyboard is a little too small for your personal tastes, you can always take advantage of the mini-laptop's three USB ports and use a different mouse or keyboard. Here's the scoop.

If you use an external keyboard and mouse with your Eee PC, temporarily turning it into more of a desktop computer, be sure to raise the mini-laptop so the screen is closer to eye level. Good ergonomic practices make a difference if you're going to be spending hours typing away.

Mice

In the mouse department, you have two types to choose from:

- ✔ **Cable** — This is the traditional mouse that comes with desktop PCs. If you've got a spare USB mouse lying around, just plug it into the Eee PC, and you're in business. In addition to larger mice, a number of companies make smaller mice designed for laptops and travel. (ASUS also makes mice in a number of different colors for the Eee PC.)

- ✔ **Wireless** — Wireless mice ditch the cable and work with radio signals that are sent between the mouse and computer. These mice either use a proprietary transmitter/receiver that plugs into a USB port or rely on Bluetooth (either built-in or as an add-on).

One of the more popular wireless mice for the Eee PC (and other laptops for that matter), is Logitech's VX Nano — shown in Figure 16-2. This mini-mighty-mouse runs on two AAA batteries and communicates with the Eee PC through a tiny dongle that plugs into a USB port. The dongle is so small that it can be stowed away inside the mouse — a handy feature to prevent loss. VX Nanos are priced around $55.

Figure 16-2:
A Logitech
VX Nano
wireless
mouse next
to an
Eee PC.

If you have a Linux Eee PC, check out this how-to information on configuring all the buttons on a VX Nano: `http://wiki.eeeuser.com/configure_logitech_vx_nano`.

Mice come with many different features such as three buttons, scroll wheels, retractable cables, and lasers for more precise tracking. For a new mouse, expect to pay between $25 and $100 depending on the features.

Wireless mice consume more power than wired mice, so if you're trying to maximize battery life, go for a mouse with a tail.

Keyboards

Until some of the latest Eee PC models with larger keyboards were available, one of the biggest grouses about the mini-laptop was its undersized keyboard. With a little practice, most people get used to small keyboard — be patient, it does take some time. But if you're just not getting the hang of the small keys, consider these three types of third-party USB keyboards:

- ✔ **Conventional** — Got an old desktop PC with a USB keyboard gathering dust in a closet? Just plug the keyboard into your Eee PC. Not the most portable solution in the world, but there are also reduced-size travel keyboards available for under $40.

- ✔ **Folding** — If a travel keyboard is still a little too bulky for you, an alternative is to get a folding keyboard. As the name suggests, these keyboards fold in half when not in use. Models range from full to travel size and are priced in the $40 to $60 range.

✔ **Roll-up** — Your last option is to forget about a conventional, hard plastic keyboard and go with a soft keyboard that rolls up. These flexible, water-resistant keyboards (as shown in Figure 16-3) are produced by a number of companies and are priced between $20 and $40. A drawback is that the soft silicone keys are silent (which takes some time getting used to) and don't have the best tactile feel.

Do a Google search for *travel keyboard*, *folding keyboard*, or *flexible keyboard* for manufacturers and dealers.

If your Eee PC has Bluetooth support, wireless keyboards are also available.

Honestly, I think toting an external keyboard around detracts from the portability and purpose of the Eee PC. If the 2G, 4G, 900, and 901 keyboards are too small for you, my advice is to go for an Eee PC with a larger keyboard.

If all your USB ports are in use and you need more, invest in a *hub*. This is a USB version of an electrical extension cord with multiple outlets. You plug the USB hub into one of your Eee PC's USB ports. This makes more ports (often four) available. Just remember, a single USB port puts out only a limited amount of power. You may need a self-powered hub that gets juice from its own power supply if you plan on using several USB devices that need power.

Figure 16-3:
Eee PC with
USB flexible
keyboard.

I saw the light

Some Eee PC users begin to develop a fear of the dark. Well, maybe not a fear but just a little dread. When the lights go out and you can't clearly peek down at the keys, the number of typos starts to go up — unless you're a very accomplished touch typist with lots of practice on the small keyboard. Yet another scary thought is using your mini-laptop for a presentation in a darkened room, and continually hitting the wrong keys to advance to the next slide — been there, done that.

To quote the Robert Cray tune, "Don't be afraid of the dark." Instead, pick up a USB powered LED light. These handy little accessories are perfect for when the lights go down — LED bulbs also don't consume much juice, so your battery doesn't take too much of a power hit when you use them.

Most lights sport a flexible gooseneck that allows you to optimally position the beam. Depending on the model and features, prices range between $5 and $20. (I'd pass on the dollar store varieties, as they often use low-quality LEDs and cheap goosenecks prone to breaking.)

Bluetooth Blues

Bluetooth has turned into the *de facto* standard for short range wireless communications. Compatible cell phones, GPS receivers, mice, keyboards, laptops, PDAs, and other devices all use Bluetooth to exchange data over radio airwaves.

When the Eee PCs were first introduced, if you wanted Bluetooth support, you purchased a Bluetooth adapter that plugged into one of the mini-laptop's USB ports. Starting with the Eee PC 901 and later models, ASUS begin including built-in Bluetooth. (You can configure Bluetooth in the Linux Settings tab or the Windows XP Control Panel.)

If you want to add Bluetooth to your Eee PC, my recommendation is to go with one of the smallest Bluetooth adaptors around, made by Mogo — see Figure 16-4 comparing its size to a Logitech wireless mouse dongle.

With any Bluetooth adaptor, if you're running Windows XP, first see if the device works by just plugging it in. If it doesn't, follow the directions that came with the adaptor and install the correct driver.

If Bluetooth doesn't come built-in, getting Bluetooth to work with a Linux Eee PC is a bit more complicated. You first enter some commands at the console and modify a system configuration file or two. You can find all the details at: http://wiki.eeeuser.com/howto:bluetoothdongles.

Expect to pay between $25 and $50 for a USB Bluetooth adaptor.

Figure 16-4:
The MoGo
Bluetooth
adaptor
(round) and
the Logitech
VX Nano
adaptor
(square) on
an Eee PC.

Personalizing Your Eee PC

In Chapter 21, I present a number of ways you can personalize the user interface of your Linux Eee PC. If you want to express yourself even more, how about sprucing up the outside of your mini-laptop? You don't need to be an artist to turn your ho-hum black or white Eee PC into a modern art masterpiece like the one shown in Figure 16-5.

The growing popularity of laptops (of all sizes) has spurred several companies to offer a variety of decals designed to uniquely personalize your PC. Commonly referred to as *skins*, these aren't cheap "slap on your car" bumper stickers, but instead are quality vinyl decals with a reusable adhesive that doesn't leave sticky goo when you pull them off. Priced around $20, they come in solid colors, fine art prints, nature scenes, you name it — you can even submit graphics files to create your own custom decals.

Figure 16-5:
A Schtickers
decal on
an Eee PC.

Here are several skin sources to check out:

- ✔ **Schtickers** — www.schtickers.com
- ✔ **DecalGirl** — www.decalgirl.com
- ✔ **GelaSkins** — www.gelaskins.com

Most companies offer skins to fit standard laptop screen sizes. If the Eee PC isn't listed, order a custom size. 8.5-x-5.5 inches should work for 700 and 900 series models, with no extra cutting required.

If you're a do-it-yourselfer and want to save a few bucks, invest in some inkjet adhesive vinyl sheets. Or take your artwork in PDF format to a commercial print shop (like FedEx/Kinkos) and have them print the file on an 8.5-x-11–inch clear adhesive label. Carefully cut the label to match your Eee PC's dimensions, and you have a custom skin for less than a couple of dollars. (Consider getting two labels, one for the skin and the other to stick over it as a protective layer.) The do-it-yourself approach works great with white Eee PCs, but leaves a little to be desired appearance-wise on the black models. If you have a black Eee PC you want to dress up, I'd recommend using opaque white labels.

Modem Madness

With wireless broadband and cable/DSL modems, dial-up modems seem like archaic relics of the past — "what's that funny screeching noise?" But depending on the location, a dial-up modem may be the only way for some people to get Internet access. If you're in that boat, read on.

Because the Eee PC doesn't have a PC Card slot like many other laptops, you need a dial-up modem that plugs into one of the USB slots. These dial-up modems are readily available and cost in the $40-to-$50 price range.

If you're running Windows XP on your mini-laptop, it's usually just a matter of inserting the USB modem and configuring it in the Control Panel — depending on the modem, you may have to install a driver.

Getting a dial-up modem to work under Linux can be more of a challenge. Most USB modems have drivers only for Windows, and if they do have Linux drivers, these typically require a lot of configuration (including recompiling the kernel).

If you regularly use a dial-up modem with your Eee PC, I'd recommend a Windows XP mini-laptop just for ease of installation and use.

If you're set on running Linux, users have found success with the Zoom 3095 V92 USB Mini modems — as shown in Figure 16-6. (It also works with Windows by the way). Just keep in mind you must do a fair amount of configuration to get it working. You can find details and a discussion of what's required at this link: `http://forum.eeeuser.com/viewtopic.php?id=7848`.

You may be able to use your cell phone as a modem with your Eee PC through a USB or Bluetooth connection. Search the EeeUser.com forums (`http://forum.eeeuser.com`) for your phone model to see if there are instructions. If not, post a message to see if anyone has gotten a similar model phone working with the mini-laptop.

Figure 16-6:
The Zoom 3092 USB modem works with Windows and Linux.

External Monitors and Projectors

In my opinion, the Eee PC makes the perfect laptop for training and presentations. It's easy to bring the mini-laptop to meetings, classrooms, or conferences; and with its VGA output, hooking the Eee PC up to external monitors and projectors is a snap.

In this section, I want to share a few tips for using external monitors and projectors — be sure to read Chapter 9, where I discuss how to change external monitor settings in Linux; for Windows, use Display in the Control Panel. I'll start with monitors first.

External monitors

Whether you're going to hook up your Eee PC to a desktop PC monitor or a big-screen TV, getting the best and most viewable display on an external monitor often is a trial-and-error process. Try a number of different monitor settings until you find the one that works the best. This is because the Eee PC supports only a limited number of screen resolutions.

Generally, a traditional monitor with a 4:3 screen ratio (square in shape) produces the best results. A more contemporary 16:9 ratio (widescreen) monitor may display a distorted image and require a bit more tweaking.

External monitor resolutions that aren't compatible with the Eee PC produce distorted images. This is because the pixels are no longer square, but are elongated or squashed.

If you get a grainy or distorted picture, try another monitor setting until you get the best appearance.

Projectors

Up until a few years ago, presentation projectors were bulky and expensive devices. Prices and sizes have fallen, and now home theater and business projectors are readily available for under $1,000.

With the Eee PC, multimedia projectors (often called PowerPoint projectors) are a bit easier to deal with than external monitors because they only support several standard resolutions. It's usually just a matter of plugging a projector into the mini-laptop so what's displayed on the screen appears on the wall.

Always connect and power-on the external monitor or projector first and then start the Eee PC. If the mini-laptop is running when the display device is plugged in, it may not work correctly with the external device.

I'll be honest with you. From a presentation standpoint, Windows XP on the Eee PC is a better choice than Linux. This is because of its full support for Microsoft PowerPoint and a little better control in selecting screen resolution and settings.

Don't get me wrong, I like OpenOffice, and it works great with basic Power-Point presentations — in Chapter 5, I tell you all about using OpenOffice with PowerPoint files. But if you have a PowerPoint presentation with lots of multi-media elements, OpenOffice can run into problems. If one of the primary uses of your Eee PC is going to be PowerPoint presentations, I'd lean toward a Windows XP model.

If you're set on a Linux Eee PC and plan on using it for lots of presentations, there is a sneaky way to successfully use PowerPoint files that misbehave under OpenOffice. You need two pieces of software:

- ✓ **Wine** — Wine (www.winehq.org) is a program that allows Microsoft Windows programs to run under Linux. I discuss Wine in Chapter 13.

- ✓ **PowerPoint Viewer** — Microsoft's PowerPoint Viewer is a handy utility that plays presentations on any computer running a copy of Windows XP (or Wine) — you don't need a copy of Office, but remember you can't create or edit files with Viewer. PowerPoint Viewer 2007 works with Microsoft Office 2007 and earlier versions of PowerPoint presentations. (You can also download older viewers that work with earlier versions of Office — they tend to be smaller if you're trying to conserve drive space.) Visit the Downloads section at http://office. microsoft.com.

After you have Wine working, run PowerPoint Viewer and then open and start your presentation. All those multimedia effects that were misbehaving under OpenOffice should now work.

Creating presentations on the Eee PC can be a bit challenging because of the small screen and cramped keyboard. I typically build a presentation on a desktop PC or a full-size laptop and then copy it to the mini-laptop.

Staying Found with GPS

GPS (Global Positioning System) is hot these days. These handy little gadgets use satellite signals to tell you where you are and the best routes for getting between Point A and B. Although you can purchase a standalone GPS device designed for your car, you can also connect certain types of GPS receivers to your Eee PC so you never get lost (I hope).

The two types of GPS receivers you can use with your mini-laptop are

- **USB** — This is a GPS receiver that connects to the Eee PC's USB port. The GPS device might not have a screen and might only send location data to the laptop. It could also be a handheld receiver primarily designed for outdoor use. GPS receivers with cables give you more latitude in mounting the device to get the best satellite reception. An example is shown in Figure 16-7.

- **Bluetooth** — If your Eee PC is Bluetooth enabled, a number of small receivers wirelessly send GPS data to your mini-laptop.

Figure 16-7:
Eee PC connected to a USB GPS receiver.

After it is connected, the GPS receiver sends location data to a map program running on your Eee PC. The program displays your current position on a map and can optionally leave a breadcrumb trail (called a *track*) that shows where you've been. Most commercial programs allow you to enter an address, and the program plots and displays the best route for getting there including spoken directions. GPS data is also used to display current and average speed, distance traveled, and your destination's estimated arrival time.

If you're thinking about frequently putting your Eee PC to work as a portable navigation device, it's easier and you have more options if you're running Windows XP., Many more digital map programs are available for Windows than Linux. Windows' popularity also ensures you can use the mini-laptop with just about any GPS receiver that can exchange data with a PC.

Older handheld GPS receivers use serial ports to communicate with PCs. The Eee PC doesn't have a serial port, so you need a USB-to-serial port adaptor if you want to use a non-USB GPS receiver.

Linux GPS resources

Although it's easier to use GPS with a Windows Eee PC, if you're running Linux, there's no need to feel lost. Here are some Linux-oriented GPS resources to steer to:

- **Tuxmobil** is the definitive source for anything (hardware or software) to do with GPS and Linux — http://tuxmobil. org/linux_gps_navigation_ applications.html.

- **Roadnav** is an open-source Linux street navigation program — http://road nav.sourceforge.net/.

- **GPSDrive** is a free program that supports street maps and satellite imagery — www. gpsdrive.de/.

- **gpsd** (as in GPS daemon) is system software that allows a GPS receiver to interface with a map program — http:// gpsd.berlios.de/.

And finally, here's a how-to tutorial that puts together all the pieces so you can get GPS working on your Eee PC — http://wiki. eeeuser.com/howto:gpsd.

There's a whole lot more to GPS than I have the pages to devote to the subject. In fact, I wrote an entire book on GPS and digital maps. If you're interested, be sure to check out *GPS For Dummies*, Second Edition (Wiley Publishing).

Chapter 17

Power to the Eee PC

*J*ust like any computer, your Eee PC needs power. No juice from a battery or an electrical outlet means your mini-laptop is now a nice, plastic paperweight, which isn't really all that useful.

Most people find the battery and wall charger that are included with the Eee PC meet their basic power needs. But what if there's no electric outlet nearby? What if you're always on the go and a single battery doesn't cut it for your computing needs?

You're in luck because that's what this chapter is all about. In it I explore ways you can power your Eee PC — both Linux and Windows varieties. I cover batteries (of all different types), charging and running your Eee PC while on the road (or in the air), and some off-the-grid options in case you're headed for some place with limited or no power.

Read on for both useful and electrifying (sorry, I just couldn't resist that pun) details.

The Juice on Batteries

Unlike a desktop PC that spends its entire life tethered to a power cord and electrical wall socket, your Eee PC is designed to go places. Thanks to its small size, you can use it just about anywhere. That is, as long as you've got a charged battery.

Battery Briefs

Here are some important facts to know about your Eee PC's battery (or any laptop for that matter):

Cells — Even though they look like it, laptop batteries aren't one big battery. They're composed of a series of cells (smaller, individual batteries) that are connected inside the sealed plastic case. More cells typically mean longer battery life, but also make the battery heavier.

mAh — This stands for milliampere-hour, a measurement of how much energy is stored in a battery. Generally, the more mAh, the longer the battery life. (Keep in mind that battery life depends on what you're doing. An Eee PC with a lower mAh battery may run longer than the same Eee PC with a higher capacity battery — if you are word processing with the wireless card off rather than watching videos with a wireless Net connection.)

Battery Memory — You may have heard that batteries have memories and occasionally need to be fully discharged. Not true with Lithium Ion (Li-Ion) batteries, which most laptops use these days. They don't have a memory (like older Nickel Cadmium batteries), and there's no need to fully discharge them. Actually, to maximize battery life, Li-Ions should be charged when they're down to around 50 percent.

Battery Life — Sooner or later, your battery is going to bite the dust. Batteries have a limited life span that depends on how many times they've been charged and how they've been maintained. As a battery starts to wear out, the amount of charge it holds slowly decreases until eventually it won't power your laptop at all. Depending on use, expect a battery to last one to three years.

In this section, I give you the juice on batteries. Maybe, after lots of use, your Eee PC's battery is starting to give up the ghost. Or perhaps you've found that one battery doesn't do the trick on those transoceanic flights, long commutes, or day outings at the beach. If you need a battery, this is where to learn about your options.

ASUS batteries

If you're shopping for a new Eee PC battery (your old one doesn't seem to last very long and you need a replacement, or you're considering a second battery so you can use your mini-laptop longer), you probably first turn to an ASUS brand battery, as shown in Figure 17-1.

This makes sense because you know a battery from the manufacturer is guaranteed to work with your Eee PC. Manufacturer batteries are also covered by warranties, whereas third-party batteries may not be.

Aside from eventually wearing out, it's rare that laptop batteries have problems — there were those exploding Dell laptop batteries in 2006, but despite all the panic, relatively few actual cases were reported.

Figure 17-1:
The Eee PC
battery.

Currently, ASUS offers the following Lithium-Ion batteries for the 2G, 4G, 8G, and 900 models (these batteries can be used in any of these models).

- ✔ **4,400 mAh** — 4 cell
- ✔ **5,200 mAh** — 4 cell
- ✔ **5,800 mAh** — 4 cell

For the 901 and 1000 models, ASUS offers this battery:

- ✔ **6,600 mAh** — 6 cell

There have been reports that ASUS will be offering higher capacity batteries in the future, but at this time there are no firm details.

Batteries come in white and black. Be sure to order one that matches your Eee PC (unless you go for two-tone colors).

Generally, the more mAh (milliampere-hours), the longer the battery will last — and the more expensive it will be. Prices tend to range from $65 to $125 depending on capacity, and it's worthwhile to shop around on the Internet for the best deal.

Although 4,400 mAh batteries are readily available as I write this, finding higher-capacity batteries can be a bit of a challenge. In March, 2008, a fire broke out at LG Chem's Ochang, South Korea battery plant. This severely impacted ASUS, Dell, and HP laptop battery availability. (An earlier fire in October 2007 at a battery factory in Japan had already caused laptop battery shortages.) Supply issues should be ironed out by the end of the year.

Speaking of batteries, don't miss out on Bonus Chapter 2 on the companion Web site (www.dummies.com/go/asuseeepcfd), where I give you tips on maximizing your Eee PC's battery life.

Third-party batteries

An alternative to using ASUS-brand batteries is to go with a third-party battery. Many generic batteries use the same components as the original batteries that come with the laptops. They don't have the brand-name on the label and are priced slightly lower because of reduced business overhead costs.

Third-party batteries typically have the same mAh ratings as manufacturer batteries, but also may be available in even higher-capacity models. For example, some third-party Eee PC batteries have a huge 10,400 mAh rating.

When buying batteries that have above normal capacity, always check a photo of the battery and its dimensions. In some cases the battery may be physically larger than the one that comes with your Eee PC — otherwise don't expect a flush fit, since the bigger battery will stick out beyond the back of the mini-laptop's case.

Before you buy a third-party battery (especially from eBay), check the EeeUser.com forums (http://forum.eeeuser.com) to learn what people have to say about a particular battery and vendor. For example, Mugen Power Batteries (www.mugenpowerbatteries.info) has received a number of favorable reviews.

Universal batteries

Instead of purchasing a battery expressly built for your Eee PC, look into getting a universal battery. These external Lithium-Ion batteries can power all sorts of electronic devices — not just your Eee PC. Plug one into the mini-laptop's power jack (where you normally plug in the wall charger), and the Eee PC runs on the external battery until it discharges. When the external battery runs out, the Eee PC automatically starts using its internal battery. Pretty slick.

My favorite universal batteries are the Tekkeon MyPower All products (as shown in Figure 17-2). Two models are available:

- ✔ **MP3450** — Provides up to 19 volts, has a USB charging port, and can be expanded with a spare battery pack. Priced around $130.

- ✔ **MP3300** — A lower cost model without all the features of the MP3450, but still providing up to 14 volts of power.

Connected to an Eee PC 4G, the MP3450 provides around three and a half to four hours of power before the internal battery takes over. (You charge the MyPower All with an included AC or DC adapter.)

Universal batteries aren't quite as lightweight and trim as the Eee PC's internal battery (they're still very portable though), but they do offer more functionality for right around the same price. They're especially handy if you have another laptop or need to power other portable electronic devices.

For more information on the MyPower Alls, visit `www.tekkeon.com/site/products-mypowerall.php`.

When I'm on the road I always carry a small, wall socket plug with multiple outlets. Public spots in airports for recharging electronic devices are always at a premium, and a multiple outlet plug lets you share the juice from a single outlet with other travelers.

Figure 17-2:
The Tekkeon MyPower All universal battery.

Getting (Car) Charged Up

A car (or truck) can power your Eee PC or charge its battery — although with gas prices these days, it's a pretty expensive generator. If you're going to be on the road with your mini-laptop, you have two options for keeping it charged; a cigarette lighter adapter or an inverter. Here's the lowdown on both.

Cigarette lighter adapters

Cigarette lighters first started appearing in cars in the 1920s — they were originally designed for lighting cigars; that's why they're the size they are. With the advent of modern automotive cigarette lighters in the 1950s, it became possible to use the 12-volt, direct current generated by a car to power electrical devices. By using a cigarette lighter adapter (CLA) like the one in Figure 17-3, you can run and charge your Eee PC.

CLAs have circuitry that converts the car's 12-volt electricity into power that's usable by the Eee PC. CLAs also have fuses to protect your mini-laptop in case a higher than normal amount of current comes through the lighter.

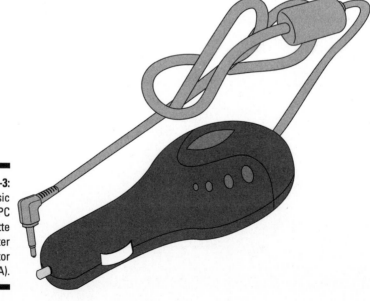

Figure 17-3:
A basic Eee PC cigarette lighter adaptor (CLA).

The popularity of the Eee PC is bringing many accessories to market, including CLAs. If you're interested in a CLA, here are several possibilities (Google *eee pc cigarette lighter* for more):

- **ASUS** — ASUS sells Eee PC car chargers for $79 — check out the ASUS e-store at `http://estore.asus.com`.

- **Brando** — Brando is a large, Hong Kong–based supplier of electronics accessories. The company offers several Eee PC CLAs (be sure you get the right one for your particular model). At $18, not including shipping, the chargers are reasonably priced and have a good reputation. The only downside is shipping to the U.S. can take several weeks. For more information on the chargers and other Eee PC accessories, go to `http://shop.brando.com.hk`.

- **Radio Shack** — If you have a local Radio Shack (`www.radioshack.com`) store, stop by and pick up a High-Power Universal DC Adapter (Model 273-1818). You'll also need an Adaptaplug C to fit the mini-laptop. Set the charger to the right voltage, and you're ready to go. (The charger is a bit pricey at $38, plus $6.50 for the plug, but you can use it with lots of other electronic devices.)

If you use a multivoltage charger, be sure you use the correct voltage for your Eee PC. The 2G, 4G, and 8G models are expecting 9.5 volts with 2.315 amps. 900, 901, and 1000 models need 12 volts at 3 amps. The mini-laptop's power supply can handle a little over and under its rated voltage, but if you use too many volts, you risk damaging the computer. You also need to ensure the power tip is the correct polarity (in the Eee PC's case, the tip is positive and the outer sleeve is negative). Always check a device's user guide or online specifications to find out about its power requirements.

Some airlines offer DC power outlets in their seats (usually business and first class). If you do a lot of flying in addition to driving, CLA chargers are available that work in both car and plane receptacles.

Inverters

Another option for powering an Eee PC while on the road is to use an inverter. Inverters convert one type of voltage to another. For example, an automotive inverter converts a car's 12-volt DC (direct current) to 120-volt AC (alternating current) — what comes out of standard United States electrical outlets.

Car inverters (two are shown in Figure 17-4) have one or more electrical outlets that work just like a wall socket. Just plug in any electrical device and you can run it from your car's electrical system. (When the car is running, its battery is being charged, so you don't need to worry about it discharging.)

Figure 17-4:
Two types
of car
inverters.

Inverters are rated at different wattages. The more watts an inverter can handle, the more it costs. Make sure you have a large enough inverter to accommodate the device(s) you plan on using. Because Eee PCs draw well under 30 watts, you can use a relatively inexpensive (around $20) 75-watt inverter.

All electrical devices have an attached label that lists their wattage. If the device doesn't show watts, but only lists volts and amps, use this simple formula:

Watts = Volts × Amps

The advantage to an inverter is you can use a variety of electrical devices with it and not need special plugs or adapters. Inverters are available in the automotive or electronics sections of most large chain stores.

Many car inverters now come with USB jacks, so you can charge MP3 players and other devices.

Off-the-Grid Power Solutions

One of the Eee PC's nicer features is its low energy use. Compared to a typical full-size laptop, the Eee PC is a frugal, gas-sipping hybrid (to continue with the analogy, a larger laptop is a mid-size economy car, and a desktop PC is a big, gas-gulping SUV).

I saw the sine

The two types of inverters are true-sine wave and modified-sine wave. *True-sine* wave inverters produce power like the kind you get from your electric company. When you look at the power wave through an oscilloscope, it appears as a smooth sine wave.

Modified-sine wave (also called square wave) inverters are the most common type of inverter. They're considerably cheaper than true-sine inverters and produce more of a squared-off looking wave.

Modified-sine wave inverters work fine for powering laptops and most household appliances. True-sine inverters are required for devices that might have problems using an electrical current with a modified sine wave. These include fax machines, laser printers, plasma TVs, and other specialized devices.

There have been a few reports of Eee PC touchpads behaving erratically when plugged into an inverter. However the majority of people using inverters and laptops have never experienced these problems. If your touchpad is misbehaving, this is likely a case of noisy power (originating from the inverter, the car's electrical system, or even the laptop). Try another inverter.

According to my trusty Kill-A-Watt meter (www.p3international.com), an Eee PC 4G uses about 15 watts of power with wireless turned on and a video playing. (It uses under 10 watts with wireless off while doing less energy-intensive tasks such as word processing). If I'm charging the battery while using the mini-laptop, I need 20 to 25 watts. By comparison, my full-size laptop consumes about twice as many watts as the mini-laptop. Even worse my desktop PC slurps an obscene ten times more power.

Low power consumption is important if you plan on taking your Eee PC to remote places without friendly public utilities that supply electricity. The Eee PC is well suited for situations like working for a humanitarian organization in the third world, living off the grid, or documenting a wilderness expedition.

In this section, I discuss renewable power sources for your Eee PC — perfect for when the closest wall socket may be a couple of hundred miles (or more) away. I focus on smaller and more portable approaches that generate a limited amount of electricity versus larger-scale technologies designed to power an entire house.

Two of my favorite e-tailers for portable renewable energy gadgets are Modern Output (www.modernoutpost.com) and Real Goods (www.realgoods.com). If you're even the slightest bit of a green geek, you'll appreciate their online catalogs.

Solar

The thought of plugging your Eee PC into a solar panel and having the little laptop powered by the sun is certainly appealing. However it's not that simple. You need to know a few things first. So here's a quick introduction to using solar with your Eee PC.

Let's start with solar panels. They come in all different sizes. First you need to figure out how big of a panel you'll need. Solar panels are rated by the number of watts they produce — the bigger the panel, the more watts. Generally, the Eee PC uses about 15 watts while running under a full load, and 25 watts under the same conditions if the battery is being charged. (The newer 901 and 1000 models use less with their frugal Atom processor.)

That means you need, at the very least, a 25-watt solar panel to directly power your mini-laptop while it's running. It's possible to use lower wattage solar panels to charge the Eee PC's internal battery with the computer turned off. I wouldn't recommend anything less than 15 watts though — the more watts the faster the charge. You can forget about small solar chargers designed for cellular phones and MP3 players because they produce well under 5 watts.

A solar panel's rated wattage is the maximum amount of power produced under the most optimal conditions. That means direct, bright sunshine. Add some clouds and the watts starts to fall off — the more clouds the less power. Higher panel wattage ratings (the more watts, the higher the price and larger the panel) increase the chances you'll get the power you need in less than optimal conditions.

Now that you know how many watts a solar panel needs to produce, it's time to select the type of panel. You have two choices:

- **Rigid** — These are traditional solar panels enclosed by a frame and encased by glass or plastic. Because of their size and weight, they're designed to be used in fixed locations. They're typically connected to the battery that you use to power your electrical devices. You can get a 30-watt panel for between $200 and $250. (Solar panel prices are starting to decline and will continue to fall due to technology advances and increased demand.)

- **Flexible** — Flexible solar panels (as shown in Figure 17-5) are designed for portability and can be rolled up or folded. They're lighter and more compact, but can be up to double the price of a rigid panel for the same wattage (for example a Sunlinq 30-watt, foldable panel is priced over $500). Most of these portable solar chargers have a female, 12-volt cigarette lighter outlet, so if you have a cigarette lighter power adapter for your Eee PC, you can directly plug your mini-laptop into the panel. Popular flexible solar panel lines include Sunlinq (www.globalsolar.com), SolarRolls (www.brunton.com), and PowerFilm (www.powerfilmsolar.com).

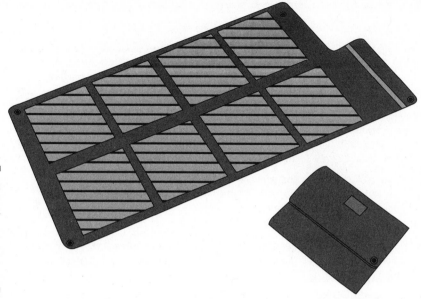

Figure 17-5:
A Global
Solar
Sunlinq
solar panel,
folded and
unfolded.

After you've decided on a panel type, you next decide how you're going to use it. The two general approaches to powering your Eee PC with the sun both require a cigarette lighter adapter.

- ✔ **Directly from the panel** — As long as you have enough sun (and wattage), your Eee PC is powered directly from the solar panel. If the watts drop below what you need, your internal battery starts supplying power.

- ✔ **From an external battery** — Your mini-laptop is getting its power from an external battery (12-volt or universal battery) that's connected to a solar panel. The panel keeps the battery charged as the Eee PC draws power from the battery.

Although it's possible to plug a 12-volt car inverter into the solar panel and then plug the Eee PC's wall charger into the inverter, I don't recommend this. Automotive inverters are inefficient and waste energy during the conversion process. When it comes to solar, waste not, want not — you want every bit of sunshine-derived power running and charging your laptop (or other devices).

If you're using a solar panel to charge external batteries, you need something called a charge controller to place between the panel and the battery. The charge controller prevents overcharging. If you don't use one, it's possible to ruin the battery by pumping too much juice into it. You can purchase charge controllers for under $30 (even Amazon.com stocks them).

Solar battery basics

If you plan on using an external battery with a solar panel to keep your Eee PC charged, here are a few tips:

✔ Use a deep cycle marine or golf cart battery. These batteries are designed for storing power, unlike a car battery that's primarily used for starting the engine.

✔ 12-volt solar batteries should never be discharged to less than 50 percent of their total charge. If you run a battery below this level, you risk permanently damaging it.

✔ f you're using a non-sealed battery, regularly check the cells and make sure they're topped off with distilled water. It's easy to kill a battery if you don't. (There's more good information on battery maintenance at this site: www.wholesalesolar. com/Information-SolarFolder/ battery.maintenance.html.)

✔ An alternative to a conventional battery is to use a Xantrex XPower Powerpack (www. xantrex.com). These are portable, backup batteries that have built-in inverters, gauges, lights, and air compressors. They can be charged with a solar panel or through a standard electrical outlet. Powerpacks come in a variety of capacities and are priced from around $75 up.

Depending on your needs, don't discount the idea of using multiple solar panels. Many types of panels can be connected (this allows you to potentially get enough electricity from two smaller panels to keep your mini-laptop powered). Also, with several solar panels you can devote one to powering your Eee PC during the day, while another charges a 12-volt battery for nighttime use.

If you're just looking to keep your Eee PC's battery charged, check out products from Voltaic Systems (www.voltaicsystems.com). The company offers backpacks and messenger bags with built-in solar panels that can charge your laptop and other electronic devices as you transport them. They're not cheap, but they're pretty cool.

Because I only have a limited number of pages to tell you about using your Eee PC with the sun, here are a few online resources for additional general information on using solar power:

✔ **Home Power Magazine** — www.homepower.com

✔ **SolarPower Forum** — www.solarpowerforum.net

✔ **OtherPower.com** — www.fieldlines.com/section/solar

Human power

Solar is hot these days (literally), but you probably guessed the technology has some serious limitations when it's dark or the skies are cloudy. If you're located in an area where you can't rely on getting power from the sun, an alternative to keeping your Eee PC powered up is to use good-old fashioned elbow-grease — by that I mean a gadget that produces electricity from you and your muscles. Here are several currently available options.

Weza

One of my favorite human-powered, electrical device manufacturers is Freeplay Energy (www.freeplayenergy.com). The company started out producing rugged, hand-crank radios for use in Africa and third-world countries. Since then, they've expanded their products to a number of different human-powered gadgets.

Of particular interest to off-the-grid Eee PC users is the *Weza* (a Swahili word that means *power*). Weza is built around a 12-volt lead-acid battery. You can charge the battery by plugging it into an electrical outlet or solar panel or by stepping on its foot treadle, as shown in Figure 17-6.

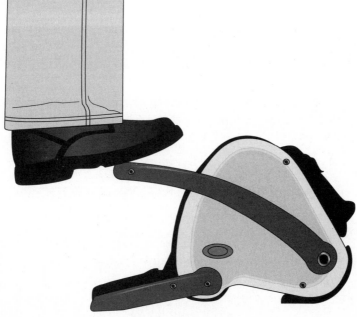

Figure 17-6:
Freeplay
Energy
Weza
foot-pedal
power
generator.

Plug an Eee PC equipped with a cigarette lighter adapter into the Weza to charge the mini-laptop's internal battery. (You need to stomp on the Weza 50 to 60 steps a minute to generate 30 watts of power. At that rate, to produce enough energy to charge a 5,200 mAh Eee PC battery, plan on an hour-and-15-minute workout.)

You probably won't want to take a Weza (weighing in at just a little less than 18 pounds) backpacking with you, but it is a very viable, compact, human-powered generator if weight isn't an issue. If you shop around, you can find the Weza in the $200 to $250 price range.

FreeCharge 12V

If Weza is a bit too large, another Freeplay product to consider is the FreeCharge 12V (see Figure 17-7). This is a small, lightweight, 12-volt hand-held generator. Attach a cigarette lighter adaptor to your Eee PC, plug it into FreeCharge, and start cranking (at 120 revolutions per minute or more).

OK, FreeCharge isn't really designed to charge laptops — its main purpose is to give cell phones a quick hit of electricity. FreeCharge's output is about half of the Weza's, so figure somewhere between two to two-and-a- half hours of cranking to fully charge an Eee PC battery. I hope you have some friends around to help (and a massage therapist to take care of your arms the next day).

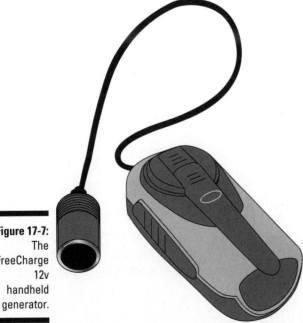

Figure 17-7:
The
FreeCharge
12v
handheld
generator.

FreePlay Energy is working on a clamp-mounted charger for the OLPC-XO laptop (attaching a clamp to the FreeCharge would make it much easier and less taxing to use). Potenco, another alternative-energy company (www. potenco.com), has developed a pull-cord power generator for the XO, which should be easier to use than a crank device. At this time, neither product is commercially available, but will be soon.

Pedal power

The least demanding human-powered way to run and charge your Eee PC is with a pedal-powered power source. This is a stationary bike hooked up to a generator. As you pedal, the generator creates electricity that you can use to directly power an electronic device or charge a 12-volt battery.

For more information on this option, check out these two sources:

- ✔ **Windstream** — This company produces a number of renewable energy products, including a bike power generator (the basic model is priced at $595). For details, go to www.windstreampower.com.

- ✔ **Pedal-Powered Generator** — If you're more of a do-it-yourselfer, David Butcher has comprehensive information and plans for building your own bike generator. His Web site is at www.los-gatos.ca.us/davidbu/ pedgen.html.

Part V
Eee PC Advanced Topics

The 5th Wave   By Rich Tennant

Good thing I had my Eee PC with me. Try turning it over now!

In this part . . .

Despite its toy-like appearance and easy-to-use demeanor, beneath the surface of the Eee PC lurks a powerful computer, ready to be unleashed by a user with a little technical inclination.

In this part of the book, I present advanced Eee PC topics. Although you can be perfectly happy using an out-of-the-box version of the Eee PC, the little computer does lend itself to tinkering — especially when it comes to the operating system.

In the upcoming chapters I present the fundamentals of backing up and restoring your Eee PC, changing the appearance of the default Linux desktop, invoking a more powerful user interface known as Advanced Desktop Mode, and using the Linux command line.

Although some of this may sound daunting, I provide clear instructions and helpful resources for the average Eee PC user who likes to experiment and wants to go beyond the basics.

Chapter 18

Backing Up and Restoring the Eee PC

*A*s you may have suspected from the title, this chapter is about backing up and restoring your Eee PC.

I know some people who are absolutely manic and compulsive about backing up their PCs, making complete copies of their hard drives every night. I also have a few *laissez faire* friends who never back up any of their files (and have yet to lose data after decades of using computers).

In my book, what you back up and how often you do it tend to be personal choices. I'm not going to get up on a soapbox and start harping about how and when you should back up your mini-laptop. That's up to you.

Instead I want to tell you about the alternatives you have for backing up your Eee PC (both Linux and Windows models). I also want to cover what to do if your system somehow experiences a serious meltdown and you need to reinstall the operating system (it can happen).

Let's start with looking at different backup strategies.

Eee PC Backup Strategies

Your primary desktop or laptop PC probably has at least a 100GB or larger hard drive. Due to the sheer volume of data, backing up these drives can be both time consuming and challenging (you may have said to yourself, "How many DVDs do I need to back up all these files?").

Thankfully, the relatively small drive size (in all Eee PCs except those with conventional hard drives) makes backing up the mini-laptop fairly quick and easy. A full backup of your system is measured in minutes versus hours and, depending on the method you use, is usually fairly painless.

Two backup approaches to consider are copying individual files and folders and imaging the Eee PC's drive. Here's the lowdown on each.

Copying files and folders

This is the most straightforward approach and best for the casual backer-upper. You just copy files you've saved on the Eee PC's drive to external storage media such as a USB thumb drive, SD card, or even over a network to a shared directory on another computer. There are two ways to do this:

- ✔ **File Manager:** On a Linux Eee PC, use File Manager; with Windows, use Explorer (the file explorer, not Internet Explorer, the Web browser). Simply select and drag (or copy and paste) the files and/or directories you want to back up.

  On Linux Eee PCs, settings and data for many programs are stored in hidden directories in the Home directory. In File Manager's View menu, select the Show Hidden Files and Show All File Systems items to see all files. You can then back up these files and folders by copying and pasting.

  If you're a Windows Eee PC user, I recommend a free program called MozBackup for backing up Firefox and Thunderbird settings and data. Download it at http://mozbackup.jasnapaka.com. Additional Windows XP backup-related tools and tutorials can be found at this site: www.microsoft.com/windowsxp/using/setup/learnmore/bott_03july14.mspx.

- ✔ **Command line:** Use a Linux shell script or a Windows command line script (depending on the operating system you're running) to automate the copying process. With scripts you can do all sorts of cool stuff like incremental and timed backups. I discuss the basics of command-line Linux in Chapter 20. For Windows, check out http://command windows.com for more information about old-school, DOS batch file–style commands.

Online backup options

With the introduction of the Eee PC 901, ASUS began offering users 20GB of secure online storage on some mini-laptop models (complete details are in your user manual). This added online storage certainly helps, considering the mini-laptop's small drive size, plus it offers another option for backing up critical files.

ASUS is not the only game in town when it comes to online storage. In fact, online backup services are big business these days. In the next decade it is estimated 70 to 75 percent of all PCs will be using some form of online storage.

If you're considering using online storage, whether ASUS's offering or another, check out a Web site called Backup Review (www. backupreview.info), which provides information and ratings on many online storage services.

After you've copied your files, you can restore them by using File Manager or Explorer (or a script if you're more technically adept) to move the copied files back to your Eee PC. Or open and edit any documents on another computer if, perish the thought, your Eee PC is broken, lost, or stolen.

Imaging the drive

An alternative to copying individual files and directories is to image your Eee PC's drive. You use a program that creates a byte-by-byte mirror image of the drive contents. If you ever need to restore your Eee PC, the program writes the saved image back to the drive. The advantage to this method is everything is saved; including files, the operating system and settings, installed programs and their settings, too. It takes a little longer than individually copying files, because every byte on the drive is duplicated, but it's the gold standard for data insurance.

Several Linux and Windows imaging programs for mirroring your Eee PC's drive are listed in the following sections.

Linux

At the present, there really aren't any user-friendly, click-a-single-button imaging programs for Linux Eee PCs. If you want to mirror your drive, here are two best bets:

✔ **dd:** dd (which stands for *Data Definition*, although many people believe it's *Data Dump*) is a utility program found in all versions of Linux. It copies and converts raw data. It is what most techies use for imaging drives. If you're mostly a point-and-clicker and aren't interested in using the command line, this option isn't for you. If you want to learn how to use dd, however, you can find a great tutorial at the EeeUser.com Wiki: `http://wiki.eeeuser.com/backup_restore`.

You can't image a drive with dd if the operating system on the drive is running. The solution is to install some other version of Linux on a USB thumb drive, use it to boot, and then run dd from the thumb drive to mirror the internal Eee PC drive. If you have enough storage capacity, USB thumb drives and SD cards work great for saving the image. I personally like USB hard drives because they offer more space and aren't as easy to lose or misplace.

✔ **EeeBackup:** If command-line dd sounds a bit intimidating, try an alternative called EeeBackup. This program installs on a USB thumb drive and has options to back up and restore full disk images or individual partition images. It also has several rescue utilities in case the backup program doesn't work. With compression, an image of a 4GB drive is around 2GB and takes around 20 minutes to make. EeeBackup has a text interface, but is simple to use (especially compared to dd). To download the utility and get more information go to this site: `www.glost.eclipse.co.uk/gfoot/eee/eeebackup/`.

There's a good tutorial for using EeeBackup at `http://wiki.eeeuser.com/backup_procedure_for_eee_with_xandros`.

Windows

If you're running Windows on your Eee PC, I recommend two drive-imaging programs:

✔ **Acronis True Image:** A number of commercial Windows drive-mirroring products are on the market, but in my opinion the best is Acronis' True Image. The program is easy to use and comes with an amazing number of features. The $49.99 price tag is cheap data insurance (a free trial version is also available). You can download and learn more at `www.acronis.com`.

✔ **Macrium Reflect:** If you don't want to shell out the bucks for True Image, check out Macrium's Reflect. It has basic features without all the whistles and bells of True Image, but it gets the job done for free. For more information, visit: `www.macrium.com/ReflectFree.asp`.

Restoring Linux Factory Settings with F9

Sometimes, installing a new program, updating the system, or poking around not knowing fully what you're doing (especially if you're a novice), can make the Linux operating system unstable (to be fair, these actions can have the same results in Windows). If this happens, don't panic.

ASUS incorporated a slick-and-easy way to restore the Linux operating system to its default, fresh-from-factory state. Just press F9 during start-up and, in less than a minute, the mini-laptop is restored to its original condition (the operating system that is — F9 isn't designed to recover your Eee PC from an accidental drop out of a second story window).

In many cases, you won't need to worry about plugging in a recovery DVD and waiting around for the operating system to be fully reinstalled, as you would with other computers.

F9 does not perform a restore on Eee PCs running Windows XP or other versions of Linux.

This magic is thanks to something called UnionFS (read the "State of the UnionFS" sidebar for details). A read-only copy of the operating system and preinstalled files are kept on the drive and are always available for a restore.

That means if you installed some new software or changed a system setting that's making your operating system misbehave, you can quickly get things back to normal by using F9.

The downside to an F9 restore is you lose all the files you've saved on the mini-laptop's internal drive, any new programs you've installed, and whatever system settings you've changed. All this data is stored on the user-space drive partition that's cleared during a restore.

Before you perform an F9 restore, make sure you save any files you want to keep. (Some users, who like to experiment with the operating system, save all their files to an SD card. Because an F9 restore doesn't affect documents on an SD card or USB thumb drive, there's no worry over losing files.)

Here's how to do an F9 restore:

1. **After you've powered on or rebooted, when the Eee PC start-up screen is first displayed, immediately press and hold the F9 key.**

   A text window is shown with three choices (use the arrow keys to choose an option and Enter to select). When this window appears, you can release F9.

   Timing is a little critical on when to press F9. If you don't get it right the first time, restart, and then rapidly (and repeatedly) press F9 when you see the start-up screen.

2. **Select Restore Factory Settings.**

   If you decide not to do the restore, choose Normal boot to continue.

3. **A message warns you that you are about to restore the Eee PC to factory settings, and all user data will be lost. Type yes and press Enter to continue with restoring.**

This is your last chance before user data is erased. If you enter something other than *yes*, the Eee PC reboots as normal with all your data retained.

4. **The Eee PC is restored to its factory settings. Press Enter to reboot.**

When the mini-laptop reboots, it's just like the first time you got the computer and turned it on. Briefly, here is what happens next:

1. **The license agreement shows.**

   If you want to use the Eee PC, you need to agree to it.

2. **Specify the keyboard layout (such as English/US).**

3. **Enter your name (or whatever you want the computer to be called).**

4. **Enter a password to use.**

   The second text box is for confirming the password in the first text box; just in case you make a typo.

5. **Specify whether you want to be logged in automatically (checked by default).**

   Uncheck this option to require a password whenever the Eee PC starts up.

6. **Enter your time zone, the correct date, and the local time.**

Your Eee PC starts up, and you're back in business.

State of the UnionFS

700 and 900 series Linux Eee PCs come installed with a file system service known as UnionFS (later Eee PC models use Aufs, which is based on UnionFS with some improvements). ASUS uses UnionFS and Aufs as part of its F9 system recovery scheme. It works like this.

Linux Eee PCs have four drive partitions. The first partition (/dev/sda1) contains a read-only version of the operating system. The second partition (/dev/sda2) is the read-write user partition which is mounted on top of the first partition using UnionFS or Aufs. (The other two partitions are small, unused Windows FAT partitions.)

Any files you save or changes you make to the operating system are written to the user partition. When you use F9, the second partition is erased (losing all your changes and files), leaving the read-only first partition still intact. It's a little like a fresh start, without needing to reformat the entire drive and reinstall the operating system.

The downside to this scheme is it consumes more drive space. Because the first partition is read-only, you can't delete any unwanted preinstalled programs to free up space. Additionally, when you update a program with a new version, you end up with two copies — the read-only original version on the first partition and the updated version on the second partition.

Using the Linux Recovery DVD

If you can't fix things with an F9 restore or your Eee PC refuses to boot, it's time to break out the recovery DVD that came with your Linux mini-laptop.

The DVD contains everything you need to perform a complete system restore (this includes reformatting the drive and installing the operating system and preinstalled programs).

You can use the recovery DVD to

✔ Create a bootable USB recovery thumb drive (this is handy if you don't have or don't want to purchase a compatible USB DVD drive to use with the Eee PC).

✔ Boot the Eee PC and reinstall the operating system (obviously you need a DVD drive for this).

The following sections give you the lowdown on each of these options.

Always back up any files you want to keep before performing a system reinstallation with the DVD or a USB recovery drive. A system recovery involves formatting the internal drive, and all files and programs on the drive are erased.

USB recovery thumb drives

With a USB recovery thumb drive, you can perform a complete system reinstall of your Eee PC without attaching a DVD drive to the mini-laptop. All the recovery files you need are copied from the DVD to a USB thumb drive. The thumb drive is formatted so it can boot the Eee PC.

You need a Windows PC with a DVD drive and a USB thumb drive (2GB or larger). When you're ready, follow these steps:

1. **Insert a 2GB or larger USB thumb drive into a PC that's running Windows XP or later.**

   All the data is erased on the USB drive, so be sure to back it up.

2. **Insert the Recovery DVD into the Windows PC.**

   AsusSetup.exe should automatically start. If it doesn't, find it on the DVD and run the program.

3. **Click the Utilities tab and select ASUS Linux USB Flash Utility (as shown in Figure 18-1).**

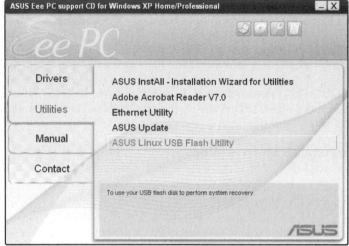

Figure 18-1:
Use the
ASUS
Support
DVD to cre-
ate a USB
recovery
drive.

4. **Choose the USB drive to copy the Linux files to, select Copy Eee PC image files to USB flash and make it bootable, and click Run (as shown in Figure 18-2).**

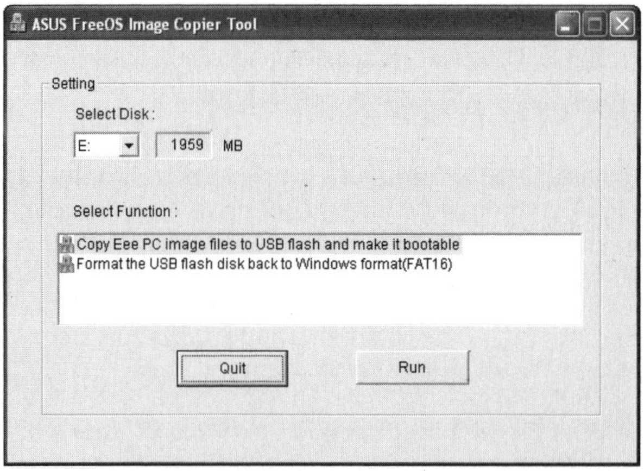

Figure 18-2:
Specifying
the USB
thumb drive
to use as
a recovery
drive.

5. **A dialog box is displayed that warns you the USB drive will be formatted. Click Yes to continue and follow the instructions.**

A few minutes go by and the utility creates your USB Linux recovery drive. You can use it immediately or store it in a safe place until you need it.

The utility formats the USB drive so that it is Linux bootable. If you want to use the drive for transferring data with another Windows PC, reformat the thumb drive. Run the program you used to create the recovery drive but select the *Format the USB flash disk back to Windows format* (FAT16) option (as shown in Figure 18-2). This reformats the drive so you can use it for storing files again.

After you've created the USB recovery drive, follow these steps to use it to reinstall the Linux operating system on your Eee PC:

1. **After you've powered on or rebooted, when the Eee PC start-up screen is displayed, immediately press and hold ESC.**

   This displays the boot device window (when you see the window, you don't need to press ESC any longer). You can select whether to boot from the internal drive, or (depending on what's plugged in) an SD card, a USB thumb drive, DVD player, or hard drive.

2. **Select the USB drive thumb drive.**

   Some status messages are displayed about Linux being loaded.

3. **When you're asked if you want to image the drive, type** yes **and press Enter to continue.**

   If you type anything else, the reinstallation ends and the system reboots normally. Otherwise, the program starts to copy data from the USB drive and writes it to the Eee PC's internal drive. (Status information about progress isn't displayed aside from a message saying the process takes about five minutes; I've found it usually takes less.)

   If you have files on your Eee PC that you forgot to back up, this is your last chance to stop the reinstallation so you can copy the files.

4. **When the reinstallation is complete, press Enter to reboot.**

   After the reboot, enter your name, password, and other information, just as you did when you powered on your Eee PC for the first time.

Recovering with the DVD

Reinstalling the operating system from the recovery DVD is the same basic process as using a USB thumb drive that I describe in the previous section. The only difference is that instead of plugging in the recovery thumb drive you created, you use the DVD directly with a DVD drive connected to your mini-laptop.

To reinstall Linux with the DVD, follow these steps.

1. **Connect a compatible USB DVD drive to your Eee PC.**

   I discuss DVD drives in Chapter 15.

2. **Insert the recovery DVD into the drive.**

3. **Turn on the Eee PC. When the mini-laptop's start-up screen is displayed, immediately press and hold ESC.**

   The boot device window is displayed (you can release the ESC key now). Select the DVD drive as shown in Figure 18-3.

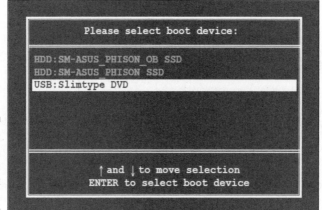

```
        Please select boot device:

HDD:SM-ASUS_PHISON_OB SSD
HDD:SM-ASUS_PHISON SSD
USB:Slimtype DVD



    ↑ and ↓ to move selection
    ENTER to select boot device
```

Figure 18-3: Selecting a DVD drive as the boot device.

4. **When you're asked if you want to image the drive, type** yes **and press Enter to continue.**

   I don't want to belabor the point, but did you copy any files on the internal drive that you want to save? If not, type something other than yes.

5. **When the reinstallation is complete, press Enter to reboot.**

   Enter your name, a password and other information, just as when you first got your Eee PC.

Using the Windows Recovery DVD

If your Eee PC came preinstalled with Windows XP, a support DVD is included with your mini-laptop. The disc has drivers, utilities, and various programs, as well as an image of the Windows operating system.

To use the DVD to perform a system recovery, you need a DVD drive to connect to your Eee PC (I discuss selecting a DVD drive in Chapter 15).

Unlike the Linux recovery DVD, the Windows version doesn't allow you to create a bootable USB recovery thumb drive.

If your Windows Eee PC crashes, it won't boot. If you have important files on the drive that you haven't backed up, consider this alternative before you bite the bullet and perform a system reinstall. Install a version of Linux on a USB thumb drive and try booting from it. In many cases you can successfully copy files from the unbootable internal drive before you format it and reinstall Windows. I discuss using different versions of Linux with the Eee PC and how to do this in Bonus Chapter 1.

The following list shows you how to perform a complete Windows reinstallation. There are a fair number of steps, but it's all pretty straight forward.

1. **Plug a USB DVD drive into your Eee PC.**
2. **Insert the Windows recovery DVD into the drive.**
3. **Turn on the Eee PC. At the start-up screen, press F2 to enter the BIOS setup.**
4. **Use the right-arrow key to display the Advanced tab.**
5. **Use the down-arrow key to highlight OS Installation and then press Enter.**

   This displays an Options window with two choices, Finished and Start.
6. **Use the down-arrow to select Start and then press Enter.**
7. **Use the arrow keys to highlight Onboard Devices Configuration and ensure all the devices all enabled.**
8. **Press F10 to save the change and reboot.**

These steps prepare the BIOS for the operating system to be installed. Now it's time to install the Windows disk image, so right after the mini-laptop reboots, follow these steps:

1. **When the Eee PC's start-up screen is displayed, immediately press and hold ESC.**

   The boot device window is displayed (you can release the Esc key now). Select the DVD drive (as shown in Figure 18-3).
2. **You're prompted to press any key to start the recovery.**
3. **A window appears and asks if you want to continue. Click OK. Another window is displayed querying you one more time if you want to proceed. Click Yes.**

   Are you really, really sure you want to continue? If you haven't backed up files that you want to keep, now is a very good time to say No.

4. **When the operating system installation is complete, you're asked to remove the DVD and restart your Eee PC. Click OK to reboot.**

You're not quite done yet though. You still need to change a setting in the BIOS, just as you did at the beginning. After the reboot, follow these steps:

1. **When the start-up screen appears, press F2 to enter the BIOS setup.**

2. **Use the right-arrow key to display the Advanced tab.**

3. **Use the down-arrow key to highlight OS Installation and then press Enter.**

4. **Use the down-arrow to select Finished and press Enter.**

5. **Press F10 to save the change and reboot.**

That does it. Windows XP has been reinstalled, and your Eee PC is now just as it was when you took it out of the box.

Chapter 19

A Real Desktop: Advanced Mode

*O*ut of the box, Linux Eee PCs come with a simple, tabbed user interface. Programs are grouped together by type in a series of tabs, and when you click an icon a program runs. You can't get much simpler than that.

This simple user interface fits with the design goal of the Eee PC being an easy-to-use computing appliance (in fact, the interface is even called Easy Mode). And although the mini-laptop doesn't use the more familiar desktop metaphor found in Windows, Mac, or other versions of Linux, it still enables you to get all your work (or play) done quickly and efficiently.

However, some users just can't get used to the simplicity of Easy Mode, and think they need more of a grown-up–looking operating system. If that sounds like you, you've come to the right place. In this chapter, I tell you about an undocumented Linux Eee PC feature called Advanced Mode.

Advanced Mode (also known as Full Desktop) gives you access to a complete KDE desktop, including a real desktop with movable icons, a taskbar with a start menu, overlapping program windows, and lots of customization options.

Read on to find out about the differences between Easy and Advanced Modes, how to install and uninstall Advanced Mode, how to use the KDE desktop. You also pick up some tips for switching back and forth between the two modes.

Differences between Easy and Advanced Modes

A picture is worth a thousand words (or something like that), so to begin explaining the differences between Easy and Advanced Modes, take a look at Figure 19-1, which shows the default, Easy Mode interface that comes with Linux Eee PCs. If you've read other chapters in the book, you should be very familiar with it by now.

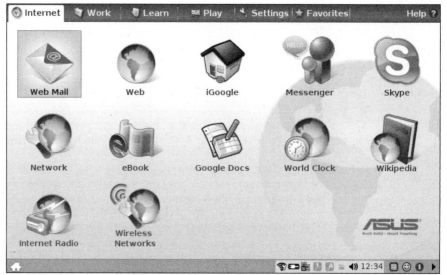

Figure 19-1: Linux Eee PC default Easy Mode.

Now cast your eyes on Figure 19-2, which shows Advanced Mode running. Wow, some difference, eh? It's a real computer!

The same Linux operating system is running and all the programs and files are the same, but the Easy Mode appliance-like user interface has been replaced by a more familiar, desktop-oriented, KDE user interface.

If the Eee PC is your first experience with Linux, most modern versions of the operating systems have full desktop interfaces that are similar to KDE in Advanced Mode. The Easy Mode interface is exclusive to ASUS Eee PCs.

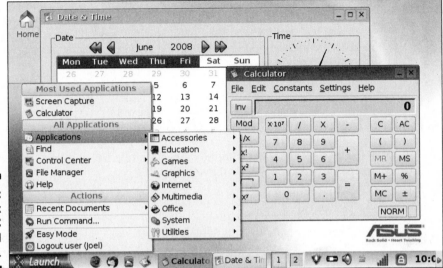

Figure 19-2:
Linux
Eee PC
Advanced
Mode.

Advanced Mode advantages

Some of the reasons to consider using Advanced Mode include

- ✔ More familiar, desktop interface
- ✔ Access to more programs and greater functionality
- ✔ Customizable background and themes

Advanced Mode disadvantages

Advanced Mode is not without its disadvantages, and you should be aware of a few of the drawbacks:

- ✔ Must be installed (although not it's not that difficult, as you'll soon see)
- ✔ Uses more memory
- ✔ Takes up a little more drive space (under 10MB)
- ✔ Requires slightly longer start-up and shutdown times
- ✔ On a small screen, the desktop metaphor gets a bit cramped
- ✔ Is unsupported by ASUS

That last item is a big one. Don't expect technical support from ASUS if you enable Advanced Mode. Easy Mode comes installed for a very good reason. If you're a Linux newbie and start playing with things that you don't understand in Advanced Mode, you can easily mess up your system, perhaps requiring an F9 system restore as I describe in Chapter 18.

Enabling Advanced Mode

If you're interested in giving Advanced Mode a try, you have two simple ways to enable Advanced Mode on your Eee PC.

Actually, there are several other methods too. If you want to check them all out, visit the EeeUser.com Wiki entry on the subject at `http://wiki.eeeuser.com/howto:getkde`.

Using pimpmyeee

In Chapter 21, I discuss customizing the Eee PC's user interface (especially in Easy Mode), and mention several tools and utilities. One of them is a shell script named *pimpmyeee* (that's not a word in a foreign language word; instead it's a run-on filename that translates out to *pimp my eee pc*).

A shell script is a like a DOS or Windows batch file. It's a text file that contains a number of commands that automate some process (you can open up the *pimpmyeee* shell with a word processor, if you'd like, and examine the commands). Shell scripts typically run in the console and have a simple text interface.

One of the features of this particular customization shell script is enabling Advanced Mode. If you don't already have pimpmyeee, you can download it with your Web browser from `http://code.google.com/p/pimpmyeee/` (right-click the file link and *Save link as*).

In addition to the shell script, you also need a connection to the Internet. After you have both, follow these steps:

1. **Press Ctrl+Alt+T to open a console session.**

2. **Enter** sh pimpmyeee-1.0.2.sh.

   Or depending on the version, whatever the filename of the latest script is. You're greeted with several options. You want the one that says F - Enable Full Desktop (KDE).

3. **Enter F as your choice.**

   Some messages scroll by and, if you are successful, the last message reads *Full desktop enabled*. It takes less than a minute for all the files to download and be installed.

4. **Press Enter to return to the shell script and then enter Q to quit.**

That's it, Advanced Mode is now installed. You can now close the console window.

Manually installing

Although shell scripts make life easy, unless you take the time to open them in a text editor, you don't know what they're doing. (I always recommend looking at a shell script before running it. As a Linux novice you may not know all the commands, but at least you have a general sense of what's going on inside.)

I want to show you how to manually install Advanced Mode. If you've read Chapter 12 on installing Linux software, some of this should look familiar. Remember, you need an Internet connection.

If you've added any repositories for installing other programs, before installing Advanced Mode I suggest you enable only the default ASUS repositories and disable any others (you can use Synaptic Package Manager to do this). This ensures you get the files you need from the right place. I tell you all about this in Chapter 12.

Follow these steps (coincidentally, these are the same commands that *pimpmyeee* uses, too):

1. **In a console window enter** sudo bash.

2. **Enter** apt-get update.

   This updates the package repository information; just in case you disabled any other non-default repositories as I suggested earlier.

3. **Enter** apt-get install ksmserver kicker.

ksmserver is KDE's session manager. When the computer starts up, the session manager launches auto-start programs and restores programs from the previous session. *kicker* is the main KDE panel that contains the taskbar and system tray. You are installing the Eee PC–specific versions of these two packages that allow you to run Advanced Mode.

4. Watch the status messages and reply Y (for yes) to any questions.

If no error messages appear, less than a minute goes by and Advanced Mode has successfully been installed.

Running Advanced Mode

After you installed Advanced Mode, you probably noticed that nothing happened. The big icons of Easy Mode are still happily staring up at you. No worries; you didn't make a mistake. Here are two ways to switch over to Advanced Mode:

✔ **In the desktop Settings tab, click the Instant Shutdown icon,**

✔ **In the taskbar, click the Shut Down icon.**

The Shutdown window appears, but a new button appears at the far left labeled Full Desktop (as shown in Figure 19-3). Yep, you guessed it. Click the Full Desktop button to run Advanced Mode — first, be sure to close any programs that are running. Well what are you waiting for?

Figure 19-3: The Full Desktop button added to the Shutdown window.

After you enter Advanced Mode and the full desktop, you can return to Easy Mode with one quick menu selection.

I don't want to sound like a broken record, but be careful with Advanced Mode. Loading it won't hurt your system; it's just the standard user interface to the same operating system. However, blindly playing with settings in this mode is probably the leading cause of Eee PC headaches and frustration for many Linux novices — and may require a F9 system restore. The Eee PC is fast and rock solid in Easy Mode (that's what I use most of the time). Do you absolutely need to run Advanced Mode to perform day-to-day tasks? The answer for most people is no.

Using Advanced Mode

I don't have the space to give you a detailed tutorial on using KDE (entire books and Web sites are devoted to subject), but I do want to give you some basic directions for getting started.

Navigating KDE

The full KDE desktop is very intuitive to use if you've had some experience with Windows or Mac. Here are a few quick tips for finding your way around.

- ✔ Double-click the Home icon to run File Manager and display your Home directory.

- ✔ Click the Launch button to display a pop-up menu with programs. This is similar to the Windows Start button.

- ✔ To access File Manager in Administrator mode, in order to perform file operations with administrative privileges, click the Launch button and select Applications⇨System⇨Administrator Tools⇨File Manager (Administrator).

- ✔ To customize the desktop (including changing colors, wallpaper, and themes), click the Launch button and select Control Center. Click the Display icon and choose Background, Panel/Taskbar, Screen Saver, or Theme to change desktop settings and appearance. You can also right-click the desktop and select Properties from the pop-up menu.

Check out the KDE Eyecandy Web site at `www.kde-look.org/` for a variety of custom themes and backgrounds. You can preview and download some of these directly from the Control Center.

- ✔ To the right of the clock in the taskbar, click the blue arrow to hide the taskbar. Click it again to restore the taskbar.

- Right-click the Launch button to edit and configure the taskbar and programs in the Launch pop-up menu.

- The two rectangles in the taskbar numbered 1 and 2 are desktops. One of Linux's standard features is multiple desktops. With multiple desktops, you can run one or more programs in one desktop and additional programs in the other desktop. This reduces screen clutter.

- To return to Easy Mode, click the Launch button and select Easy Mode.

- To shutdown or restart, click the Launch button and select Logout user.

To access KDE's online help system, click the Launch button and then select Help (look for the lifesaving ring icon). Or, for much, much more detail on using KDE, check out the official User Guide at `http://docs.kde.org/development/en/kdebase-runtime/userguide/index.html`.

Booting into Advanced Mode

After installing Advanced Mode, if you want to automatically boot into it instead of Easy Mode when your Eee PC starts up, here's how:

1. **Return to Easy Mode.**

2. **In the Settings tab, click the Personalization icon.**

3. **Under Login Mode, select Full Desktop Mode.**

   This option (as shown in Figure 19-4) is only available when Advanced Mode is installed. You won't see it otherwise.

4. **Click OK.**

Figure 19-4:
Setting up
Full Desktop
Mode in the
Personal-
ization
dialog.

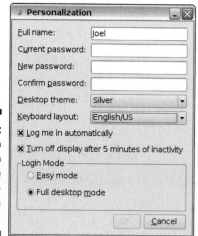

The next time you turn on or restart your mini-laptop, Advanced Mode loads and runs. If you decide you'd rather start up in Easy Mode, just go back into Personalization and change the Login Mode setting.

Two small drawbacks to this technique are that, first, the system double boots; it starts Easy Mode and then it loads Advanced Mode. That means slower start-up times. The second issue occurs if you move any file icons onto the desktop in Advanced Mode. Each time you reboot, the icons disappear (the files are still on drive though). The way to address both of these problems is to modify certain system configuration files. For instructions on how to do this, go to the EeeUser.com Wiki at http://wiki.eeeuser.com/howto:getkde. If you visit the site with your Eee PC, you can easily copy the required changes from the Web page and paste the text directly into the system files you need to edit.

Uninstalling Advanced Mode Files

In the event you want to uninstall the Advanced Mode files (let's say you find you aren't using the full desktop very much), it's a simple process. Here's how:

1. **Return to Easy Mode.**

2. **Press Ctrl+Alt+T to open a console session.**

3. **In a console window enter** sudo bash.

4. **Enter** apt-get remove ksmserver kicker.

   This removes *ksmserver* and *kicker* which are required for Advanced Mode to run.

5. **Enter** Y **to continue.**

   Status messages appear and in less than 10 seconds Advanced Desktop is no more. To double check, shut down. The Full Desktop button should no longer appear in the Shutdown window.

There is an uninstall version of pimpmyeee called unpimpmyeee, but it doesn't remove the Advanced Mode files.

If you ever perform an F9 system restore or have to restore your Eee PC from the recovery DVD, you must reinstall the Advanced Mode files.

Chapter 20

Command-Line Linux

*W*hen dinosaur operating systems ruled the earth, you instructed a computer what to do by typing in commands at a terminal keyboard (before that you used punch cards, but we're not going to set the Wayback Machine that far back today).

In those days, UNIX, DOS, and just about every other operating system didn't have user-friendly desktops. Instead, they had a Command-Line Interface (CLI), which required you to memorize all sorts of arcane commands. Thankfully, those days are long gone, and the CLI has been replaced by familiar mice, menus, and windows.

Although the command line is for the most part a dusty relic of the past (you can happily use your Linux Eee PC and never have to worry about entering text-based commands), it's still available, and you actually have some compelling reasons for knowing a little about it.

In this chapter, I gently introduce you to command-line Linux on the Eee PC. My goal is not to turn you into a keyboard Linux guru, but to explain the basics of using the command line just in case you want (or need) to put it to use.

Conquering the Console

To begin with you must know exactly where to enter Linux commands. You use a dedicated window called a *console* (it's also known as *shell* or *terminal*).

You type commands in the console, ending each line by pressing the Enter key. The Eee PC then executes the commands. If the Eee PC doesn't understand the command (let's say you made a typo), it displays an error message.

So why use the console when you have a perfectly good touchpad or mouse for clicking icons and menu commands? There are some good reasons for using the console, including

- ✔ It's faster for navigating the file system and entering commands.

- ✔ It teaches you more about what's going on behind the scenes.

- ✔ It offers a consistent way of entering commands when dealing with different Linux user interfaces.

- ✔ You can create and run shell scripts (the Linux version of a DOS or Windows batch file) to automate tasks.

- ✔ You can impress your friends, family, and coworkers with your *3l33t skillz* (that translates out to *elite computer skills* for you non-hackers).

When you hear people talking about *bash,* it's not necessarily what they want to do to their Eee PC when it misbehaves. Instead they're referring to the Bourne Again Shell (BA Shell, get it?). Bash is the default shell on most Linux distributions. It interprets and processes console commands. Bourne is Stephen Bourne who wrote the original Unix shell, which was called *sh.*

Let the Console Session Begin

The version of Linux installed on the Eee PC does a pretty good job of hiding the console from you. You won't find a console, terminal, or shell icon in any of the desktop tabs. This makes sense, in a way, because the Eee PC is designed to be a simple computing appliance — ASUS limits the ways a novice Linux user can possibly get into trouble.

That said, two versions of consoles are available on the Eee PC (both are preinstalled). Here's a little about each, as well as how to start them.

Consolation prize: xterm

When you press Ctrl+Alt+T, a console window is displayed as in Figure 20-1. This is a version of console named *xterm* (the underlying windows system for Linux is called X Windows, thus xterm, as in terminal).

You don't need to be at the desktop to open an xterm window. You can be in most any program, and Crtl+Alt+T will pop up a console session.

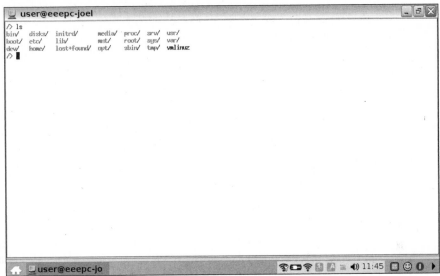

Figure 20-1:
The xterm
console.

Each time you press Ctrl+Alt+T a new console window opens. You can have multiple consoles open at once.

xterm is a very basic console, and Linux novices may find several limitations in using it, including

- ✔ Small text size
- ✔ Fixed text and background colors
- ✔ Difficulty in copying and pasting between programs

Although it's possible to change xterm settings, it's not straightforward for a Linux newbie. To learn more about xterm settings and options, visit its manual page at www.xfree86.org/4.0.1/xterm.1.html.

After the xterm window is displayed, you can start entering commands. If you want to try out a simple console command now, type *ls* and then press the Enter key. The contents of the current directory are shown, and the console waits for the next command. (I describe more commands coming up.)

To close an xterm console window, you have two choices:

- ✔ Click the window close box (the red square with the white X in the upper right corner).
- ✔ Type **exit** in the console.

Komputing with Konsole

The other console available in Linux Eee PCs is called Konsole. Konsole is KDE's default console (it's shown in Figure 20-2). Compared to xterm, Konsole looks more like a real program. It has menus, dialog boxes, and windows. It's more user-friendly and has many features, including

- Bookmarking for frequently used commands
- Easy copying and pasting between programs
- Variable text size and fonts
- Vertical scrolling for when more than one screen of information is displayed
- History with searching for previously entered commands

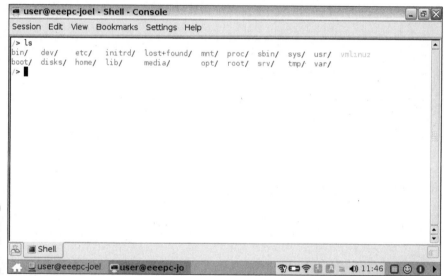

Figure 20-2:
The Konsole console.

Konsole also has a number of advanced features. To learn about them, select Konsole Handbook in the Help menu. Or visit the program's home page at: http://konsole.kde.org/.

There are two ways to run Konsole. The first is to use the xterm console. (I know, using a console to run another console sounds a bit silly.)

1. **Press Ctrl+Alt+T to open a console.**

2. **Type** konsole.

The other method is to run Konsole from within the File Manager.

1. **In the desktop Work tab, click File Manager.**
2. **In the Tools menu, select Open Console Window.**

The Konsole window appears, and you can start entering commands.

When you're done with Konsole, in the Session menu, select Quit.

Which console to choose?

Choosing a console is a lot like choosing a flavor of ice cream. There is no right answer, so try out both consoles to see which works best for you.

If I want to enter some quick commands, I use xterm. It's fast and gets the job done.

If I'm going to be using console for awhile, I switch to Konsole. It's easier on the eyes, copying and pasting is simpler, and I have quick menu access to advanced features.

You can change a setting with the TweakEEE utility that changes Konsole to the default console when you press Ctrl+Alt+T. I describe how to do this in Chapter 21.

Console Concepts

Now you know about the consoles you can use with the Eee PC. But before I show you some basic Linux commands, I want to briefly cover a few fundamental console concepts.

The first and most important thing to remember is that when it comes to commands, Linux is case-sensitive. If you type **Konsole** to run the program, you get an error message. If you type **konsole**, the program runs. Pay attention to capitalization or lack thereof.

The second point is that many Linux commands are simply programs. If you start nosing around in directories with the console, you find these programs in the /bin directory. If you know the name of a program, you can run it by entering its name while using the console.

When you type a command in the console, press the Enter key to run the command. When I talk about commands in this chapter, assume Enter is pressed unless I tell you otherwise.

If you don't know what you're doing at the console, you can really mess up your system. Although the Linux Eee PC is incredibly easy to restore if you make a bad boo-boo at the console, I encourage you to take the time to understand what commands mean before you blindly start typing, copying, or pasting commands shown on Web sites or forums.

Command help

Even though console is text-based, it does have a fair amount of online help available. If you want to learn more about a Linux command when you're using the console, use a command named *man*.

man is short for manual — as in the user guide variety. Enter **man** (followed by a space) and the command you want help with. For example, to find out about the pwd command (which displays the name of the directory you're currently in), type: **man pwd**.

After help is displayed, several keyboard commands enable you to view and navigate through the manual information. Here are some of most common keyboard commands:

- ✔ **Space** or **PgDn** shows the next screen of text.
- ✔ **PgUp** shows the previous screen of text.
- ✔ **Up- and down-arrow keys** moves up or down a line at a time.
- ✔ **Q** exits the manual.

Information displayed with man tends to be terse and sometimes not the easiest to understand. If something doesn't make sense, head to Google. Many Web sites provide in-depth and easy-to-understand explanations of Linux commands including examples.

Arguments

If you use the console long enough, at some point you will enter a command and things won't work out as you expected. You're certain that you're right and the computer is wrong. But that's not the type of argument I'm talking about here.

Many commands have arguments (sometimes called switches). This is an optional bit of text added to a command that changes its behavior. Typically, arguments are distinguished with a hyphen.

Here are some simple arguments you can try:

- ✔ **ls** shows the contents of a directory.
- ✔ **ls -a** shows the contents of a directory, including invisible files and directories.
- ✔ **ls -1** shows the contents of a directory in long listing format, including filenames, creation dates and permissions.

Use man, which I discussed in the previous section, to see what arguments are available for a selected command.

Sudo

Computer geeks tend to like science fiction, but *sudo* has nothing to do with Mr. Sulu from Star Trek. Instead, sudo is an acronym for *Super User Do*. Here's what this command is all about.

In order to run some Linux commands and programs, you must have administrative privileges. These commands and programs relate to activities such as changing the operating system or how it runs — typically tasks that only a system administrator can perform.

When you start a console session, it's running in a nonprivileged state, so to execute certain commands you need to type **sudo** (followed by a space) before you enter the command. This gives you the privileges you need to execute a command or run a program.

For example if you want to run File Manager in a privileged state (let's say you want to customize the user interface, as I describe in Chapter 21, and add your own icons to a system directory), at the console you enter

```
sudo XandrosFileManager
```

When it comes to sudo, "with great power, comes great responsibility." With administrative privileges you can modify and delete system files you normally couldn't. Be careful out there! Sudo should not be used for everything.

In other Linux distributions, you supply an administrator password with sudo. This is not the case with Xandros and the Eee PC. Some people believe this is a bit of a security flaw.

Directories and files

You can use the `cd` and `ls` commands at the console to connect to directories and list their contents. In addition to File Manager, two undocumented programs also enable you to view everything on your drive.

Konqueror

Konqueror is the default KDE file manager (as shown in Figure 20-3). Its menus, icons, and windows are intuitive and easy to use (online help is available), and it offers full access to the Eee PC file system.

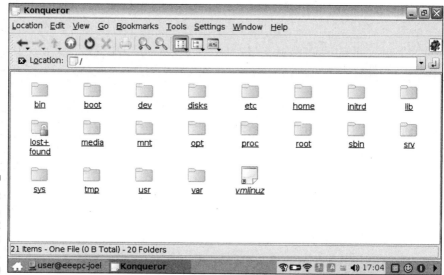

Figure 20-3: Konqueror, the default file manager.

To run Konqueror, at the console type **konqueror**.

Midnight Commander

Midnight Commander is a Linux, text-based file manager that you can use to view files and directories on your Eee PC (all well as copy, delete, and rename files, and do other things, too). Use the cursor to run commands and move through the directory structure. Midnight Commander is shown in Figure 20-4.

To run Midnight Commander, at the console type **mc**.

If you're new to Linux, please only use Konqueror and Midnight Commander for exploring. Avoid the copy, delete, rename, and other power commands that might get you in trouble if you don't know what you're doing.

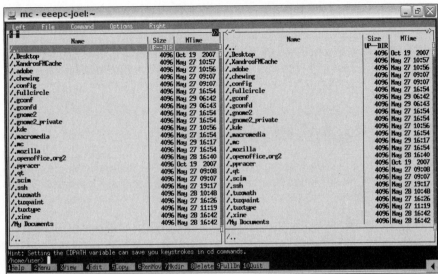

Figure 20-4:
Midnight
Commander.

Wondering what all those /bin, /etc, /sbin, and /usr directories are? Here's a link that explains and describes Linux's directory structure: www.tuxfiles. org/linuxhelp/linuxdir.html.

Redirecting and piping

Many Linux commands send their outputs to the screen. If you want to save the contents of command output to a file, you can redirect the output, using the > character.

For example, to save the contents of a directory listing to the file mydirectory.txt, you enter

ls > mydirectory.txt

Two > characters (>>) append command output to a file. For example ls >> mydirectory.txt adds the directory listing to existing data in the text file, whereas a single > overwrites the file with new data.

The pipe command also redirects output, but to other commands or programs instead of files. The | character (Shift+\) pipes the output of a command to another command.

For example if you use the ls command to view the contents of a large directory, and the files fly off the screen before you can see them, you can use piping like this;

```
ls | less
```

This redirects the directory listing output to a program named less. Less is normally used to view text files, but can also process text output from commands. You can now leisurely browse through the directory listing, using less to display a screen full of files at a time.

Keyboard shortcuts

The console (specifically, the bash shell) has a number of keyboard shortcuts to make life easier when you're using it. Here are a few useful shortcuts to know:

- ✔ **Ctrl+A** — Goes to the beginning of the line you're typing.
- ✔ **Ctrl+C** — Cancels the command that is currently running.
- ✔ **Ctrl+E** — Goes to the end of the line you're typing.
- ✔ **Ctrl+K** — Clears all text after the cursor.
- ✔ **Tab** — Auto-completes a command, file or directory name.
- ✔ **Up- and down-arrow keys** — The bash shell keeps a history of previously entered commands; the arrow keys scroll through them.
- ✔ **Right- and left-arrow keys** — If you're typing a command and notice a typo, use the right- or left-arrow keys to move the cursor to the character after the mistake. Fix the typo by using Backspace and entering the correct text.

Here is a link to a complete list of bash shell keyboard shortcuts: www. bigsmoke.us/readline/shortcuts.

More on command-line Linux

There's much more to using command-line Linux than I have the pages to describe. Here are some excellent, online learning resources:

- ✔ http://linuxcommand.org/ — A great tutorial and reference site
- ✔ www.tuxfiles.org/linuxhelp/cli.html — Linux command line tutorials for newbies

- ✔ www.freeos.com/guides/lsst/ — Linux shell scripting tutorials

The Eee PC is a perfect computer for experimenting with and learning Linux. Don't be intimidated by command line Linux. It's not that difficult to master if you spend a little time with it. The return is definitely worth the investment.

Console Commands

I end this chapter with Table 20-1, a short collection of common Linux commands with brief descriptions. If you want to experiment with these commands in the console, use man to learn about them first.

Many more commands are available. Refer to the sidebar "More on command-line Linux" for additional resources to consult.

Table 20-1	Common Linux commands.
Command	*Function*
cat	Displays file contents
cd	Changes directory to the specified directory. cd .. moves up one directory level.
pwd	Displays the current directory
chmod	Sets file permissions
clear	Clears the screen
cp	Copies file(s)
date	Sets or displays the date and time
diff	Compares two files
df	Displays free disk space
exit	Exits the shell
free	Displays free and used memory
fsck	Checks the file system
grep	Searches for file(s) with given string
history	Displays a list of your most recent commands
less	Displays a text file
ls	Displays directory contents
find	Searches for a file
mkdir	Makes a directory
mv	Moves or renames files or directories
rm	Deletes/removes a file(s)
rmdir	Removes a directory
sort	Sorts files

Chapter 21

Customizing the User Interface

· ·

In This Chapter

▶ Learning about simpleui.rc

▶ Editing tabs and icons with Launcher Tools

▶ Modifying IceWM preferences

▶ Tweaking the interface with TweakEEE

▶ Changing desktop themes with Theeemer

▶ Other customization tools

· ·

In Chapter 9 and the section about personalizing your Linux Eee PC, you see that aside from being able to change the background color, you can't do much else to customize the Eee PC's desktop.

ASUS wanted to keep the Linux Eee PC simple and sweet, so it doesn't provide a control panel for personalizing the mini-laptop. Or at least that's how it appears on the surface. But I'll let you in on a little secret.

You actually can add a touch of personality to the Easy Mode desktop interface and even do a little tweaking to make it easier to use. It's not that hard if you know a few simple tricks and employ some easy-to-use tools written by several Eee PC users.

In this chapter, I fill you in on what you need to know to modify the default Linux desktop interface. I show you how to add program icons and tabs, bring back icons that mysteriously disappeared, modify the taskbar, change backgrounds, and use different themes.

simpleui.rc Explained

First, some background to help you understand how the Eee PC works. The mini-laptop uses a file named *simpleui.rc* to store a number of Linux desktop settings. This text file contains information about the desktop tabs and which program and folder icons are found inside each of the tabs. A program named AsusLauncher uses the settings in simpleui.rc to create the Eee PC desktop.

By editing simpleui.rc, you can customize which programs appear in the tabs — changing their icons and even adding new tabs. (Remember, if changes to simpleui.rc make your Eee PC misbehave, you can always use an F9 restore that I describe in Chapter 18 to get back to normal.)

simpleui.rc can sometimes get corrupted when you add or update software — this is what causes program icons to disappear. You can restore vanished icons with the Launcher Tools programs that I discuss later in this chapter or keep a backup copy of simpleui.rc to replace a corrupted copy.

If you're a techie and like to do everything by hand, check out this how-to on backing up and modifying simpleui.rc: `http://wiki.eeeuser.com/ howto:backupsimpleui`. Keep in mind that simpleui.rc may be installed in different locations depending on the Eee PC model. Do a search for simpleui.rc in the `http://forum.eeeuser.com` forums for more information.

You can back up simpleui.rc with console commands and edit the file with a text editor (the data elements in the file are called *parcels*). However several programs make the job much easier — even for Linux gurus. I tell you about them next.

Adding Icons and Tabs with Launcher Tools

If I want to modify the Easy Mode Linux desktop, the first place I turn is Launcher Tools. Launcher Tools is a collection of programs (shown in Figure 21-1) that includes

- ✔ **SimpleUI Editor** — A graphical user interface tool for editing the simpleui.rc file

- ✔ **Iconifier** — An application that creates desktop icons from graphics files

- ✔ **Reload GUI** — A program that reloads the desktop so you can view changes without restarting your Eee PC

- ✔ **Uninstall** — A utility that removes all the Launcher Tools if you don't need them any more (a nice feature because of the limited drive space on many Eee PC models)

Figure 21-1:
Launcher
Tools
installed
in the
Favorites
tab.

To install a copy of Launcher Tools, follow these steps:

1. **With your Eee PC Web browser, go to www.3eportal.com.**

   Click the Downloads button at the top of the page. Go to the Launcher Tools information link.

2. **Download the latest version of altools (right-click the link and Save Link As).**

   This saves a copy of *altools* (the Launcher Tools installation file) to your My Home directory.

3. **With File Manager open, right-click the *altools* file, and select Install DEB File from the pop-up menu.**

   The installation program runs. Follow the instructions.

A copy of Launcher Tools is now installed in the desktop tab you specified. Click the Launcher Tools icon to display the programs.

After installing, you can also run the SimpleUI Editor from Launcher Tools by typing *suieditor* at the command line.

You can make many changes to the desktop using SimpleUI Editor, but here I want to focus on a few basic customization techniques. SimpleUI Editor is pretty simple to figure out, and you'll be personalizing your desktop in no time.

Changing a program's icon

If a program icon in a tab doesn't suit you, you can easily change its appearance with SimpleUI Editor. Run the program and then follow these steps:

1. **Select the program icon you want to change, right-click, and choose Properties from the pop-up menu.**

2. **In the Icon drop-down list box, select an icon.**

   A list of preinstalled icons is displayed.

3. **Click Apply.**

4. **Click Save Changes at the top of the window.**

   Whenever you save changes, SimpleUI Editor always makes a backup copy of simpleui.rc. In the Save Changes dialog box, the program tells you how to revert to the backup file.

5. **Click Reload AsusLauncher at the top of the window.**

A new program icon is associated with the program.

Desktop icons are saved in PNG format in the */opt/xandros/share/ AsusLauncher/* directory — you need administrator privileges to add files to this directory — on later Eee PC models the icons may appear in the */var/ lib/AsusLauncher/* directory. See Chapter 20 for more information. For a quick tutorial on creating your own icons, visit http://wiki.eeeuser.com/ customizeeasymodeicons. You can also use the Iconifier program that comes with Launcher Tools to create icons from existing PNG files.

Adding a program icon to a tab

If you just installed a program on your Eee PC and want it to appear in one of the desktop tabs, run SimpleUI Editor and follow along:

1. **Right-click in the tab area (not on a program icon) and select New Program in the pop-up menu.**

2. **In the dialog box, select the tab you want the program added to.**

3. **Enter the program name you want to appear in the tab.**

4. **Select an icon to associate with the program.**

   A number of preinstalled icons are available.

5. **In the Command text box, enter the program's path.**

If you don't know the exact path, try entering the name of the program and press the Enter key. SimpleUI Editor searches directories where programs are commonly installed. If it finds a match, it uses that path. Remember, Linux is case-sensitive, so the program and path must be capitalized correctly.

6. **Click Create.**

7. **Click Save Changes at the top of the window.**

8. **Click Reload AsusLauncher.**

A new program icon is now available in the desktop. Click the icon to run the program.

You can also use the same steps to create folders within tabs. In Step 1, choose New Folder from the pop-up menu instead of New Program.

To delete a program or folder icon from a tab, run SimpleUI Editor, select the icon, right-click, and choose Delete from the pop-up menu.

Restoring a vanished icon

In the simpleui.rc file, each desktop icon has a link to a program that runs when you click the icon. If the link is blank or points to a program that doesn't exist (often an incorrect path), the icon won't be displayed in a tab.

This is a frequent culprit in the case of the vanishing icons. Link information accidentally gets changed when you run Add/Remove Software, and the icon disappears. To restore the icon, SimpleUI Editor is your friend. Follow these steps:

1. **Select the tab containing the vanished icon.**

2. **Select the program icon that disappeared, right-click, and choose Properties from the pop-up menu.**

   The Item Properties dialog box is displayed as shown in Figure 21-2.

3. **In the Command text box, enter the full path of the program.**

   If the path is blank or it says *Invalid Command!* underneath, there's your problem! If you don't know the program's full path, type in the program's name (for example, FBReader) and press Enter. This auto-searches for a program with that name's correct path. (Remember, Linux is case-sensitive, so use exact uppercase and lowercase spelling.) If *Valid Command!* appears under the path, you're set.

Figure 21-2:
Properties
for a pro-
gram icon
in SimpleUI
Editor.

If you don't know the name of a program, refer to the chapters in Part II of this book where I discuss each desktop tab and its respective program. Program names and paths for preinstalled programs can also be found here: `http://wiki.eeeuser.com/doc:icewmstartmenutemplates`.

You may notice icons for programs you've never seen before. These may have been added when you ran Add/Remove Software. You can delete any unused icons (which is good housekeeping) or leave them alone.

4. **Click Apply.**

5. **Click Save Changes at the top of the window.**

6. **Click Reload AsusLauncher.**

The program icon should now be restored to the desktop, and you can happily use it again.

Adding a new tab to the desktop

If you're a little bored with the standard Internet, Work, Learn, Play, Settings, and Favorites tabs, why not add a tab of your own? It's simple. Use the Tab Management menu in SimpleUI Editor.

1. **Select New Tab from the menu.**

2. **Specify a JPG background file to use.**

Backgrounds are saved in JPG format and are stored in the */opt/xandros/ share/AsusLauncher/* directory (or */var/lib/AsusLauncher/* in some Eee PC models).

3. **Give the tab a name.**

4. **Choose an icon for the tab.**

5. **Provide a Tab ID.**

   It can be the same as the name — as long as the ID is unique.

6. **Specify where you want the tab to appear.**

   You can choose if it appears before one of the existing tabs or after the Favorites tab.

7. **Click Create.**

8. **Click Save Changes at the top of the window.**

9. **Click Reload AsusLauncher.**

You now can use SimpleUI Editor to add program icons to your newly created tab.

To change the properties of an existing tab, including the name and background image, select Properties Current Tab from the Tab Management menu. You can also delete tabs with this menu.

Chilling with IceWM

IceWM is a Linux window manager that's popular on PCs that don't have screaming fast processors and lots of memory — it doesn't require many system resources. That's one of the reasons it's used by the AsusLauncher program to display the Eee PC's desktop interface.

IceWM is very customizable. It uses a preferences file for storing information about elements of the window manager desktop and how the elements appear. Like simpleui.rc, you can modify settings in this preferences file to change your Linux Eee PC's default user interface.

You have two options. Modify the preferences file by hand (here's a tutorial with some basics: http://wiki.eeeuser.com/howto:icewmstartmenu); or if that's a little intimidating, change settings with the TweakEEE and Theemer programs that I tell you about coming up next.

For everything you always wanted to know about IceWM but were afraid to ask, visit the project Web site at www.icewm.org and check out the IceWM user manual (www.icewm.org/manual/icewm-1.html).

Tweaking the Interface with TweakEEE

Launcher Tools is great for modifying the tabbed desktop, but if I want to make even more changes to the interface I use a nifty all-purpose utility called TweakEEE (as shown in Figure 21-3).

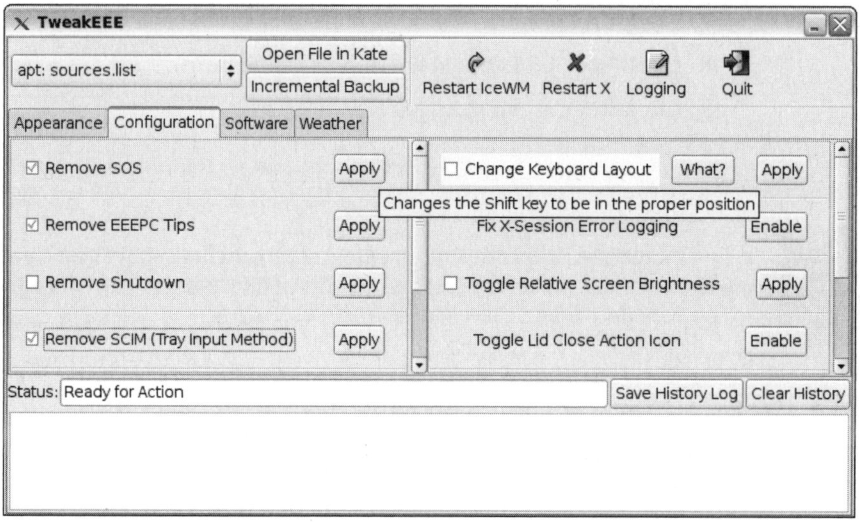

Figure 21-3:
Customize the interface with TweakEEE.

To install a copy of TweakEEE, follow these steps:

1. **With your Eee PC Web browser, go to www.infinitedesigns.org/archives/195.**

2. **Right-click the download link and Save Link As.**

   This saves a copy of TweakEEE to your My Home directory.

3. **With File Manager open, right-click the TweakEEE file, and select Install DEB File from the pop-up menu.**

   The installation program runs. Follow the instructions.

A copy of TweakEEE is now installed in the desktop tab you specified. Click the TweakEEE icon to run the program.

In addition to modifying the interface, TweakEEE can also download and install a number of popular programs, back up interface-related files, change the default console, add extra repositories, and perform a number of other Swiss-army-knife–like tasks. Spend some time exploring the program to learn about all its features.

Showing the Start button

If you're a Windows user, you're certainly familiar with the Start button in the lower-left corner of the Windows taskbar. TweakEEE can add a similar button to the desktop interface, making it easier to navigate programs. Run TweakEEE and then

1. **In the Appearance tab, check Show Start Menu and Menu Template.**

2. **Click Apply.**

A Start button is added to the taskbar as shown in Figure 21-4. Use it to run installed programs.

Figure 21-4: Add a Start button to the desktop.

Changing the taskbar clock format

By default, the clock in the taskbar displays the time only in a 24-hour format — with no apparent way to change it to the more familiar AM/PM format. At least not until you use TweakEEE.

Click the Appearance tab and then scroll to the bottom until you come to the Clock Format option. You have a choice of

✔ Time displayed in 24-hour format (13:00)

✔ Time displayed in AM/PM format (1:00 PM)

✔ Time and date displayed numerically (7/12/08 - 01:00 PM)

✔ Day of the month and time displayed (12 - 01:00 PM)

✔ Month, day and time displayed (July 12 - 01:00 PM)

Select a format and click Apply. The taskbar clock now reflects the new setting.

Removing taskbar icons

You may not use certain icons in the Linux desktop taskbar very often, and so they just take up space. These icons include the following:

✔ **SOS** — Runs the Task Manager. You can also run SOS from the Shutdown dialog.

✔ **EEEPC Tips** — Displays a brief list of Eee PC-related tips in the browser.

✔ **Shutdown** — Runs the Shutdown program. You can also run Shutdown by clicking Instant Shutdown in the Settings tab or pressing the power button.

✔ **SCIM** — Switches between Chinese and English as the input method.

✔ **Num and Caps Lock** — Shows whether the Caps Lock and NumLk keys are depressed.

To turn off these icons in the taskbar, click the TweakEEE Configuration tab, choose the icons you don't want displayed, and click Apply. (You may need to click the taskbar to refresh it.)

To turn an icon back on, uncheck it and click Apply.

Custom Themes with Theeemer

Downloading themes (or skins) is a popular way to personalize a PC. A program, written by the author of Launcher Tools, lets you do just that with your Eee PC.

Theeemer (Th-Eee-mer, get it?), as shown in Figure 21-5, can modify a number of different IceWM settings to give you a custom user interface.

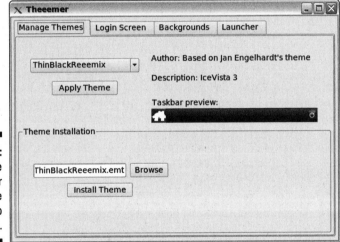

Figure 21-5:
Use
Theeemer
to change
desktop
themes.

When you run the program, four tabs are displayed. Click a tab to see options for making changes to various user interface elements.

✔ **Manage Themes** — Select a theme from the drop-down list box (a preview appears, showing you what the taskbar looks like using the theme). Replace the current theme with the selected one and click Apply. A sample theme is shown in Figure 21-6. To add additional themes (files with a `.emt` extension), use the Browse button and click Install Theme. That theme now appears in the drop-down list box.

Notice that many themes don't show a preview taskbar. That's because these themes are more generically suited for Linux PCs. There aren't many custom themes designed specifically for the Eee PC yet (the ones that are available show the preview taskbar). You can get several Eee PC themes on the Theeemer download page (`www.3eportal.com`). Look for more themes in the future and for programs that make it easier to create and save themes.

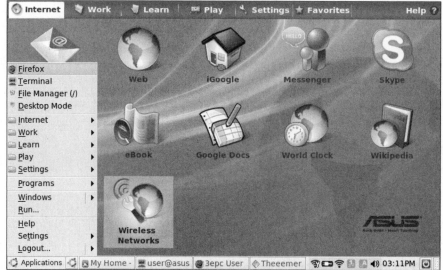

Figure 21-6:
The Mock
Ubuntu
theme
applied to
the Eee PC.

✓ **Login Screen** — This option lets you replace the default login screen at start-up with a JPG graphics file of your own. (There are convenient Restore and Default buttons, just in case.)

✓ **Backgrounds** — Similar to the Login Screen option, this selection is for replacing the background of a desktop tab with a JPG file of your choice.

✓ **Launcher** — With Launcher you can change individual elements of the taskbar. Move the cursor over an element to display pop-up information about the image name (a PNG file) and its dimensions. Right-click an element to change its color or replace the image with your own. (It's quick and easy to go back to the default settings in case you're not happy with your changes.)

As with other programs, the best way to learn about Theeemer is to spend some time experimenting. To install a copy of the program, follow these steps:

1. **With your Eee PC Web browser, go to www.3eportal.com.**

   Click the Downloads button at the top of the page. Go to the Theeemer program information link.

2. **Download the latest version of Theeemer (right-click the link and choose Save Link As).**

   This saves a copy of Theeemer to your My Home directory.

3. **In File Manager, right-click the Theeemer file and select Install DEB File from the pop-up menu.**

   The installation program runs. Follow the instructions.

A copy of Theeemer is now installed in the Settings tab. Click its icon to run the program.

If Theeemer didn't appear to install or if nothing happens when you click the program icon, open a console session (by pressing Ctrl+Alt+T) and enter: **theeemer**. If you get an error message about no valid themes, enter this command at the console to copy themes into a required directory: **cp -rf /usr/ share/icewm/themes ~/.icewm**.

Questions about Theeemer? Post them in this EeeUser.com forum thread: `http://forum.eeeuser.com/viewtopic.php?id=15049`.

Using Other Customization Tools

In addition to Launcher Tools, TweakEEE, and Theemer, you can use several other tools to customize your Eee PC's user interface.

Pimpmyeee.sh

Pimpmyeee (pimp-my-eee) is a shell script for customizing your Eee PC. You can download it with your Web browser by visiting `http://code.google. com/p/pimpmyeee/` (right-click the file link and choose Save link as).

With the script, you can do the following:

- ✔ **Enable Advanced Mode desktop.**
- ✔ **Disable SCIM input and remove its taskbar icon.**
- ✔ **Install several themes.**
- ✔ **Remove SOS and Eee PC Tips from taskbar.**
- ✔ **Enable extra repositories.**
- ✔ **Enable all codecs.**

After you've downloaded Pimpmyee.sh, follow these steps to run the utility:

1. **Press Ctrl+Alt+T to open a console session.**
2. **Enter** sh pimpmyeee-1.0.2.sh.

   Or depending on the version, whatever the correct filename is. You're greeted with several options. (You need an Internet connection for some of the choices).

3. **Select the interface option you want to change.**

4. Press Enter to return to the shell script and then press Q to quit.

There's also an Unpimpmyee.sh utility to revert some of the changed options to original form.

Shell scripts are just text files. You can open them with a word processor to see the commands that are being executed. Anytime you work with a shell script you should do this.

Easy Mode Editor

Easy Mode Editor (also known as EM Editor) is another program for modifying simpleui.rc. It has a different interface than SimpleUI Editor, but shares many of the same features. To download the program and learn more about it (including seeing some screen shots of the utility), visit `http://download.projectsakura.com/eeepc/emeditor.html`.

In this chapter, I focus on how to modify the Easy Mode desktop. However, if you're using Advanced Mode (the full desktop), you don't need to hand modify preferences files or use third-party programs to personalize your Eee PC. Many customization options are available in the KDE Control Center. I tell you how to install Advanced Mode and access the Control Center in Chapter 19.

Part VI
Part of Tens

The 5th Wave
By Rich Tennant

SEVERAL HOURS PASSED BEFORE WAYNE DISCOVERED THAT HE WAS LOOKING AT HIS SCREEN SAVER AND NOT OUT THE SUBMARINE'S PORTHOLE

"It's incredible! I'm seeing life forms never before imagined!! Bizarre, colorful, almost whimsical!!!"

In this part . . .

All Dummies books have a part called The Part of Tens, and this one is no exception. This is a rather eclectic collection of Eee PC–related information. You find a chapter devoted to troubleshooting common Eee PC problems and another one that presents essential Internet information sources.

Chapter 22

Ten Eee PC Troubleshooting Tips

*T*he Eee PC is a reliable little computer, but every now and then gremlins can creep in and cause some trouble.

In this chapter, I list ten Eee PC ailments you may run into some day. For each problem, I describe the symptom and then provide one or two possible solutions. (Some of the solutions involve using the Linux console and entering text commands, but I walk you gently through the process.)

It's always convenient (and sometimes justified) to blame the Eee PC, its operating system, or a program for a problem you're encountering. Before you do this though, take a minute to ensure it's not a PEBKAC situation — that's Problem Exists between Keyboard and Chair.

My Icon (s) Disappeared!

Symptom: You used the Add/Remove Software program to update your Linux Eee PC, and now one or more icons have gone missing from the desktop.

Solution: Elementary, Watson. The *simpleui.rc* (which contains information about desktop icons) has gotten corrupted. If you've backed up this file, as I discuss in Chapter 21, simply replace the corrupted file with your backup.

You can also use an icon utility such as SimpleUI Editor (part of Launcher Tools) or Easy Mode Editor to bring the icon(s) back. I tell you all about these tools and how to use them in Chapter 21.

The last resort solution is to perform an F9 recovery. This restores your Linux Eee PC to how it came from the factory. The one gotcha with this technique is that any data you've saved on the Eee PC's drive (including new programs, files, and operating system settings) are deleted. Be sure to back up your files onto an SD card or USB thumb drive. I tell you all about performing an F9 restore in Chapter 18.

My Touchpad Has Problems Scrolling

Symptom: When you use the touchpad you need to exert a lot of pressure to move the cursor, or you barely brush the touchpad and the cursor goes flying.

Solution: Touchpads work by using sensors to measure the electrical charge in your finger. Your touchpad can be working fine, but suddenly starts misbehaving because something changes the way the electrical charge (known as *capacitance*) is measured. This could be increased heat, humidity, or even sweat on your skin. To remedy the problem, change the sensitivity settings to make the touchpad more or less sensitive. With Linux, use the Touchpad program in the Settings tab; with Windows, go to the Control Panel and change the Elantech touchpad properties.

If you run Windows XP and continue to have problems with the touchpad, try installing the latest touchpad driver from the ASUS support Web site (http://support.asus.com).

My Web Cam Doesn't Work

Symptom: You try to use your Web cam, but it doesn't work.

Solution: First, determine if this is a hardware or software problem. Is it just one particular program that won't work with the Web cam or all programs? For example, the version of Skype that originally shipped with Linux Eee PC 4G may need to be upgraded to a later version to work with the Web cam.

In Windows, make sure the Web cam is enabled in the Eee PC tray utility.

If you installed your own copy of Windows XP and used nLite or a similar utility to shrink the size, be sure you didn't remove the Windows Image Acquisition (WIA) module. The Web cam needs these files to function.

If the Web cam doesn't work with any programs, there's a chance it somehow has become disabled in the BIOS settings. Here's how to re-enable it:

1. **Turn on or reboot your Eee PC.**

2. **At the start-up screen, press F2 to enter the BIOS setup.**

3. **Use the right-arrow key to go to the Advanced tab.**

4. **Use the down-arrow key, select Onboard Devices Configuration. Then press Enter.**

5. **With the down-arrow key, select Onboard Camera. Make sure it is marked Enabled.**

   If it's not, press Enter, select Enabled from the menu, and press Enter again.

6. **Press Esc to return to the Advanced tab.**

7. **Use the down-arrow key to select OS Installation. Make sure it's marked Finished.**

   If it's not, press Enter, select Finished from the menu, and press Enter again.

8. **Press F10 to save your changes and exit.**

The Eee PC reboots, and your camera should now be working.

Speaking of Web cams, I need to make a pitch for a cool little open-source program called Dorgem (`http://dorgem.sourceforge.net/`). Dorgem turns your Windows Eee PC's Web cam into a stealthy security monitor with motion detection code that snaps a photo when the camera detects movement. This is the perfect tool for spying on your cats when you're not home.

My Eee PC Suspends When I Close the Lid

Symptom: You close the lid on your Linux Eee PC, go off to do something, and when you come back, the battery has drained.

Solution: By default, when you close your Linux Eee PC's lid, it goes into a Suspend state. A reduced amount of power is still being used during suspend, and the battery can fully drain — depending how much of a charge it has and how long you leave it sitting.

There is a way to have your Linux Eee PC shut down instead of suspending when you close the lid. (Sorry, there's no way to do this with Windows; you can only change settings to have the Eee PC suspend or do nothing when you close the lid.) To shut down instead of suspend, you modify a shell script. Here's how:

1. **Open a console by pressing Ctrl+Alt+T.**

2. **Enter** sudo kwrite /etc/acpi/lidbtn.sh.

   This loads the shell file you need to change.

3. **In the file, look for the following lines:**

```
if [ $LID_STATE = "closed" ] ; then
        /etc/acpi/suspend2ram.sh
```

4. **Change the lines to read:**

```
if [ $LID_STATE = "closed" ] ; then
        # /etc/acpi/suspend2ram.sh
        /sbin/fastshutdown.sh
```

   The # in front of the line turns it into a comment so the command isn't executed. The added line that follows is an instruction to run a shell script that shuts down the Eee PC.

5. **Save the file and quit the word processor.**

Your Eee PC should now shut down when you close the lid. Give it a try.

For other ways to control a Linux Eee PC's behavior when the lid closes, check out this how-to: http://wiki.eeeuser.com/close_lid_shutdown.

I Forgot My Password

Symptom: You forgot your password and now can't log in to your Eee PC. Ouch!

Solution: First, make sure Caps Lock isn't on when you log in, then read on.

Windows

If you're running Windows XP and forget your password, you can log in to a PC in several ways. Check this handy how-to for one simple method that involves booting into Safe Mode as Administrator: www.wikihow.com /Log-on-to-Windows-XP-if-You-Forget-Your-Password.

After you're logged in, change your account password to something more memorable (and consider writing it down in case there's a future memory lapse).

Linux

If your Eee PC is running the default version of Linux, ASUS officially says you're out of luck if you forget your password — you must do an F9 system restore (which will erase all your files).

However, what ASUS doesn't tell you is that you have two sneaky ways to access a password-protected Eee PC without losing all your data. If you promise to use these methods only for good, and not evil, I'll share them with you.

✔ **Boot from another version of Linux** — Most computer users don't realize that if someone has physical access to a PC he or she can easily bypass an operating system start-up password — this holds true for both Linux and Windows. Instead of booting from the internal drive (which prompts you for a password), boot from a different operating system on a CD/DVD, USB thumb drive, or SD card. Presto! You've got access to the contents of the hard drive and can copy files or reset the password (to learn more about this, Google for *Linux root password reset*). If you want to try this approach, I tell you all about using other versions of Linux with the Eee PC in Bonus Chapter 1 on the companion Web site.

✔ **Use console commands** — Using another operating system to breech a PC's security, is a tried-and-true technique. But there's a faster and easier method to get around the password prompt. You can use an undocumented method to put your Eee PC into a special console mode at start-up. In this mode, you can enter certain commands to bypass the password prompt and then reset your password.

Here's how to use the console commands:

1. **Immediately press and hold F9 when you see the start-up screen.**

   This displays boot loader options (the program running is called Grub, by the way).

2. **Press the e key to select the Normal Boot option.**

   This displays different boot commands.

3. **Use the arrow key to select the line that starts with *kernel* and press the e key.**

   You can now edit the boot command line.

4. **At the end of the line, type a** space, **then** XANDROSBOOTDEBUG=y.

   This puts the Eee PC in debug mode when you reboot.

5. **Press Enter.**

   You're back at the main boot loader screen. Make sure the line starting with *kernel* is selected.

6. **Press the b key.**

   The boot command executes, and the BusyBox command prompt appears.

   BusyBox is a small program that provides versions of several essential Linux commands. It's known as the Swiss army knife of embedded Linux and is found in a number of Linux hardware devices.

7. **Enter the following commands:**

```
mount /dev/sda2 /mnt-user/
      cd /mnt-user/home/user/
      rm .AsusLauncher/requireLogin
      exit
```

These commands mount the Eee PC's drive and delete a configuration file responsible for requesting a password at start-up. The mini-laptop reboots and no longer asks you for a password.

With the start-up password bypassed, you're halfway there. You still need to deal with that pesky password you forgot (the Personalization program in the Settings tab won't let you change your password unless you know the old one). Here's how to do a password reset from the command line:

1. **Open a console by pressing Ctrl+Alt+T.**

2. **Enter** sudo passwd user.

   This changes the user password. Type in a new password (write it down this time) and press Enter. If you're prompted to enter the password a second time, do it.

3. **Enter** sudo passwd.

   This changes the root password. Use the same password that you just entered.

4. **Close the console window.**

Whew, that was kind of a pain. But if everything went okay, you're back in business with a new password and all your files intact.

Although this procedure is as smooth as silk on an Eee PC 4G, I can't guarantee it works on other Eee PC models. (There's always a possibility ASUS could change the location of the password prompt configuration file.) You can learn a little more about using the BusyBox console and the Eee PC here: http://wiki.eeeuser.com/howto:installrescuemode.

If you set a BIOS password and forgot it, you have two options. Open the Eee PC case (your mini-laptop should be powered off, not connected to power) and remove the BIOS battery — it's similar to the type used in watches and calculators. This clears BIOS settings. Wait a few minutes, reinstall the battery, put your Eee PC back together, and power on. The other option is to install a new version of the BIOS as I discuss in Chapter 12.

My Wireless Connections Aren't Working

Symptom: Your Eee PC's wireless connection unexpectedly stops working, won't reconnect, or you've never been able to get a connection.

Solution: Wireless problems can be both tricky and mysterious to resolve (I once had networking troubles that I swear were related to the phase of the moon). Usually the culprit is a setting that was inadvertently changed or a temporary glitch in the wireless card, router, or either's interface software. You can try a number of things if you run into wireless difficulties. Check out the following:

✔ Is wireless enabled on your Eee PC? Is the blue light on? If it's not, wireless is disabled. Press Fn+F2 to enable your wireless and wait for a connection.

✔ Is your wireless router/access point to blame? If you have another laptop, can you successfully get a Net connection? If not, reboot or turn the router off and on again. Wait about a minute until it reconnects to the Internet and then try connecting again with your Eee PC. (Typically, I'll power my Eee PC off and then restart it after the wireless router's status lights indicate there's a connection.)

Check which version of firmware the wireless router is running. If it's not the most recent, upgrade to the latest version. Check your user manual or the manufacturer Web site for details.

✔ Does your router have any security settings (such as MAC address filtering, WEP or WPA) that may be preventing the Eee PC from connecting? Some Linux Eee PC's have difficulty connecting to a wireless router using WPA encryption when the required password contains a space — use a different password.

✔ Are you having troubles connecting to just one access point? Try connecting to a free public WiFi network (at a library, coffee shop, or college). If you're successful, delete the problem connection and create a new connection (I tell you how to do this in Chapter 3). There's a chance something in the settings got corrupted.

Some Linux users have reported that upgrading to the 1.05 desktop with Add/Remove Software resolved their wireless issues. I discuss upgrading your Eee PC in Chapter 12.

My Eee PC Hangs at Shutdown

Symptom: You shut down your Eee PC, but it stays on. The shutdown screen may stay displayed or the screen goes black.

Solution: Press and hold the power button until the Eee PC turns off. The operating system got a little confused about something during the shutdown process and is stuck in a loop. Restart your mini-laptop and see if it shuts down normally.

If shutdown woes continue, try upgrading to the latest version of the BIOS as I describe in Chapter 12.

I Can't Write to an SD Card or a USB Drive

Symptom: On a Linux Eee PC, you can't save, move, or delete files on an SD card or a USB thumb drive. Your mini-laptop displays cryptic messages and won't let you write to the card or drive.

Solution: First, check that the write protect tab isn't switched on (all SD cards have this as well as some USB thumb drives). If the write protect tab is flipped on, switch it to the other position and you're in business.

If that doesn't do the trick, there's a good chance the volume permissions are set to read-only, so any write operations to the device are being denied. The first thing to try is

1. **Start a console session by pressing Ctrl+Alt+T.**

2. **Enter** sudo XandrosFileManager**.**

This runs File Manager with administrative privileges. Try copying, moving, or deleting files you previously had trouble with it. If you're successful, great!

You don't want to be using File Manager with administrative privileges all the time, however, so make some changes to a configuration file that has permissions settings. Here's how:

1. **Open a console by pressing Ctrl+Alt+T.**

2. **Enter** sudo kwrite /etc/udev/rules.d/50-xandros-udev.rules.

   This loads the configuration file you need to change.

3. **In the file, find this line:**

   ```
   BUS=="usb", KERNEL=="sd[!0-9]", NAME="%k",
   MODE="0660", GROUP="floppy", SYMLINK+="disks/
   Removable/%k", RUN+="/usr/bin/usbstorageapplet
   zip %k"
   ```

4. **Change MODE from "0660" to "0666".**

   This sets permission for all users to read and write to the device. Change MODE to "0777" to allow read, write, and execute (run programs).

5. **Save the file.**

6. **In the console enter** sudo /sbin/udevstart.

   This last step reloads the changed configuration file. You should now be able to write files to your SD card or thumb drive.

My Eee PC Isn't Working Right

Symptom: Your Eee PC just isn't working correctly and seems to be suffering from some mystery ailment.

Solution: The first question to ask is always: "What did I do right before my Eee PC started misbehaving?" Did I install a new program, upgrade to a later version, or make a change to the operating system? Nine times out of ten the answer provides an important clue.

With Linux, the default Easy Mode is pretty stable. When you start using Advanced Desktop, make undocumented changes to the operating system, or enter commands at the console (especially if you don't fully understand what you're doing), you risk making your system unstable. The solution is to perform an F9 restore (which I describe in depth in Chapter 18). If that doesn't work, do a full reinstallation of the operating system with the recovery DVD.

Windows is a little more forgiving when it comes to making system changes (unfortunately, however, there's no F9 system restore). The first thing to try is reinstalling any Eee PC drivers for the devices (touchpad, Web cam, or keyboard) that may be giving you problems. The drivers are on the DVD that came with the mini-laptop, or you can visit the `http://support.asus.com` Web site to get the latest versions.

If you used nLite or a similar program to try to reduce the size of Windows XP to save drive space, make sure you didn't delete something that was required. (I talk nLite and shrinking Windows in Chapter 11.)

If you're still having problems, the last resort is to perform a complete system reinstallation.

Whether you're running Linux or Windows, you did back up any important files before doing a system restore, didn't you?

My Eee PC Is Dead

Symptom: I saved the worst case scenario for last. You turn on the power and nothing happens. Or maybe the green power and blue wireless LED status lights come on, but the screen is black. Your Eee PC seems to be, to quote an old Monty Python skit, "pushin' up the daisies."

Solution: Don't panic (panicking really never gets you anywhere, anyway).

First, try plugging the Eee PC into an electrical outlet. There's a chance the battery has completely discharged, and there's no power left.

If that doesn't work, with the mini-laptop still plugged into the wall charger, read Chapter 18 for instructions on restoring your system with the DVD that comes with the Eee PC.

No luck with that? It sounds like it's probably a hardware or BIOS problem. If it's a failed motherboard or power supply, there's not much you can do (unless you're handy with a soldering iron and know your way around the insides of a PC, in which case you probably don't need this chapter for advice).

If the BIOS has somehow become corrupted (say you tried to upgrade it, but something happened), you've got a last-resort option. Check out your user manual or this Wiki entry for information on installing a new copy of the BIOS: `http://wiki.eeeuser.com/howto:updatebios`.

Failing that, cross your fingers that your mini-computer is still under warranty and contact ASUS (defective Eee PCs are replaced rather than repaired).

Chapter 23

Top Ten Eee PC Internet Resources

Traditional paper and ink books like this one are handy references — especially because they don't require electricity and are pretty easy to tote around just about anywhere. However, a tremendous amount of information and shared collective knowledge can be found on the Internet.

In this chapter, I list and describe what I consider to be the top ten (well, maybe more than that, but who's counting) Internet resources for the Eee PCs. Here you find official and unofficial support and download sites, blogs devoted to the Eee PC, and other indispensable links.

The Official Word

Let's start with two Web sites hosted by ASUS. Drum roll please!

✔ **Eee PC** (`http://eeepc.asus.com/`) — This is ASUS's official Eee PC Web site. You find product information, news, and announcements related to the mini-laptop. It's a bit sparse and some of the unofficial Web sites provide more and better information, but it's still a good place to visit.

✔ **ASUS Support** (`http://support.asus.com`) — This is the general support site for all ASUS products. Here you can access official FAQs, download updates and utilities, and contact support staff.

Because ASUS is an international company, it has a presence in many countries. I've found Eee PC information (including downloads) can vary between ASUS country Web sites. If you feel like doing a little globe-trotting and exploring, check out ASUS's main site at www.asus.com and then click a country link.

A lesser publicized ASUS resource, but incredibly useful if you know what you're looking for (such as Windows drivers, user manuals for different models, and other utilities) is the company's FTP site at:

```
ftp://ftp.asus.com/pub/ASUS/EeePC/
```

Directories are organized by model, and you can click a folder to view available files. The descriptions are nonexistent to minimal, so this site is more for the advanced user with some technical savvy. To download a file, move the cursor over the name, right-click, and use your browser's Save Link As pop-up menu command.

Answers to Just About Any Question

If I have a question I need answered or want to keep up-to-date with what's happening in the technical part of the Eee PC world, the first place I turn to (even before the ASUS sites) is the EeeUser community at www.eeeuser.com.

Put together by an Eee PC enthusiast who goes by the name of Ant, this is the most widely used and read Web site devoted to ASUS' wee wonder. The site made its debut months before the Eee PC was publicly available and has turned into the definitive online Eee PC information resource — ASUS customer support is even known to steer users to the site.

Pay special attention to two parts of the EeeUser community:

✔ **EeeUser Forums** (http://forum.eeeuser.com/) — An extensive series of forums, organized by subject, where you can post questions and get answers from experienced Eee PC users from all over the world. There's quite a bit of information-sharing that goes on in the forums, so don't be shy about registering for a free account and participating. (Or if you're shy, just sit back, lurk, and soak up lots of Eee PC knowledge.)

Most forum members are friendly and helpful, but they ask you to do two things before posting a question. First, use the Search command at the top of the window and see if your question has already been discussed. Second, visit the Wiki. What Wiki you say? The one I talk about next.

✔ **EeeUser Wiki** (http://wiki.eeeuser.com/) — If you're not familiar with the concept of a wiki, it's a Web page where anyone can contribute knowledge and information. The EeeUser Wiki is devoted to sharing tips, tricks, and techniques related to the Eee PC. It offers a large number of how-tos and tutorials, ranging from novice guides to technical instructions for experienced Linux users. The Wiki is indexed and searchable. I highly recommend this resource because it covers a variety of advanced topics that I don't have room to discuss in this book.

In addition to the EeeUser forums, two other forum sites exist that, while they don't quite get the large volume of traffic, still have good information. You can find them at `www.eeeplace.com` and `www.eeeasy.com`.

Best of the Blogs

If you want to stay up-to-date on all the latest news about Eee PCs (including new product releases, reviews, rumors, and general gossip), a number of blogs are devoted to your favorite mini-laptop. In alphabetical order, my top blog picks include

- **All About Eee** PC (`www.allabouteeepc.com`) — This blog started in February 2008, and so far is one of my top picks — mostly because it's frequently updated and, in addition to news and views, contains a number of how-to articles.

- **ASUS EEE Hacks** (`http://asuseeehacks.blogspot.com`) — Another one of my favorite daily reads, with fresh news and useful information.

- **Blogeee** (`www.blogeee.net`) — This is an Eee PC blog from France that has posted a number of exclusive news stories including yet to be released, upcoming Eee PC models. Because I've forgotten most of my high school French, I use Google's translation service at: `www.google.com/translate_t` to see what the Web site has to say.

- **Eee Guides** (`www.eeeguides.com`) — This blog doesn't get a lot of updates, but it does have some excellent tutorials.

- **EEE PC Unofficial Blog** (`http://eeepc.net`) — Primarily an Eee PC news blog with good content and frequent updates.

- **EeeUser** (`www.eeeuser.com`) — Home of the EeeUser forums and Wiki that I mentioned earlier in this chapter. Ant and other contributors also run this blog devoted to, you guessed it, the Eee PC.

- **JKK Mobile** (`http://jkkmobile.com`) — A great site covering ultra-mobile computers with an emphasis on the Eee PC. In addition to typical blog entries, the hosts also post a number of review and technical information videos.

- **Liliputing** (`www.liliputing.com`) — Another site devoted to small laptops. Lilliputian computing, get it? A good resource for the latest ASUS news as well as coverage of Eee PC competitors.

Index

• *I* •

• U •